THE
AGE
OF
WELLINGTON

THE AGE OF
WELLINGTON

THE LIFE AND TIMES
OF THE DUKE OF WELLINGTON
1769–1852

By Leonard Cooper

LONDON
MACMILLAN & CO LTD
1964

MACMILLAN AND CO LIMITED
St Martin's Street London WC 2
also Bombay, Calcutta, Madras, Melbourne
THE MACMILLAN COMPANY OF CANADA LIMITED
Toronto

To Mark Hamilton

Printed in Great Britain

Apologia

ANY AUTHOR who undertakes to add yet another book to the corpus of Wellingtonian literature, vast as it is, may justly feel that he has a need and a right to account for his temerity. Not, I would firmly add, to apologize for it. An apologia is not the same thing as an apology, being simply a speech or writing in explanation of and in defence of some action or policy.

I am not trying to write a life of Wellington, a task which has been performed often and adequately by many writers and superbly by Mr. Philip Guedalla. Nor am I attempting a "background book," since that field has been thoroughly covered by such writers as Sir Arthur Bryant and Miss Carola Oman. What has been in my mind is an attempt to tell the story of an age, especially as it was the setting for one of its greatest figures. Because it was an age of change and unrest it can perhaps be best seen in all its sharp contrast with the story of a man who hated change, ignored unrest and remained, to its and his own end, perfectly satisfied with the value of the time in which he had begun his life.

It may seem absurd to talk of any age as one of change, since all of them are that. Yet there are periods in history when the demands of new thought and the reaching out to a new good—quite apart from the question of whether what is attained is really either new or good—seem unusually urgent and dramatically vivid. And, of such periods, Wellington's time and our own stand out as glowing examples. Indeed, the more that one looks at them the more one is impressed by the likeness between them. In both cases a man who has lived through them or through a good part of them may be pardoned if he wonders whether he has not been dragged into a world utterly different from the world of his childhood. Those of us who are not yet old can only look back with amazement on the simplicities of our youth. We can remember when it took more than three weeks to get to America and less than three days to finish a Test Match; when soldiers walked abroad in the scarlet of the line or in cavalry blue; when it was an adventure to have a ride in a motorcar and an unbelievable thrill to be taken to see a flying machine; when beer cost—was it twopence a pint?—and tobacco sixpence an ounce; when Europe was still the unquestioned preserve of a few inter-related royal families; above all when we in Britain slept peacefully at night, in the knowledge that the British Fleet ruled the seas and pre-served the peace of the world.

The contrast between the world of 1769, when Wellington was born, and that of 1852, when he died, was no less complete and dramatic. In 1769 France was still a monarchy and the dominant power in Europe, where the Holy Roman Empire still survived, though only as a shadow of its former greatness. Britain was still almost entirely agricultural and her electoral system was that which had happily sufficed her since the Glorious Revolution of 1688. Education meant Latin and Greek for the upper classes and nothing at all for most of the lower; there were no railways, no income tax and no trade unions. The Army still marched in the uniforms and fought with the tactics which had sufficed for Marl-borough. India was a trading station, the Thirteen Colonies of North America a profitable satellite, already in the process of detaching itself from its parent body. Mozart had only lately finished a season as a child prodigy in London, and the horrible modernity of Beethoven lay in the unimagined future. God still blessed the Squire and his relations, while Roman Catholics and Dissenters were barred from nearly every sphere of activity, having much more prospect of entering the Kingdom of Heaven than Oxford University or the House of Commons.

When Wellington died, both of these denominations were enfranchised, railways sprawled across the green face of Britain, and her people had far more say in electing their own members of Parliament. France had entered on her perennial course of dissolving governments and changing constitutions; the United States was on the way toward becoming a world power. Popular education was spreading throughout a Britain whose young of the upper classes were nourished, by grace of Dr. Arnold, on a diet no longer confined to the classics but enriched by moral uplift, compulsory games and the prefectorial system. *Tannhäuser* and *Lohengrin* had been produced in European opera houses, and their composer was on the point of visiting London to conduct the Philharmonic con-certs.

Only the Army, the last stronghold of Wellingtonian tradition for many years yet to come, would soon set out for the Crimea in uniforms as uncomfortable and impractical and with weapons and tactical training as obsolete as its commander, Lord Raglan, who still lived in a Peninsular dream and habitually referred to the Russian enemy as "the French."

In Wellington's lifetime, as in our own, Britain had stood out, often almost alone, against foreign tyranny and had lain under threat of invasion. In both she had fulfilled the younger Pitt's proud boast that she had saved Europe by her example and might yet save herself by her efforts. From both struggles she had emerged triumphant, battered and impoverished to face a period of commercial uncertainty, political unrest, penal taxation and world-wide ingratitude. Wellington's Britain surmounted her difficulties and emerged stronger, richer and more powerful than before. What the outcome of our own tribulations may be lies yet in the unknown future. Because we are still the men and women of the breed which Wellington knew we have neither the right nor the cause to despair of an equally happy outcome.

The War of 1914–1918 drained us of much of our material wealth and all too much of our nation's youth—of the men to whom we should ordinarily have looked to guide and lead us in the coming years. We had hardly recovered from our grievous losses when we were sent reeling again by the sufferings inflicted in the Second World War. We emerged from that, poorer than ever in men and money, poorer still by the loss— the temporary loss, we must hope—of a certain confidence in ourselves and of something of our national fibre which had been at the foundation of our greatness. Ever since 1918 our problem has been that of husbanding our diminished resources, material and spiritual, and keeping up our end against competition from other nations into whose hands has passed the wealth and authority on which we had looked as our unquestioned right. In short, though our lighthearted way of dissipating our national resources would hardly suggest that we fully realize it, our business now is to make do with what we have got left.

No man in our history knew more about making do than the Duke of Wellington, who throughout his life was generally short of everything that he needed for doing his job. In his personal career he began without many advantages. His family were poor, he had little influence in an age which was dominated by privilege, his education was cut short because of the family poverty, and he was given to understand that not much was expected of him in comparison with his brilliant elder brother. He was, as his mother said, "food for powder" and nothing more.

In his active life, even when he was commanding Britain's army in the Peninsula, he was still short of things that he most needed. He never had enough cavalry or enough money or enough competent subordinates. The penury of the Treasury denied him the siege train which would have opened for him the way out of Portugal into Spain, so that he had to take

Badajoz and Ciudad Rodrigo by assault at the price of hideous casualties—casualties which he could not afford, since, as he said, he was
commanding Britain's last army which, if he were to dissipate, he could
not replace. Nor had he ever enough influence with the home governments to insist on the appointment of senior officers whom he wanted
nor to avoid that of men who were of no use to him but had to be found
jobs because of their influence and connections. He said of his divisional
generals in Spain that he could echo Lord Chesterfield's remark, in an
earlier war, that he only hoped that the list of their names would frighten
the enemy as much as they frightened him. The only commodity which
he never lacked was that of foreign allies, and with these he would gladly
have dispensed, since the Spanish Army, he remarked, were chiefly distinguished by a habit of disappearing on the eve of battle and of "re-
assembling later in a state of nature." And, it must not be forgotten, he
was fighting against a war machine which was never short of anything
which could be given to it by its commander, who was also the undis-
puted governor of all the resources of his country.

When Napoleon lost an army in Russia, he built another and was in
the field again within a year. If Wellington had lost his army he would
never have got another. He would have lost at the same time his cause
and the safety of his country. As it was, he only just achieved what he
had to do. It was, as he remarked to Creevey in Brussels after Waterloo,
"a damned nice thing—as near a run thing as ever you saw," adding,
characteristically, "By God, I don't know that it would have done if I
had not been there."

But he always was there. Having small resources and little skilled help,
he did everything himself. Napoleon worked with a huge and highly
trained staff. Wellington was his own Chief of Staff, his own Quartermaster-General, Judge-Advocate and Paymaster. As he once said, "The
reason why I succeeded in my campaigns was that I was always there
and saw to everything myself." He calculated before a campaign what
would be his exact needs in food, clothing, transport, equipment, and he
would not move until he was sure that he had enough. When his army
was on the move he personally checked their consumption of food, ammunition, fodder, boot leather and saddlery. When he brought them to
action he was there in the middle of them, ready to take advantage of an
opportunity or to rectify a mistake, assuring them by the mere fact of his
presence that he had the situation in his grip. One of his cavalry briga-
diers, Robert Long, overheard at Albuera an old soldier asking a comrade, "Where's Wor Arthur today?" and, when his friend said that he
had not seen him, adding, "I wish he wor 'ere." The confidence which
he gave to his men was immeasurable, in spite of the fact that they did

not really like him nor he them. To him, they were "the scum of the earth—they have enlisted for drink, that is the simple truth." Even after the triumph of Waterloo he could find nothing better to call them than "the most infamous army I ever commanded."

He never praised them or thanked them, though they served him as few commanders have ever been served. When they deserted he shot them; when they looted he hanged them; and, perpetually and on the smallest excuse, he flogged them.

They never loved him—it would have been a miracle had they—as Marlborough's troops or Montrose's Highlanders loved their leaders. But they trusted him. To them he was "Wor Arthur" and "the long-nosed bugger that beats the French." They knew that he was careful of their lives and saw that they were well fed, clothed and armed, but they did not flatter themselves that this was because of any affection he felt for them. It was his job to look after them, and he did it and they knew that he would always do it. In the same way he never praised or rewarded them, though he scarified them lustily if they failed him. It was their job to be brave and beat the French and no man ought—such was his simple creed—to expect praise or reward for doing his duty.

No man of his or of another time had a higher conception of his duty, carried it out more thoroughly and said less about it. Only in casual conversations by carelessly dropped remarks did he confess his entire devotion to it and his acceptance of it as the whole end of a man's life. "I am 'nimmukwallah,' as we say in the East," he said once. "I have eaten the King's salt and I conceive it to be my duty cheerfully to serve him wherever he may call upon me to go." In one of his rare moments of emotion, on the evening before Waterloo, he said to Uxbridge, who had asked him some question about the coming battle, "One thing is certain, Uxbridge—that is that you and I will do our duty."

Later, in civilian life, he accepted from George IV, whom he hated and despised, an invitation to form an administration for no better reason than that other men had tried to do the same and had failed. At the height of the struggle for the Reform Bill in 1832, he again obeyed the King, William IV, though he knew that he had no chance of getting together a cabinet and that, even if he had, it would not last a week. As he said, "The King's Government must be carried on," and if no one else would try, it was his duty.

In his active life he had little rest from the eternal struggle to balance his duty against his resources. In his private life and in his secret soul he was as conscious of his own shortcomings and applied to them the same heroic remedy. He was a poor speaker and he knew it, so "I never make speeches if I can help it." He admitted once that his rules about public speaking were never to speak unless the subject were one about which he knew something and never to quote Latin.

He could be lively in conversation, logical and terse in argument, fluent and offensive in rebuke, but he could never be inspiring in public speech and still less could he be persuasive. So he was never regarded as a great national leader as William Pitt in his day and Sir Winston Churchill in ours were justly regarded. Wellington's absorption in the idea of his duty and his disregard of the claims of men who thought of reward or personal power were admirably suited to his needs as long as he was a soldier, as surely as they were inadequate and self-destructive when he became a politician. He hated politics, he confessed, because he had to waste so much of his time in "assuaging what gentlemen call their feelings," and he had little regard for feelings whether his own or anyone else's.

Many people, indeed, declared that he had no feeling, no heart and no humanity, but they were men who had not heard him sobbing over the casualty lists at Badajoz or seen him sitting all night, white-faced and grim, over the list of those killed at Waterloo. Once he revealed himself to a woman, Lady Shelley, when he told her, "There is nothing worse than a defeat except a victory." Of course, as he would have said, he had feelings like any other man but they were his own affair. They had nothing to do with the job or his duty.

No doubt he was wrong and the release of a little generosity and human feeling would have made him a less forbidding man and a less disastrous Prime Minister. But, in civilian life, he could not realize that other men were less swayed than he by the thought of their duty or that, if they were, it was anything but discreditable. He might have had the sense to recognize that Britain meant to have parliamentary reform and have been spared the colossal blunder of his famous speech in the House of Lords in 1831 which ruined his party and went near to causing a revolution. He could surely have realized how dangerous and foolish was his remark, under the threat of internal upheaval, that "The people of England will be quiet, and if not, there is a way to make them." Of course, there is always a way and he had spent the best years of his life fighting against its chief exponent.

Soldiers seldom make good politicians and Wellington was one of the worst, yet there was room then, as there will always be, for the qualities which were his especial strength. At the Congress of Vienna and in command of the occupying forces of the Allies in Paris, he was pre-eminent not only on account of his immense prestige and his integrity but because he was free from any desire for revenge.

He came back to a country which loaded him with honours and wealth but which, as is the way of the British, soon showed that they had tired of him, as they always tire of their heroes of yesterday. They still needed him. It was his misfortune that he was forced into the foremost position where he had need of other qualities which he did not possess. He was out of touch with a country in which he had spent hardly a month during the last seven years and out of sympathy with men who dealt in words and half-promises and who seemed to have ends other than those of their country to serve—ends of party or self, which he despised and did not even try to understand. His single-minded devotion to his duty seemed a quaint anachronism, though they were glad to turn to him for counsel and strength when it seemed that England faced revolution and London destruction at the hand of the Chartists.

In the age of change, the pace was quickening to a mad whirl like the spinning of a driving wheel when the belt is broken. Wellington was unchanging and unchangeable, increasingly obstinate and testy, a man from an earlier time who had outlived his welcome and lingered on, a memorial of values with which the age had done and of which it had no desire to be reminded.

But the values, too, lingered on, as unwelcome yet as unshakable as their personification. It might be that the world would once again discover the need of them. It may even be that the world of our day is sick for the values which the world of 1832 rejected. If so, yet another telling of Wellington's story is justifiable. And, unless the world is on the verge of that discovery, it matters little what tale is told.

Acknowledgements

I owe a great debt of gratitude to the Leeds Library and to its Librarian, Mr. Frank Beckwith, M.A., who has constantly guided my researches and helped to solve my problems; I am also most grateful to all the staff of the Library and especially to Mr. Bumby and Mr. Walker for their ready and pleasant co-operation.

As ever I am grateful to my agents, Messrs A. M. Heath and Co., and among them chiefly to my friend Mark Hamilton who has been kind enough to let me dedicate this book to him. I must also thank John Cooper, my son, for his help in reading and compiling the index.

L.C.
1963

Illustrations

Plates

Maps

Drawn by William Bromage from the author's original sketches

PART I

1769-1797

I

The family name had been Colley (or Cowley) and was now Wesley. Soon it would be Wellesley, and the boy who was born in the Merrion Street house in Dublin on April 29, 1769, would add the final metamorphosis by becoming Lord Wellington. His father, the second Baron Mornington, had recently been advanced in the Irish peerage to an earldom, with the viscounty of Wellesley of Dangan, and is still remembered as the composer of some charming glees and part songs and a moderate output of church music. Just before the boy Arthur's birth, his father had been given a doctor's degree in music at Trinity College, Dublin, and elected to the vacant professorship. This seems to have given him more pleasure than any viscounty or earldom, since music was his passion and he devoted all his spare time to organizing choral and orchestral societies in Dublin. There was always plenty of good music there, and it was less than twenty years since Handel had directed the first performance of *Messiah* in the Fishmongers Hall. The English had, no doubt, done some terrible things in Ireland—so, for that matter, had the Irish—but they had made of Dublin a city of lovely houses and thriving culture.

Lord Mornington was far from being a rich man and found it difficult to manage on the meagre salary of his professorship. Like so many parents before and after him, he was perpetually worrying about his sons' education, though its beginning presented no difficulty. There was a family house at Dangan in County Meath and both Richard, the eldest, and Arthur went to a little school in Trim. That would do well enough for a time, but Richard was growing up fast and his parents had already discerned in him signs of genius. For that reason and because he was the heir, nothing but the best was good enough. He must go to Harrow and from there to Christ Church. Even there he must wear the gold tassel of a gentleman commoner.

Arthur suffered the fate of a younger son in a family who believed strongly in the rights of the first-born; so strongly indeed that all the family assumed that Arthur was not only less important than Richard but also much less intelligent and less likely to profit by a good education.

They were determined to do their best for Richard, as long as the money lasted; and when he was seven, they moved to England to save the expense of the journeys and also perhaps to come a little closer to the place where positions, commissions and sinecures were distributed. They settled down in Kensington, and Richard, having had the benefit of both Harrow, from which he was removed after taking an active part in a rebellion, and Eton, went up to Christ Church and assumed the gold tassel. He was, his mother insisted, "likely to make a figure in the world from his great abilities," but, of course, nothing much was to be expected from Arthur or from his younger brother Gerald. Still, they had to be educated, though money was now harder to find than ever and Richard, at Oxford and already preparing to enter political life, was always needing more. Lord Mornington, like so many artists, was not an accomplished money-earner, though from time to time he produced new and brilliant schemes for becoming rich without the disagreeable necessity of working. He was engaged on the last and wildest of them, a lottery in 1781, when he died, leaving only a bare subsistence for his family, unless Richard's allowance could be cut to leave something for the younger children. But of this Lady Mornington would not hear. In her determination to hold out as long as she could, she sent Arthur and Gerald off to Eton, trusting to luck that she might be able to keep them there.

In later years Wellington said little about his life at Eton, which lasted only two years before the bills became intolerable. Certainly he never made the foolish remark about winning Waterloo on the playing fields of Eton, which has been attributed to him, because there were none. The boys played a little cricket and some fives, but it was all in a disorganized fashion, and there seems to have been no football of any sort. The first Eton and Harrow match was played probably in 1800, though the date is not quite certain, and the first official record is of a game played at Lords in 1805 when Lord Byron was in the Harrow XI.

The amusements of the Eton boys at the time when Wellington was there were much more individual and considerably less innocent. The Eton of those days was in no sense like the public school system which Dr. Arnold instituted at Rugby. There were no prefects and, blessedly for many boys, no compulsory games. The boys spent much of their spare time roaming over the countryside, bird's-nesting, chasing sheep, annoying farmers and drinking in public houses. Since there were no senior boys charged with the duty of maintaining discipline and decency, bullying was frequent and inconceivably cruel. Young Charles Milnes Gaskell, in a letter from Eton, told a horrifying story of big boys putting on sharp spurs, mounting on the backs of little boys and riding them till they dropped bleeding and exhausted. George Brummel remembered that for almost a whole term he never got any dinner, because the leg of mutton which was allowed for each "mess" was only enough to feed the seniors, and the small boys could think themselves lucky to get a taste of gravy on their bread.

The birch was in constant and savage use and could be applied for the little matter of one false quantity or concord, while for serious offences there was almost no limit to the number of strokes or of new birches for their administering. (An early Lord Halifax recalled having been birched every day for a week and twice on Saturday.) It may be that this constant flagellation contributed something to Wellington's later insistence on retaining the lash as a military punishment.

It is hard for us who know only the humane schools of today to realize that such things went on; harder still to understand parents who could condemn their children to endure them. It is never fair to judge the acts and feelings of an age by the standards of a later one, and the late eighteenth and early nineteenth centuries were not sensitive about human suffering. Even fighting with another boy, a practice which was prevalent and highly popular with spectators, had its serious risks. One of Lord Shaftesbury's sons died after a fight, though his death was not so much attributable to the punishment which he took as to the copious streams of brandy which his second considerately poured down his throat between rounds.

There is, unfortunately, very little on record of Wellington's days at Eton. He went through the ordinary course of classical studies without distinction, unlike his elder brother Richard, who had become a very competent Latinist and more than adequate in Greek. Latin was then the basis of a gentleman's education and was held in greater regard than Greek if only because not many years had passed since it was used in diplomatic correspondence. As late as the year 1730 all pleadings and indictments in the law courts were in Latin. Arthur would never be one of those boys of brilliant promise, like Charles Townshend, founder of the Eton Society, and others who were early marked out for a career in politics and whom ministers of the Crown would occasionally visit while they were still at school to inquire into their progress. The trouble was not so much that Arthur could not aspire to Richard's standards as that he was hard put to it to keep ahead of Gerald, his junior, though Gerald was no genius. It was, perhaps, Arthur's lack of success in Greek and Latin which led him to formulate, in after life, his two rules for public speaking: "I never," he said, "speak about something I know nothing about and I never quote Latin." It was a wise precaution as he must have realized on a later day when, as Chancellor of Oxford University, he startled his audience in the Sheldonian Theatre by giving false quantities to the o's in Jacobus and Carolus.

Of his athletics at Eton he left no record except that once, when he revisited the place, he asked to be shown a ditch over which he used to jump and remarked that perhaps some of his spirit of enterprise owed its origin to the tricks which he used to play at school. He did not even appear to have retained those memories of marbles, pegtop and Puss-in-the-Corner on which the poet Gray looked back with affection.

Few boys in their early years at a public school have much time or thought to spare for the affairs of the great world, being almost wholly occupied in holding their own in their new surroundings. The senior boys at Eton had exceptional opportunities for getting reliable information about such things. The distance from London was not too great to allow short visits or week ends, and there were few weeks in any half when some old Etonian of distinction was not to be seen in the college or entertaining parties of boys at his hotel or lodging.

Since it was almost obligatory in those days for the King's first Minister to be an Etonian, party managers and patronage secretaries kept a regular watch on Etonians who were reaching leaving age; and Townshend's Eton Society had from the beginning made a practice of debating on political subjects. Whatever affairs of state or of world interest were occupying the public mind at any time, there was almost certain to be an Etonian mixed up in them, so that the boys felt themselves linked to the outer world as members of a family may feel about their distant relations.

In 1781, when there were Wesley boys at Eton, a boy named Cornwallis was already there. His father was fighting a hopeless battle at York Town but finding time to write to his son, "I do as much work in a week as you do in a whole half at Eton and I never get a half-holiday." The war with America, which British statesmen had made and which British generals were losing, was near its end. The British, having begun to acquire an empire, were now apparently determined to lose it or throw it away, through the fault of their statesmen and the blind obstinacy of their King. Even the British Infantry, who had won so fine a reputation at Blenheim and Dettingen and Minden, seemed—though the fault was not theirs—to be men of lesser stature than their fathers and were bitterly criticized for failing to cope with civilian forces under the amateur command of Washington, though in fact their real enemies were a stretched line of communications, a shortage of practically everything and the incompetence of their commanders. The boy who was now in the classroom at Eton would, before long, show the world that "that astonishing infantry" had lost none of its vigour and courage when it was properly led.

The Wesleys were not a family of importance in the political world, and since there were other children to be educated and Richard seemed to cost more every year, in 1784 Lady Mornington came to the decision that Arthur must leave Eton, as another of her sons was of the age to go there. He had not shown any promise or talent which would justify her in denying the other children for the sake of completing his education. Richard, now the head of the family and always a little inclined to undervalue any talents but his own, concurred in the decision, but while that was easily taken, there was a new problem in what to do with him in the immediate present. He was only fifteen, and he had so far shown no particular signs of aptitude for anything except by a pale reflection of his father's love for music and a moderate skill on the violin.

Lady Mornington decided that, for the present and largely in the interest of economy, it would be well to keep Arthur with her and for both of them to spend most of their time abroad wherever the rate of exchange was favourable. There were good schools on the Continent where the fees were less than half those at Eton, so that his education need not suffer too badly. He had shown no great aptitude for ancient Greek or Latin, but perhaps he would take more kindly to modern French.

They settled down in Brussels for the first twelve months. Arthur discovered a new fondness for his violin, which had not prospered in the atmosphere of Eton. It was a dull year for all of them, but for him it was valuable because he learned to write and speak French fluently, an accomplishment which he was to find invaluable later when he had dealings with Talleyrand and Metternich and while he represented his country during the interminable debates of the Congress of Vienna.

But he was soon tired of Brussels, where there was no occupation for his leisure hours. He was at the awkward age of puberty, when a boy's voice wavers between a shriek and a growl and his limbs seem out of control. He needed exercise, and since they could not afford to keep a stable, he often hired a horse and rode out alone down the rather dreary road which leads to the Forest of Soignes, crosses it and goes forward till it descends the gentle slopes between the farms of Hougomont and La Haye Sainte. Then he would ride back again, often entering Brussels by a street of which he forgot the name but which he recognized nearly thirty years later when the windows of a great building were all lighted up and there was the music of violins—violins which went on playing while one after another the officers unobtrusively left their partners and went back to their billets to make ready; went on playing, dimly heard through the wall of a room where the Duke sat with his maps and his staff officers and placidly remarked, "Bonaparte has been humbugging me, by God! He has stolen twenty-four hours on me"; violins which at last wavered and died into silence when from the street below came the rattle of drums, the skirl of Highland pipes and the tramp of feet as the battalions marched out on the road to Quatre Bras.

II

THERE WERE two more rather aimless years abroad, most of which Arthur spent in the once-famous military academy at Angers, whose curriculum had by now dwindled into a tedious alternation of riding school and fencing or dancing lessons. Academically he learned nothing there, but Angers can hardly be held to blame for that, since he was not an intellectual and would not have acquired much more knowledge anywhere. The two years were not wasted. Arthur improved his French, though his accent would never be really good, and learned something about the state of Europe, about the aspirations and fears of European statesmen and about the new theories which were troubling the calm of Europe's political thinkers and students. It was easier for him to make a life of his own because Lady Mornington had gone back to England to attend to family business, and he tasted for the first time the exciting, though sometimes alarming, sensations of being able to go where he liked and do more or less the same.

His choice did not include more than he could help of the riding school or the *salle des armes,* and, with admirable good sense, he made a habit of visiting the French families to whom his fellows at school introduced him and of mixing with the officers of the regiments which were stationed in the district. He dined with the Duc de Brissac, where he met a brother of Talleyrand, and with the Duc de Praslin, where an excitable little Abbé called Sieyès talked to him at some length and quite incomprehensibly about something called the *tiers état.* And afterward he always swore that he met Chateaubriand, though he could never remember what he looked like or what he talked about. He found the company of the officers of the garrison more congenial and they seemed to like him.

He was only sixteen, but boys grew up quickly in those days when a child of twelve often commanded a boat's crew of grown men, and Arthur had always been a little solemn for his years. He was growing into a man and leaving his gawky and awkward youth behind him, so that the men in the messes where he was a guest accepted him as one of their own sort and talked freely to him and in front of him. There could be no better way of learning for a boy who did not like books, and he had the sense to keep quiet and listen when his seniors talked among themselves after dinner—when the wine was going round and the men lounged in their chairs with as much ease as their tight tunics allowed. Arthur had already noticed the tendency of French officers to wear their uniforms in public on every possible occasion and he did not like it. It seemed to him purely ridiculous that a man should dress himself in a constricting tunic with skintight leathers on his legs and trail an immense sabre into every café or inn or private house which he entered. When his own chance came he rigidly enforced the wearing of plain clothes by officers at all times and in all places except when and where they were actually on duty, and he set the example both at home and abroad, as he did when he drove out to the field of Waterloo with his uniform neatly packed in a valise and stowed away in the boot of his carriage. Yet even Wellington was slightly staggered to see Picton appear at Quatre Bras wearing a civilian frock coat and top hat and carrying an umbrella to which he obstinately clung throughout the day.

Wellington was always grateful in later years for the chance which had thrown him so much into the company of French officers and their friends, finding it always easier to make contact with them and to follow their thoughts than did many of his contemporaries. From the talk now in the unguarded hours he began to get his first view of European problems and to understand that other nations beside his own had troubles and ambitions and even that, to them, the British were foreigners.

Most of all he heard about France, though the officers were more guarded when they spoke of her, and the Abbé Sieyès had been more earnest than enlightening. Arthur Wesley sat and listened and thought and pieced together the disconnected words and half-understood allusions, and as he did so, he began to realize that something in her economy or her constitution was deadly sick and that no one could find an acceptable remedy. The disease was easy to diagnose and there was a simple and obvious course of treatment, if only France would follow her doctors' advice and live sparely and work hard until she was well again.

The plain fact was that France was on the verge of ruin for very simple reasons. She had been grossly overspending her national income for years to support the magnificence of Louis XIV and the extravagance of Louis XV. She had undertaken a seemingly endless series of wars and the bills were coming in. That there was no money to pay them was the fault of that strange fiscal system under which the only people who were expected to pay taxes were those who had nothing to pay them with. The nobles and the clergy were exempt from taxation and not even King Louis dared to suggest an alteration or to admit the defect when his visiting experts pointed it out to him. The peasants had to pay their *taille* and *gabelle,* the tax on their salt; this was the imposition which they most bitterly resented, having, for the most part, no other relish even when they had bread. The court of Versailles was the most luxurious and magnificent in Europe, and the nobles who attended it were chiefly men of great wealth with large estates in the country. They could have well afforded to pay their share of taxation, but tradition was strong and selfishness stronger still. So a slightly dreary procession of financial experts, economists and Swiss bankers examined the accounts, put their fingers on the weak spots and were shown the door. The wheels were running down in France for lack of money to keep them going, and the services— even the army in which France took such pride—were months, sometimes years, in arrears with their pay.

It is possible that Arthur Wesley was less shocked and surprised by this evidence of penury than were the Frenchmen who revealed it to him, for though he was not yet a soldier, it was a notorious fact in England that officers and men were very lucky if they saw their pay at all. The British Army was paid in accordance with a simple system which anyone could understand but by which only the lucky few could profit. At the top of this system stood the Paymaster-General to the Forces, who received and signed for the total sum due to the Army for pay. It is easy to understand why the Paymastership was one of the most eagerly sought after offices. Several very respectable fortunes had been based on a few years' tenure of the post, the highest achievement in this line having been, by common agreement, that of the first Lord Holland, the father of Charles James Fox, who readily helped his father to dispose of his gains. There are no known figures of Lord Holland's peculations, but at one stage of his career he was able, in addition to his other expenses, to pay off his son's gambling debts, which then amounted to about £140,000. When this and the other charges had been disposed of, anything that was left over went to the colonels of regiments, since there was no permanent organization into divisions or brigades and a colonel owned his regiment

as much as if it were his shop or his business. The colonels, after the
Paymaster had parted with the residue of the pay, recouped themselves
for what they had spent on their men and on equipment, uniforms and
food, and found that the most satisfactory way of accounting for their
expenditure was to carry on their strength some two or three hundred
men who had no other existence except as names. If after that there was
any money left, the troops sometimes got some of it. And if it is objected
that the government's auditors should have spotted and stopped the
fraud at its source, the true, though appalling, explanation is that the
government auditors whose duty it was to examine the Treasury's accounts were the Treasury themselves. Sometimes the opposition or some
powerful body would threaten to impeach the Paymaster, but it was seldom more than a gesture. Tradition was in favour of the system, and
Cabinet ministers must live. In any case the opposition hoped or expected to get into power themselves sooner or later. They could hardly
be expected to take a step so drastic as to curb their own opportunities.

There were other things which the French officers discussed with less
knowledge and with a certain alarm. All the world over soldiers have
grumbled about their pay and have half-enviously cursed the peculators,
but this was something strange and menacing, this talk of ideas and
movements and the unfamiliar names which men were beginning to recognize and to use—names like Descartes and Grotius, Hobbes and Locke
and above all Rousseau. An army mess is not the most fertile soil for
intellectual uprisings and few men in France—certainly fewer in England
—could give a coherent account of such new doctrines as The Social
Contract, Locke's "Laws of Nature," Grotius' "Lex Talionis" or Rousseau's "Return to Nature." But they were there, making themselves felt
perhaps in small and subtle ways, in a touch of insolence from a shop-
keeper or black looks from a few peasants. They left an uncomfortable
feeling that the old familiar ways were threatened and that new hands
were reaching out for power. The threat was somewhat clearer to a mind
like that of Edmund Burke, always half a prophet, who had said as early
as 1769, the year of Arthur's birth, "There is some extraordinary con-
vulsion in the whole system the effect of which on France and even on
all Europe it is difficult to conjecture."

Now, however dim the threat, the same spirit of rebellion, these dangerous theories about the rights of man, was spreading in Europe. France
had been sympathetic toward the Thirteen Colonies, and Frenchmen had
crossed the Atlantic to fight for them against the British. Some of them,
it might be, had been impregnated with the ideas and would infect others
at home. It was all very vague as yet; there was nothing that a man
could point to and say, "That is an act of treachery" or "This is the

beginning of revolt." Yet, in a way, the revolt had been alive for many years, and one of its sources, improbable though it might sound, was Britain, which had defied the power of the Pope, had killed one King and would have killed another if she had caught him. It would be absorbingly interesting to know what impression of the state of Europe young Arthur Wesley took home with him.

He was a serious-minded boy and must have gathered, as others did, the impression that Europe was only waiting for a new order of things, that she had been drained by dynastic wars until she was beginning to question whether there was much to be said for dynasties. France was on the point of financial ruin. Prussia, under Frederick the Great, had just given the first demonstration of the methods which were to make her the greatest menace to civilization in the twentieth century. The Holy Roman Empire was even now justifying Voltaire's famous sneer ("neither holy nor Roman nor empire") and degenerating into the Empire of Austria-Hungary. The wretched Poland had in 1770 been ravaged by a pestilence which killed more than a quarter of a million of her people and, only two years afterward, had suffered the first of many partitions at the hands of Russia, that greatest of all pestilences, for which the world has yet to find a cure.

Spain, though considerably better organized and having far sounder finances than had the other great Catholic power, France, had lately ceased to carry much weight in European affairs, being much occupied with internal organization and still firmly under the heel of the Church. Spain had had her great days and was still formidable but she had passed her peak. France seemed to be passing hers—no one dreamed of her greatness to come or took much notice of a starved-looking artillery subaltern called Bonaparte who had just been posted to his first battery. The American colonies had thrilled the large part of the Old World which hated Britain by their courage and successful resistance, but America was far away and did not count in European counsels. The nation with the most hopeful future was undoubtedly Great Britain, with her increasing wealth, her sea power and her adventurous traders who would go to ends of the earth in search of goods and leave behind them a few years later a fragment of Empire. To European ways of thought, Britain was an eccentric form of democracy, blandly indifferent to political theorizing, loyal to the Crown and intermittently disrespectful to its wearer. A queer, cold-hearted nation they seemed, living in a perpetual drizzle, eating cabbage or dumplings, playing their incomprehensible national games and incessantly despising the rest of the world.

However much or little Arthur Wesley had learned about Europe, it was time for him to go and learn what he could about his own country, which he was to serve for the rest of his life. So far he knew the green hills and weeping skies of Ireland, the water meadows round Eton and the grey dignity of Windsor, with a casual knowledge of a small part of London.

He left Belgium in 1786, when he was seventeen, and now he knew what his life was to be. Lady Mornington, having mourned his awkwardness and vowed to God that she did not know what to do with him, returned to her original opinion that "he was only good to be food for powder." Richard, after a successful career at Oxford, was establishing himself in political life and was able and willing to bestir himself to help his tiresome younger brother to a start in life, which start could not be made too soon to please him. It was too soon to please Arthur, who did not want to start, but he knew—he would always know—his duty, and if his mother had him marked down for a soldier, then a soldier he would be. But, as others were soon to find, he was seldom at the end of his resources, however dark his prospects might seem, and he had a knack of extricating himself from the most nipping of pincers. He would be a soldier, but he had no intention of doing any soldiering. Having got a job, he at once proceeded to ensure that it would give him the minimum of trouble and work, and above all that it would not whisk him away on foreign service.

It might be possible, with the help of Richard's growing influence, to find a congenial occupation for the hours which he did not propose to spend with his regiments. At any rate he would look about him. It was always as well to know what was going on at the other side of the hill.

III

ARTHUR WESLEY came back in 1787 to an England which still, to all appearances, was tranquilly enjoying the eighteenth century and was in no hurry to move on to the nineteenth. She was still almost entirely an agricultural country, though the next few years would change all that with the Industrial Revolution. Where other European nations were facing political changes, under the influence of modern doctrines, and would in the future change the form of their government, England still seemed content with a King who had set himself to defy Parliament and with a government which had lost the best part of an empire. Her electoral system had been revised in 1688, the year of what the Whigs called the Glorious Revolution, as well they might since they had been in power practically ever since. It was completely out of date and irrelevant to the times in which it existed, since it left the real power of the country in the hands of the large landowners and country gentlemen and ignored the growing population of the towns. The system, like most British systems, was illogical but had so far worked fairly well. It was obviously unfair that Cornwall should contain sixteen parliamentary boroughs, each returning two members, and that the whole of Yorkshire should return only two: but when it became so unfair as to be intolerable someone would probably think of a way to alter it and deal the cards afresh.

It is easy to understand why the British, as politicians, have always been an enigma and a source of irritation to more forensically minded nations. They had no written constitution and did not appear to feel the lack; their law was, or appeared to more rigid minds to be, based entirely on what some judge had said about what some other judge had meant. They would put up with almost anything and were the despair of revolutionary agitators till the moment when some comparatively trivial burden would suddenly prove too much for them, like the twenty shillings which would not have ruined Mr. Hampden's fortune; and then they would utter the phrase with which they generally prefaced action—"Look here, this won't do"—and act with surprising promptness and vigour.

In the years before the American Revolution, Benjamin Franklin, who had crossed the Atlantic as often on his own or his country's business as had any of his fellow countrymen, fretfully observed of the English, ". . . in all sorts of people a want of attention to what passes in such remote countries as America, an unwillingness to read anything about them if it appears a little lengthy and a disposition to postpone the consideration even of the things they know they must at last consider, so that they may have time, for what more immediately concerns them, and withal, enjoy their amusements."

Those amusements were very important to the English, and since they were still a nation of countrymen, it was natural that they should find their pleasure in the traditional sports of their countryside. Roads were few and bad, unpleasant in summer and impossible in winter, so that there were hardly any great gatherings for sport, which consequently remained local and intimate. Yorkshiremen played "knur and spell"; Cumberland and Westmorland men wrestled in their own traditional way and ran races across the fells. Cricket had taken hold more firmly in the south than in the north, and the Marylebone Cricket Club was founded about the year of 1744, though it did not take up its permanent headquarters at Lords till 1824. The men of Hambledon were playing on their grounds at Broadhalfpenny and Windmill Downs in 1750, and the Hambledon Club continued to play matches against Kent or All England till 1791. Other counties had their own form of football or wrestling, sometimes playing mammoth football matches in which the whole population of two villages turned out and the game might last for three days.

All over England the chief winter sport was hunting, which had not yet become expensive or exclusive. Many a squire up and down the country kept his own small pack and hunted fox or hare in the nearby district, which often had to be determined in consultation with the adjacent owner of a pack. Large corporations like those in Manchester and Birmingham kept their own packs, which were usually followed by twice as many men on foot as were mounted.

Almost every possible form of cruelty in matching animals against each other was practiced and thoroughly enjoyed, in country market places or in open spaces in towns or, more often, as feeling against such cruelty grew, in stables or derelict buildings where the men would sit enthralled to watch dog against bear, bull against three dogs, or any combination for which the means were available. It was not a squeamish age, and men who saw nothing amiss in hanging or transporting children for a petty theft or in flogging a soldier almost to death for a minor military offence were not likely to shed any tears for a mangled dog or a tormented bull.

It is always a mistake to underestimate the importance of sport in the history of eighteenth- and nineteenth-century Britain. It had much to recommend it, since it filled up what little leisure a farm labourer or apprentice had and strengthened his limbs. It may or may not have taught him the principles of fair play, as has been claimed for it, but the probability is that so self-conscious and earnest an attitude came in later with organized sport and compulsory games at schools. The importance of the genuine country sports in that age was that they formed an immensely strong link between one class and another and gave men the feeling that, in spite of superficial differences in income, in accent, in luxury of living, there was fundamentally no difference between one man and another. The Squire could take a toss in the hunting field as easily as his groom; a Duke was as susceptible to a fast yorker as was his gardener. However arbitrary and overbearing about his rents or repairs a landowner might be, there was an authority above him just as arbitrary and not to be argued with. When the umpire said he was out, he was out.

Because of this attachment to the countryside and to its sport and its life, the English landowners were never separated from the workers on their estates or the colliers in their mines as were the French aristocrats from the peasants. The result was that when the revolution came to France in 1789, the French aristocrats paid dearly for their withdrawal from ordinary life into the artificial existence of Versailles and, when the people became their judges, had no one to speak for them or to remember them with kindness; but when England was on the verge of it in 1832 it was the Whig party, who fought for the Reform Bill, forced it through Parliament and compelled the King to accept it.

When the day came, the Duke of Wellington was to be the most stalwart and immovable opponent of reform, but when he reached London from Belgium at the age of eighteen there was no hint of future greatness about his life or his prospects. All the greatness in that family was the prerogative of Richard, the elder brother who so kindly helped him to get a commission—any commission as long as he got it soon. He was not a landowner nor had he any prospect of becoming one, since the

Wesleys had left their old home in Ireland and were rootless and impoverished in London, where Lady Mornington proposed to stay until her children were launched into the world.

London at the end of the eighteenth century was little more than a very much enlarged country town from which a man could ride in less than an hour to a meet of the hounds in any of the Home Counties. Every morning great wagons rolled in from the country bringing its produce to the city, and in open markets women sat by their stalls offering fruit which had been picked in the early hours of the same morning and eggs which had been laid but a few hours before. There was even one woman in St. James's Park who sold drinks of milk from her cow: her customers, if they came at the right time, could see her draw it. The old cries of "Fresh Lavender" and "Cherry Ripe" were heard in the streets, and the long-distance coaches arrived with their horses' heads decorated with flowers which the ostlers would have put in at Tottenham or wherever the last stage had been.

In the theatres and concert halls there were definite signs of a change of taste, though the pleasure gardens at Vauxhall and Cremorne and Ranelagh kept their attraction for thousands of Londoners, and there were startling equestrian displays to be seen at Astley's Amphitheatre. The Theatre Royal, Drury Lane, remained faithful to its dramatic tradition, though Garrick had retired in 1776 and no longer played Lear in contemporary satin with dress sword and diamond-heeled shoes. Playgoers who mourned his loss were beginning to speak hopefully of the young Kemble who had made his debut in *Hamlet* in 1783 and appeared to be willing to perform Shakespeare's plays as Shakespeare had written them and not with an altered ending in which a revived Hamlet married a restored Ophelia or the Macbeths retired into the Highlands to lead a simple and virtuous life. That had been the fashion only a few years before, but now the public taste did not seem to require it and was content to let their tragedies remain tragic. The greatest change was in the operatic and musical world, which had turned away from the traditions of Handel within twenty years of his death. In the first half of the century Italian opera had obsessed London audiences, but the craze had passed and Mozart quickly captured them with the London productions of *Seraglio* in 1782 and of *Figaro* and *The Magic Flute* in 1786 and in 1791.

But the supreme entertainment and pursuit of the governing classes was, and for a long time would be, politics. The great houses in London were becoming the strongholds and rallying points of one party or another and their hostesses showed as much keenness and did as much manoeuvring as the men. Holland House, where the formidable Lady Holland ruled, was the home of Whigs, especially of the more extreme young Whigs who followed Charles James Fox. Devonshire House was Whig, but Whig of the old tradition, which was hard to distinguish from the Tories at Lansdowne House, since both parties were led and dominated by the same type of landowner and there was little to distinguish between their actions when in office, other than the freedom with which they abused each other. The Whigs had had things more or less their own way since the Glorious Revolution but with so little opposition and such assured majorities that they had become less united and threatened to break up into small sections still nominally within the Whig party. Men were talking of the "Rockingham Whigs" or the "Bedford Whigs" (of whom it was unkindly said that you could buy them in bulk but not individually), and there was a possible threat of a third section, to be led by Charles Fox with intermittent help from Edmund Burke, whom the horrors of the French Revolution were so soon to turn into a passionate worshipper of the rule of the British aristocracy and to restore the fire and fervour which had languished since he had had the cause of the Thirteen Colonies to maintain.

The political world of London, which had grown a little weary and despondent with so many years of Whig supremacy, came sharply to life as internal squabbles threatened the unity of the party and seemed to hold out promise of a return to Tory government. Above all and in both parties there was at first curiosity and then indignation when it was known that the new King was not content to follow the strict constitutional lines which had been imposed on his predecessors, but was interfering actively in politics and forming a third party of his own, who were soon known as "The King's Men." With these friends, whom he bought or bribed, he was determined to influence Parliament, and to restore to the Crown all the power which the rebels of 1688 had so wisely restricted and carefully controlled. The English wanted no more of the Divine Right of Kings, having heard it expounded at length by the Stuarts, who were better at theory than practice, and having seen it exercised by the Tudors, who were good at both but preferred practice—their exposition of the doctrine had never gone to much greater length than Elizabeth's, "Must is a word not used to Princes." They were not going to stand a revival of it by a member of a family whom they had installed on the throne for the express purpose of laying the ghost of a dead doctrine.

For some years after 1688 the Tory party had suffered from the suspicion, which was sometimes justified, that they were Jacobites at heart, and the prejudice lingered for years, even after the last hope of the cause had perished in the mists of Culloden Moor. Now forty years later, the Tory party could surely be considered purged of any trace of Jacobitism and so might hope for a return to office. Indeed, the day of their return was not far off, for the French Revolution, which changed so many lives and fortunes, swept them into power and kept them there for many years. When their time of success was drawing to an end, their leader in the Lords would be the Duke of Wellington, who now, as Arthur Wesley, was in London, without much money and without the entrée to any of the great political houses, hoping for nothing more than a commission as an ensign and more or less resigned to his family's opinion of him as "food for powder and nothing more."

IV

TILL THE END of his life Wellington would continue to defend the system of purchasing commissions, by means of which he first entered the Army in 1787. It was a system which hardly admitted of any defence, so illogical was it and so much harm had it done to the Army. Any young officer who had the money to put down could buy a step in rank as soon as there was a vacancy, even if there were men, his senior by years in his own regiment, who were much better fitted for promotion. If an officer had not enough capital, all that he could do was to wait for a vacancy for which he would be eligible without payment. In peacetime this was a very rare occurrence, and almost the only prospect lay in what was called "augmentation" when a battalion which had been stationed at home was ordered on foreign service. In such a case there were sometimes vacancies to be filled for which no purchaser offered, especially if the battalion were ordered to an unpopular or unhealthy station abroad. But such vacancies were too infrequent to be of help to many non-purchase officers, and their only other chance lay in the hazards of war, with the possibility of promotion in the field to replace casualties.

Wellington's support for the system was not wholly based on his characteristic reverence for tradition and horror of change, though they, no doubt, sustained it. His reasoned argument for purchase was that it kept the command of the Army in the hands of men of estate and family, men who understood the traditions of service and soldiered because it was what their families had always done and what men in their position

B   (21)

were expected to do. He believed that this ensured loyalty to the established order of society and removed all danger of control of the Army by ambitious career officers who would think only of themselves and, if they became powerful, might attempt to use the troops to set up a military dictatorship. It was a fear which had prevailed in England ever since the time of Cromwell, when the standing Army had been a menace to the whole country and when Cromwell's system of military government under his major-generals had given England a shock from which she had never recovered. The memory of that time was at the bottom of nearly all the typical British distrust of the Army and the habit of regarding the private soldier as a criminal in a scarlet coat. Wellington, in spite of his long years of service and his position in the Army, was always a most scrupulous respecter of constitutional rights, as he showed when, toward the end of his life, he was asked to prepare a plan for the protection of London against the Chartists. In doing so, he insisted that the troops must be kept out of sight, and control left to the police and special police until it was certain that only the use of troops could restore the situation.

Fortunately the British, after their experience of Cromwell, have never been inclined toward that particular form of lunacy, the military dictatorship, but the world of our own day has seen so many instances of it in Europe and South America that Wellington's foresight has been amply justified, however small the danger may have been at home. His feelings on the subject must have been both genuine and strong, since he never pretended to think that the officers with whom the existing system provided him were ideal or even passable. His Peninsular dispatches are full of railing at their indolence, their ignorance and lack of training, their failure to read orders and their tendency to apply for home leave while on active service. Even all this, it would seem, he was prepared to put up with rather than run the risk of encouraging the career officer, whose efficiency might be put to selfish and evil ends.

The Duke had only to look back on his own career to realize how useful the system had been to Arthur Wesley, then eighteen years of age and just gazetted ensign in the 73rd Foot. The 73rd was a Highland regiment and he had no Scottish connections, but since he did not mean to spend any time with them, that did not very much matter. At the moment he was less in control of his own destiny than the obedient chattel of a self-elected family committee consisting of Lady Mornington and Richard. Between them they had got him into the Army, but that was only a first step. He had no private means and what little money the family had was always needed for Richard's really important career. Since a subaltern of Arthur's standing could hardly be expected to live on his pay it was obvious that some additional employment must be found for him.

There were various posts which a young officer could combine with military duty. As it happened one of them presented itself almost at once, and by a stroke of rare good fortune it was in Ireland, of which Lord Buckingham had just been appointed Governor-General. He had need of an aide-de-camp, and Lady Mornington, who knew him, had no difficulty in securing the post for her son. So Arthur left a London in which the politically minded were just anticipating the trial of Warren Hastings and the musical were beginning to whistle or hum the melodies from *Don Giovanni* and Gluck's *Orpheus* to take up his duties in Dublin. It was only a minor disadvantage that the 73rd was just then ordered on foreign service, and he overcame it by purchasing a promotion to a lieutenancy in the 76th. His family was already thinking of the next step for him and was exploring the possibility of his becoming a member of the Irish parliament. Richard's career necessitated his permanent residence in England, and the family borough of Trim was at present represented by a still younger brother, William.

Richard, intent on moving his pawns about in the game of family advancement, had almost decided that William had better follow him to England, where no doubt a seat in the British Parliament could be found for him. It would be most convenient for Arthur, as his duties as aide-de-camp would keep him in Ireland, to become member for Trim, and there were then no regulations which forbade a serving officer to be a member of Parliament. To achieve this it was obviously necessary for Arthur to remain in Ireland, whatever might be the destination of his regiment, so he embarked on the rapid series of transfers and promotions by purchase which were to carry him through seven regiments in the same number of years. The ensign who joined the 73rd Foot in 1787, became, by way of the 76th, 41st and 58th of Foot (with a divagation into the 12th Dragoons), a major in the 33rd Foot in 1793 without having seen a shot fired in action and with only a minimum amount of regimental service to his credit. He bought his captaincy in the 58th Foot in 1789, the year when the Paris mob went roaring through the streets to the Bastille prison, and he was still in attendance at Dublin Castle when another Paris mob stormed the Tuileries and butchered the Swiss Guard. (Lieutenant Bonaparte of the Artillery watched them, muttering to himself that they were "vile canaille" and remarking to a friend that "a whiff of grapeshot" would have blown them off the streets.)

In London, Fox had hailed the taking of the Bastille with a cry of joy. "How much the greatest thing it is that had ever happened and how much the best," while Burke reflected gloomily, "This Revolution begins very ill," and saw no assurance that "a thing which had been so violent in its beginning would not be bloody in its ending." Events in Europe were moving at a speed too headlong to be controlled, as the powers, headed by Austria and inspired by Marie Antoinette's desperate plea for help, began to concert steps first to save and then to avenge the King and Queen of France and were misled into publishing a manifesto which suggested, if it did not threaten, destruction of France if any harm should come to their King and Queen.

The young Republic went to war. The first armies of Revolutionary France, ill-equipped, half-clad and hardly organized, streamed toward the frontier. Danton called for more and more men. Then Britain was drawn in and the French Army lay on the heights above Toulon, where the British Fleet was in harbour to supply the town and to take off survivors, should resistance become impossible. (Major Bonaparte was passing near on his way to Italy and was drawn into the defence to help with the siting of guns.)

At last it was time for Major Wesley of the 33rd to begin real soldiering, since duty as an aide-de-camp was well enough for peacetime but no occupation for a soldier whose regiment was to go abroad on active service. He had been elected to the Irish Parliament as member for Trim and had met and fallen in love with Miss Kitty Pakenham, though there was nothing more between them than a mild understanding that someday they might marry. The 33rd was under orders for foreign service, though it was not for some time that the men were told that their destination was Ostend. By then another promotion had come to Major Wesley who went out as a lieutenant-colonel commanding his regiment.

The campaign which followed is of no interest to any but military historians and of very little to them. The triumphant march of the Allies, which was to have taken Paris and ended the Republic, had never got far beyond the frontiers, and as the winter of 1794 drew nearer, it lost all its impetus. The war in the Low Countries turned into a series of disjointed operations with the British perpetually manoeuvring round Ostend and Antwerp. Colonel Wesley and the 33rd did not arrive in Belgium with the first force under the Duke of York but followed a few weeks later and were ordered to attack Ostend. Soon afterward they were moved by sea to Antwerp for its defence. Colonel Wesley found himself at the time commanding his own and another regiment and subsequently a brigade of three battalions.

In January of the new year operations were stopped by a terrible period of snow and frost, and the British suffered more loss by frostbite and sickness than they had or would have in action in the whole campaign. But, if the campaign had little military value, it gave to Arthur Wesley his first experience of war and it taught him a lesson which he was never to forget. As he himself said afterward, "I at least learned what not to do and that is always something." Even his inexperienced eyes could see the basic causes of the failure in the weakness of the strategy and the absence of direction from whoever was supposed—if anyone was—to be commanding the combined forces of Austria, Holland and Britain, with a small detachment of Germans in British pay. The grand strategy had been laid down by the combined general staffs of Austria and Prussia with a little help from Britain, but while it had included a triumphant march on Paris, it had made no provision for any alternative, so that the combined forces became bogged down in the Low Countries with no further orders than their own commanders could give them.

In the British force, communications broke down almost completely and each brigade or regiment had to fend for itself until orders arrived. When they arrived they were often out of date, owing to the time which it had taken to transmit them to units of whose whereabouts Army headquarters had only the vaguest information.

The Duke of York, who commanded the British, was, like one of his royal predecessors, the Duke of Cumberland, a soldier whose talents were administrative rather than tactical. The problem of command soon became too much for him; nor were his subordinates any happier. It was a campaign of regimental officers with no formation greater than a brigade in action at once. "I was on the Waal, I think," Wesley wrote afterward, "from October to January, and during all that time I only once saw a general from headquarters." So disgusted and disillusioned was he with his first sight of the British Army in action that several times he wrote home to Richard announcing his intention of returning to Ireland as soon as the French saw fit to go into winter quarters. It was a strange resolve for the man who was to complain so bitterly in the Peninsula when his officers asked for home leave on urgent private business. Wesley never got the opportunity. The French were a young and uninstructed army who had not been taught the eighteenth-century rules of war and continued to fight throughout the winter, even in the frost and snow of that January. Under the impact of that bitter cold the British Army fell to pieces, and as they trailed wearily northward across Holland, thousands of them died of exposure and hunger. When at last they reached the Ems, a general reported to the Duke of York, "Your Army is destroyed. The officers, their carriages and a large train are safe, but the men are destroyed."

Colonel Wesley never forgot the lessons of that retreat or the sight of an army which suffering and lack of discipline had reduced to a stumbling rabble. It may often have been in his mind when he himself commanded an army and, having learned what not to do, successfully avoided it. Worst of all was the lack of orders. To his mind, the reason for it was that headquarters were far too distant from the fighting troops, so that they could neither control a situation nor take advantage of any favourable opportunity. He wrote bitterly, "We had letters from England and I declare that those letters told us more of what was passing at headquarters than we learned from the headquarters themselves." He believed that a commander's battle headquarters should be so far forward that he could control the actual line of battle himself and give oral orders as the position varied from hour to hour. It was from a forward position that he fought all his great Peninsular battles. As he later said, "The real reason why I succeeded in my own campaigns is because I was always on the spot—I saw everything and did everything myself." It was in Belgium that he learned that lesson and in Belgium again twenty years later that he triumphantly demonstrated his mastery of it, when the troops who lined the ridge at Waterloo saw him riding among them and sometimes heard his voice in a sharp order—"Go on, Colborne, go on! They won't stand." To a returning cavalry brigade, "Gentlemen of the Household Cavalry, I thank you." And to an advancing infantry regiment, "There, in you go, my lads, and let's see no more of you."

If that was the most important of his lessons, the one to which he referred most often in later days was the problem of supply. It was a problem to which few armies had given serious attention and in the British Army no corps or department existed for feeding and supplying active troops, beyond the employment of civilian contractors who were often dishonest and, not being under military discipline, were hard to control. A Wagon Train was in existence as part of the Army, to whom they were known as "The Newgate Blues" on account of the colour of their uniform and their reputation for thievery, but their duties were only to carry supplies. They had nothing to do with the baking of bread or killing of animals for meat, for which there were no arrangements except what were made within the regiments themselves.

In the winter of 1794–1795 the supply arrangements broke down completely, and troops in the lines were almost reduced to starvation during the worst months of the coldest weather. Wellington had seen the battalions under his command on the Waal frozen and starving, all discipline gone and with no idea but a purely animal need for food and warmth and rest. Whatever delay it might impose and whatever criticism it might occasion, he would never again, whenever it was humanly possible to avoid it, subject his men to such unnecessary suffering.

The last important lesson which he afterward remembered and instilled into his own commands was the importance of the regimental officer's maintaining discipline and looking after his men. He had observed, as had the general who reported on it, that among a shattered and retreating army the officers were paying more attention to their own safety and to their own baggage and vehicles than to their men. Among the men who stumbled and crawled homeward were carriages belonging to officers, loaded to the roof with their private luggage, their wine and special food. These carriages were drawn by horses which would have been much better employed in the traces of the guns or the ranks of the cavalry. (All armies were alike in this. In 1812, the Emperor Napoleon gave orders that all officers' private carriages found in the column were to be pulled out and burned.)

In all Wellington's dispatches, especially in those from the Peninsula, he never ceased to complain of the indolence or carelessness of the regimental officers except when they were in action. When his Army was in retreat from Burgos in 1813 his orders spoke repeatedly and fiercely about the junior officers' lack of care for their men and of their disregard of orders. No one could find fault with their courage in action. What they lacked was the sense of responsibility for their men at all times—in barracks, on the line of march, in camp, in their time of leisure. It was not really the fault of the officers, who had been given little or even no training before commanding a unit in action. It was the fault of the system which, though he railed against it, he did nothing to improve even when, as Commander-in-Chief, he had the opportunity.

It would appear that there was one lesson of this campaign which Wesley only dimly apprehended and which no other British general perceived at all. It is evident that, when he writes of going home as soon as the French have gone into quarters for the winter, he and all his fellow officers are thinking in terms of the past century and of the last war. It was no blame to them, for with the French Revolution had come something new into the world, which no contemporary mind could absorb at once and which had its effect in every department of national life. It is difficult even now to realize what must have been the feelings of an average man as the news of the Revolution reached him, a little at a time and slowly, as news travelled in those days. It must have been a sensation of bewilderment as though some power not of this world had broken loose and had destroyed all normal human values.

The military mind is perhaps inclined to rigidity and to a taste for looking back for precedents or upward for authority. When the officers knew that fighting was imminent they would naturally be occupied with training their units, organizing and equipping their formations and, for want of other guidance, doing it as they had done it all their lives and as they expected the enemy to be doing at the same time. All European nations were organized as they had been before the Seven Years' War and had no anticipation of any other sort of campaigning. They did not realize that the French by virtue of their Revolution had broken with all tradition and that their Army knew no rules except such as they would make for themselves. They could not be expected to understand that among the horrors which the Revolution had unloosed on the world was the concept which was to become known to a later generation as Total War. Still less could they guess that the flood of unrestrained enthusiasm and awakened hope which had carried the first armies of the Revolution to victory would shortly be harnessed and directed by the one man who would have the genius to temper the fierceness and control the enthusiasm without abating either of them, but would direct the rushing waters of France into the dark channels of his own ambition.

V

WITH THE SUCCESSES of the French Revolutionary Army in the Low Countries and the whirlwind campaign of General Bonaparte's Army in Italy in 1796, modern war may be said to have begun. The wars of the eighteenth century had been fought on strictly military principles which had become almost as formal and regular as the steps of a minuet. It was partly because the Austrian and British troops in the Low Countries had been trained on these principles that their failure was inevitable from the start.

Frederick the Great's victories had impressed the rest of Europe with the military strength of Prussia. The Allies suddenly found themselves faced with an entirely new type of war based on no principles which had yet been expounded by military experts and, indeed, they began to think, on no principles at all. In this they were right, since the French tactics at this early stage of the Revolution were wholly experimental and seemed to have as their object the seeking out and destroying of the enemy. To the mind trained in the school of Condé and Vauban, this was rank heresy, for the object of eighteenth-century tactics was to avoid a pitched battle for as long as possible. Marshal Saxe had written that a capable commander might well get through a whole campaign without having to fight a battle.

Considering the composition of the armies of that century, it was a prudent ambition, if only on economic grounds, since all the armies concerned were highly trained and extremely expensive professional soldiers, who were the personal possessions of their kings and were not to be considered as what a later generation would call "expendable." Frederick's famous grenadiers, for example, were recruited and trained at enormous cost, lavishly clothed and equipped and were generally regarded as the finest infantry in Europe. Frederick knew very well that if his grenadiers were to suffer heavy casualties it would take a long time and cost a fortune to bring the regiment up to strength again.

It was chiefly for this reason that the vulgar expedient of the pitched battle was excluded from orthodox tactics and that the fortress became of so much importance. War was to be purely a business of manoeuvre, with fortresses as objectives and the cutting of the enemy's lines of communication taking the place of battles. Manoeuvres were further restricted by the system of supply, which was to set up food stores in certain defined places within the area and to use these as pivots of manoeuvre. Since such supplies were often stored in fortresses, it was a further reason for regarding the fortress as the basis of strategy and tactics. When both sides knew and adhered to these rules, war became a dignified and predictable process with opposing commanders making move and countermove like opponents in chess.

It sometimes happened that, in spite of all skill in manoeuvring, two armies met head-on with no alternative but to fight it out. When this happened, the reason for manoeuvring to avoid battles and casualties became apparent, for casualties in battle were enormous in comparison with the number engaged. Tactics on the actual field of battle were as rigid as in the previous movements. Armies fought for the most part in line, being meticulous in preserving their dressing and reserving their fire as long as they could be taught to, with the final object of firing a volley at a range of no more than a hundred yards. At anything above this range the contemporary musket was hopelessly unreliable, but at close quarters the weight of the bullet alone ensured that any man who was hit was either killed or so badly disabled as to be unable to take any further part in the battle. Naturally an attack of this sort needed troops who were not only very brave but rigidly disciplined. It was an ordeal for the advancing line to come on without firing, probably under cannon fire, keeping their dressing and their steady pace and seeing before them the ranks of the enemy from whom at any moment there might come a volley to blast them before they could fire a shot. It was even more of an ordeal for the troops who stood on the defensive to watch the oncoming line, silent except for the drums which were marking the pace, and to hold their fire until the order was given.

The whole story of Wellington's campaigns from 1794 until 1815 is really the story of the old tactics, especially of the line and the volley against the new methods of the French, whose way it was to attack in column covered by a screen of sharpshooters. The French Revolutionary armies adopted the column formation in attack as soon as they went into their first battles. Its invention is usually attributed to Carnot, an engineer officer who had just become Minister for War and was shrewd and experienced enough to estimate the caliber of the new armies and the formations which they could be trusted to adopt. He knew that for them to attempt an attack in line would be to court disaster, and the formation which he laid down for them was the column. It had the great advantage for raw troops that in it they were closely massed together and that all but the leading ranks were less exposed to enemy fire and gained confidence from the feeling of having comrades in front, beside and behind them. The front of the column, being narrow, would only be vulnerable to such of the enemy as were more or less immediately in front of them, though—and this was one of its great dangers—the whole column would become vulnerable on either or both flanks if the enemy were able to bring forward troops to enfilade them. A further disadvantage was that when the column came within musket range only a small party of their firepower could be used against the enemy lines, and the muskets in the centre and rest of the column could not come into play until the front of the column broke up or was destroyed. Carnot realized this but, being convinced that a column was the only formation possible for armies with the sort of training which his could be expected to attain, devised a widening of the front of fire by adding a screen of extended sharpshooters to cover the column in its advance, to keep down enemy fire and then to withdraw and let the column go through to the attack.

It was the classic formation in which Napoleon fought all his great victories, and he has often been credited with its introduction into the French Army; but Carnot's orders are clearly the origin of it, and Napoleon adopted it because his troops were used to it and because he found that when the enemy's front was shaken the column had the advantage of great penetrating power. He kept almost invariably Carnot's screen of sharpshooters but improved on the original idea by protecting the flanks of the attacking column with other units moving in echelon on one or both sides or else with cavalry or advanced batteries. It was especially in his use of cavalry and still more of artillery that he departed from established rules and showed his own genius.

The eighteenth-century tactics had made almost a fetish of dividing guns and cavalry when drawing up a line of battle. It was customary to have a body of horse on each flank and another in reserve in rear of the main body of infantry and to use them by single regiments as the necessity arose to follow up a successful infantry attack or to counter-attack when the enemy had failed to penetrate the defence and were retreating to reform. Guns were generally placed in small groups at intervals in the infantry line of battle and dealt with targets in their immediate area.

Napoleon believed that unless artillery concentrated their fire they would lose half of their effect. His principle was always to allot as many guns to one part of his front as he could spare and never to split them up into half-batteries or sections which could only give a weak and largely ineffective curtain of fire along a whole front. In the same way he early began to keep his cavalry concentrated and eventually held practically the whole of them in a cavalry reserve, under Murat's command, and used the whole weight of them in one stroke at some crucial point in the battle, to complete a victory or to retrieve a failure. Moreover, in this way he had them concentrated and under his own hand when the moment came to launch the pursuit of a beaten enemy, which was one of his most effective strokes and which, as at Austerlitz and Jena, completed the enemy's discomfiture and turned a more or less orderly retirement into a panic-stricken flight.

One of the most fatal results of the Russian Campaign in 1812 was the complete destruction of his cavalry, for complete it was. Of the 60,000 horsemen whom he led into Russia not one serviceable horse returned, and only a handful of his trained horsemen. He knew the extent of the loss especially in horses, since good troop horses cannot be trained in a matter of months. All through the campaigns of 1813 and 1814 he was weak in cavalry and had to economize in their use. Even at Waterloo, where his cavalry were relatively strong, there were too many half-trained men and green horses among them. Wellington, unlike so many British generals before and after him, was an infantryman, and it was with infantry that he won nearly all of his fights. The British infantry when he joined the Army had earned for themselves a great name in earlier wars on the Continent, since the eighteenth-century tactics were particularly suitable for their methods and their greatest strength, which lay in their fire control.

Individually they were not particularly good marksmen, though this was largely the fault of their famous musket, Brown Bess, which, like any other musket of the day, was only accurate up to about a hundred yards. It was their volley firing which had gained them such a name when they fought under Marlborough and later at Dettingen and Fontenoy and Minden. So strict was their discipline and so constantly were they exercised in the volley that it was said by European critics that they could hold fire longer and fire more closely in unison than any other infantry of their time. That had always been their way, even before they took to the musket. The fire orders which launched the British volley were echoes of the master-bowman's "Shoot wholly together" at Crécy and Agincourt. It would still be their way before Ypres in the autumn of 1914 when German officers refused to believe that the British infantry who held the line at Geluveld were not all armed with automatic rifles, so rapid and sustained was their rifle fire.

But the army with which Colonel Wesley first saw service was very different from the veteran army of the Seven Years' War. At no time had Britain's military reputation stood higher than after the exploits of Wolfe's men at Quebec and of the six British infantry regiments which had charged and broken the French cavalry at Minden. But since then they had declined in numbers and in quality, and their more recent actions in America suggested that not only was their leadership incompetent but the troops themselves had fallen off in training and in endurance. The first cause of the decline was the inevitable reduction of strength at the end of the war.

No nation wished to carry a larger standing army in peacetime than was necessary, if only on account of the expense, but the British aversion to the idea of the standing army at all—another legacy from Cromwell—always impelled them to reduce its strength without any relation to the tasks which, even in peacetime, it was called on to do. The whole story of the British Army had been one of sudden expansion for war and over-drastic reduction after it. Politicians who preach economy are always on safe grounds when they suggest a reduction in the Army Vote. Even more dangerous has always been the tendency to starve what few troops are kept of everything that they need for training, so that every time they have been called on to fight, they have begun each war with obsolete equipment left over from the last. It can never be easy to recruit enough good men into a body which is the subject of general dislike in the country, and in the army of 1780 and the following years the quality of the men was very poor. Wellington himself said later of his own army that they were the "scum of the earth—they have enlisted for drink, that is the truth." To "go for a soldier" in those days was looked on by the soldier's fellow countrymen as the final step toward degradation. "Its rank and file," Sir Arthur Bryant writes, "were unemployed artisans, jailbirds and village bad-hats who had exhausted every other resource but enlistment in a despised calling. They had no continuity of employment, no interest in their profession save regimental pride and little hope of gratitude from the community they served. For England still regarded with jealousy a force which might be used to increase the power of the Executive."

The way in which this army was officered was another scandal. The purchase system was bad enough in itself, but it was made even worse by the cynical way in which it was abused for personal ends. Every regiment carried on its strength a few officers whom it did not know by sight because they had never done a day's duty with it. Some of these purchase officers were children for whom their parents had bought a commission before they were out of the nursery, so that if the children wanted to soldier when they grew up, they would start with many years' seniority over men who had served with their regiments and been, perhaps, in action. It is said that a nursery maid in a great Scottish house was once ordered to "leave what you're doing, now, and take the Colonel's porridge and the Major's bread and milk up to the nursery." That this was sober truth and not exaggeration is proved by one of the first actions of the Duke of York on his appointment to the Command-in-Chief in March 1795. He sent out to all units a circular calling for a return of all captains under twelve years of age and all lieutenant-colonels under twenty.

Undoubtedly many of the officers who really did serve at home and abroad were excellent leaders of men, and almost invariably they were brave in action; but they were appallingly ignorant about their profession, and in peacetime at home, when they should have been learning the elements and getting to know their men, they devoted nearly the whole of their time to hunting, racing, gambling and drinking and only put in token appearances with their units. Whatever may have been the Duke of York's merits as a commander it was he who first tackled the problem of training a peacetime army, especially of ensuring that officers knew and did their duty. He instituted the system of confidential reports which is still in use today. Commanders-in-Chief had left the training of their men entirely to the regimental commanders, but the Duke issued training schedules for all units, and his inspectors saw to it that they were observed. One of the greatest debts which the Army owes to him was the idea of special training colleges for officers which came to reality in Sandhurst, Woolwich and the Staff College.

After the Seven Years' War the British Army was reduced to a total establishment of 45,000 men, of whom only 15,000 were at home. The rest were scattered all over the world on various stations. The normal strength of the French before the Revolution was half a million. As soon as war broke out in 1793, Pitt introduced a bill to raise 25,000 recruits for the Army and to embody 19,000 additional men in the Militia. He dared not resort to compulsion, which the country, even in a bellicose mood, would have resented, and the results of appeals for volunteers were so meagre that the government was compelled to resort to the undignified expedient of bribing men to accept commissions on condition that it would enlist a certain number of men to serve under them. With every 450 men added to the strength of a battalion, one major could acquire a lieutenant-colonelcy for £600 and two captains majorities for £500 to £770. Companies were sold to any bidder for £2,800 and the price of recruits per head rose to £30. This squalid scheme succeeded in raising 30,000 men at very little cost to the public, but that was its sole benefit.

The men were useless, since anything that could walk on two legs was considered good enough to qualify as a soldier. They were unfit, diseased, mentally unsound, capable neither of marching nor of using weapons. The officers whom this scheme added were no improvement on the men, since commissions were given simply in exchange for recruits without any inquiry as to the fitness of the applicant to command men and carry a sword. Once again it proved a useful investment for fathers on behalf of their sons, and the least damage was often done when these were children in the nursery, since at least they did not interfere. The real menace was the young man who had no hope of getting a commission in the normal way, when even a purchase officer must be accepted by the colonel of his regiment as suitable. Now money was the only criterion, and there were some unhappy regiments where officers of many years' service found themselves under the command of a lieutenant-colonel with neither knowledge nor breeding but with the cash necessary to buy himself in at that rank. It was well for the country that the Duke of York took a firm line directly he became Commander-in-Chief, for these panic measures had done the Army infinite damage and had come near to ruining it. Not all traces of the harm had been removed when Wellington took command in the Peninsula.

VI

IT WAS THE YEAR 1795 and the war against the young French Republic was over. The British and their allies had retreated in different directions after a campaign in which the British had been engaged at La Cateau, Ypres, Poperinghe, Furnes, had made a fighting withdrawal from Dunkirk and had, at last, been taken off in transports and sailed for home escorted by the indomitable Navy. The Channel ports were in enemy hands; the Army which returned was weary and disillusioned, and had lost much of its arms and equipment. England, having jeopardized the small Regular Army after having all but ruined it for the sake of economy and political advantage, was belatedly rearming. The country swarmed with hastily formed and ill-armed units for home defence in case of invasion. The government, after having nearly been defeated on a vote of confidence, was broadening its basis and turning itself into a coalition by allotting a few of the minor posts to members of the opposition.

Yet anyone reading of Britain's position in 1795, without knowing the year, might be excused for taking it for another crisis more than a century and a half later. And, to emphasize the comparison, in that early spring of 1795, the voice of a great Prime Minister spoke for Britain and rallied her courage and energy. Pitt admitted the greatness of the reverse which they had suffered but wrote, "It ought to have the effect of increasing if possible our exertions." A week or two later, he said in the House of Commons, "It has pleased inscrutable Providence that this

PART I : 1769-1797

power of France should triumph over everything that has been opposed to it. But let us not therefore fall without making any efforts to resist it. Let us not sink without measuring its strength." He then turned his attention to strengthening Britain's alliance with any other country which would undertake to stand with her against the common enemy. (For recreation he would send for his maps and produce ambitious schemes by which the enemy could be surprised and defeated by landings on inaccessible beaches or attacks from impracticable directions, schemes from which he had to be gently dissuaded by his more skilled advisers.)

The British took their loss calmly, since they had never been much in favour of the venture to the Low Countries and also since they have always had a tendency to regard a skillful retreat as identical with a victory. The country was not frightened but it was excited and bellicose. If the variety of new uniforms which sprang up all over the counties could have frightened the French, then the invasion was a danger past. Yeomanry, Hussars, Volunteers, Militia, turned out to drill on the village green and marched swinging down the roads between hedges just beginning to grow green with spring. Each new unit that was raised tried to excel its predecessors in dress which rivalled the brightest colours of summer. A vast number of patriotic songs were written and sung to rapturous applause; a wealth of patriotic oratory was expended to stimulate recruiting. This was—as she would be again—England "standing alone" and rather pleased with herself in consequence, the confidence of a nation which had never been invaded, a little boastful perhaps and with a regrettable tendency to see the enemy as ridiculous rather than menacing. This was England at her best, as she had been before and would be again when in mortal danger.

But, as before and to be again, there was also Britain at her worst—a little frightened, even if she neither knew nor admitted it, a little over-generous in making sacrifices which might be difficult to restrain and, above all, jolted out of her traditional tolerance into a suspicious and cruel mood against possible enemies within her own limits. It was the sort of tension in which race riots or persecutions are born and flourish and in which the short view takes precedence of any long-term project. Worst of all, it is a mood of which advantage can easily be taken by those who wish to subject their fellows to their own principles or their own ideas of how the country should be governed, the mood which in France follows the cry of *"La Patrie est en danger."*

In such a situation the more generously minded will, on impulse, surrender or endanger certain of their liberties in the belief that they will be restored when the crisis is over. But there are always men who are ready to take advantage of an impulse of this sort to further their own ideas and who, having once restricted a liberty or imposed a restraint, will fight to keep it after the necessity has passed. Particularly is this a danger when the restrainers have already been on the watch over a certain movement or temper among the people and see their opportunity to curb or crush it. So William Pitt in the crisis of 1795 seized his opportunity of attacking certain liberties of speech and writing and of crushing the growing demand in the country for Parliamentary reform. The method was the usual one of prolonging a temporary restriction. In 1795 Parliament suspended habeas corpus and it was to remain suspended till 1801.

The suspension was immediately followed by the Treasonable Practices Act and the Seditious Meetings Act. One vastly increased the number of offences which could be classed as treason and dispensed with overt proof of any treasonous act; the other banned public meetings of more than fifty people without the superintendence of a magistrate. Both bills were passed with a large majority which encouraged Pitt to go on to the Combination Act of 1799, which dissolved all existing trade unions or associations and made it a criminal offence for two or more men to concert together for the purpose of asking for higher wages.

As soon as these various bills became law the government instigated a number of prosecutions, most of which were of writers or speakers who had criticized the government or had spoken approvingly of the French. But Pitt, in his youth and inexperience, had miscalculated the temper of the nation, which was indeed frightened and vindictive enough, but not so much as to be forgetful of all sense of justice and men's right to a fair trial. Many of the prosecutions in England miscarried, notably those of Tooke and Thelwall, two radical campaigners who were put on trial for high treason, though the jury found the accused guilty of only some technical offence connected with the holding of public meetings. They served a short term of imprisonment, but the acquittal on the main charge was a heavy defeat for the government. Not for the first time the integrity of a jury and the impartiality of a judge had defended the rights of the people. Pitt and his advisers had sense enough to take warning and brought no more such prosecutions in England, though they prospered better in Scotland largely because of the ferocity of Lord Braxfield who presided at some of the trials.

Pitt was undoubtedly a great Prime Minister and probably the best handler of government finance since Robert Walpole. His courage and persistence kept Britain's allies in the battle with France until Napoleon was defeated. In home affairs he made great and beneficial changes in the Poor Laws, and in spite of the cost of war and especially of the subsidies which he paid out to the allies, he kept Britain solvent. He was in fact, though not nominally, his own Chancellor of the Exchequer; his budgets, which even when Prime Minister he often introduced himself, were held to be models of economy and prudence. But he bears a heavy load of guilt for the persecution which he instigated and encouraged of men whose only fault was that their opinions differed from his. "The habit of repression," Sir George Trevelyan writes, "begun by Pitt against a majority in time of war had become the custom of the country and was continued by Pitt's successors in time of peace. The partisanship of government against the poor and against those who attempted to plead their cause, however natural during the French Revolution and the French war, distorted and embittered the social processes of the Industrial Revolution and left marks which were never entirely healed in the remedial period that followed."

VII

COLONEL WESLEY'S first campaign, in the Low Countries, was nearly to be his last, in such a disillusioned mood did he return to England. He had seen, he said, "the way in which commands are given out," and he did not like it. He had seen the Duke of York, at the age of twenty-eight, in command for no better reason than his birth, and subject to the control and advice of a few senior officers, most of whom were senile or incompetent. He had seen, above all, the importance which the Horse Guards, the office in England which controlled commands and promotions, attached to seniority and the indifference with which they regarded efficiency and initiative, so that competent officers like Lord Moira were sent home, to be replaced by nonentities who happened to be a few years senior to them. Finally he had seen the whole tragic confusion of an army thrust into a campaign without direction or objective, with allies but no common plan and with grossly inadequate transport and supplies. He had commanded a brigade, not without success, but there was no honour or promotion for him. In fact, there were few honours of any sort awarded or deserved, though the Duke of York, who had mismanaged the whole affair, was rewarded by promotion to Commander-in-Chief. The French had begun to stimulate their commanders to greater efforts by guillotining a few of the more unsuccessful of them, beginning with a General Custine, but the English were more merciful or expected less of theirs. After the Seven Years' War, Lord George Sackville, who had been court-martialed for failing to take the cavalry into action at Minden in 1759, was appointed Secretary for War for the Colonies, in which capacity and under the name of Germaine he mismanaged the American War of Independence. In the same way, H.R.H. the Duke of York went to the Horse Guards as Commander-in-Chief, though, unlike Sackville, he proved to be most efficient as an administrator.

Wesley came home from Holland in April 1795 determined to abandon his army career, though he hoped to retain his rank and pay in addition to such new posts as he might find. He was beginning to worry about his debts, and there was the pleasing though not immediate prospects of marrying Miss Pakenham. A lieutenant-colonel's pay, together with the allowances of an aide-de-camp, which he still was, amounted to little more than £500 a year, to say nothing of the necessity of saving a sum of capital to buy further promotion. His nephew, Long Wellesley, is supposed to have remarked that no man could live like a gentleman in London under £10,000 a year. Even in Ireland a married man could hardly be said to exist on £500, so there was urgent need for some other occupation.

The 33rd Foot were in camp in Essex but their commanding officer was not at the moment interested in them. They would be looked after by somebody or other but his own need was urgent and his thoughts turned first to Ireland. He was known there and he was already an aide-de-camp to the Lord Lieutenant, but unfortunately for him there had been considerable changes since last he saw Dublin Castle. Colonel Wesley was now to learn the uncomfortable truth that places and preferment go to the man who is on the spot when the vacancy occurs and that a man who is away for a few months might as well have been away for the same number of years for all the memory that he leaves in official minds.

There were always places or sinecures or pensions to be had in Dublin for men who knew how to get them. Bad as was political bribery in England, it was nothing to the wholesale corruption of Ireland under British rule in that century. The Irish Parliament was dominated by members from privately owned boroughs, who voted without question for the man who had put them into the seat. It was all part of the cynical opportunism with which England governed Ireland purely for England's own benefit. But, Wesley was to find, though there were many gratuities there were even more applicants, and since most of the patronage in the country was in the gift of the Lord Lieutenant and his staff, no one who was not well known to them had much chance of getting any of it.

There had been two changes in the Viceroyalty of Ireland since Colonel Wesley had last been in that country. The new Viceroy, Lord Camden, knew nothing about him and in any case was too busy in trying to rectify the eccentricities of his predecessor, Lord Fitzwilliam, one of the best intentioned and least discreet rulers known to Irish history. Fitzwilliam had grievously offended Pitt by announcing his acceptance of the position before Pitt had made public the offer and had aggravated his offence by publishing his intentions to grant full emancipation to the Irish Catholics. Pitt was not against the proposal but knew that it must be introduced by degrees and had already persuaded the Irish Parliament to pass an act enfranchising the Catholics in 1793, though they were still prevented from serving in the Army as officers and from becoming members of the Irish Parliament or holding any office under the Crown. It was a ridiculous situation, when more than three-quarters of the population were Catholics, that the Protestant Church should be established by law and that all public offices should be in Protestant hands. There had not been a Catholic Viceroy since Lord Tyrconnel in the time of James II.

Pitt would willingly have gone a long way further toward complete emancipation but was hindered by the obstinacy of the King, who was convinced that to agree to it would be a violation of his coronation oath. It was one point on which Pitt knew that it would be impossible to persuade him, especially as his first attack of madness had been accompanied by a fierce struggle between the Irish and English Parliaments about the regency. Pitt honestly believed that the idea of emancipation, if it were pressed on the King, might result in a further attack and had promised that he would never consent to its introduction while the King lived. But he meant to work for the benefit of Irish Catholics by degrees so that, when the day should come, he or his successor would without difficulty be able to free them from all restrictions.

There was still some Jacobite sentiment alive in Ireland and the idea of a landing by the French to help the Irish regain their liberty had been in all their minds as a possibility and a pious hope. In the years which followed 1789, there grew up a crop of more or less secret societies, a form of activity always dear to Irish hearts, calling themselves by such names as "The Steelboys," "The Peep o'Day Boys," "The Orangemen" and "The Ribbonmen." At first these sprang up in the predominantly Protestant north, but they were soon copied in the Catholic south. Their main and avowed object was to drive out the English and restore the historic Island of the Saints, but, as a secondary aim, they were quite content to fight each other till it was time to combine against the English.

The Revolution in France renewed every hope that Ireland had ever had, and in 1791 Wolfe Tone, Thomas Russell and Napper Tandy, with some less well known patriots, formed the Irish Society, which denounced all previous treaties with England and demanded the establishment of a separate Irish Republic, by negotiation if possible but, failing that, by force. The hope of negotiation was plainly little more than a gesture, for Tone was soon going to and from Paris, pleading for armed support for a proposed rising. Conspirators are not generally at their best when they come to the details of their schemes, and the synchronization of rising and French help was at fault by two years. In 1796 a French force under General Hoche got as far as Bantry Bay but were scattered by a gale and were either driven back so far that they lost touch with the rest of the fleet or were wrecked. The rising, which should have taken place at the same time, misfired and, after several postponements, began in 1798. It was an abject failure from the start, since the first thing that the Catholics did was to hunt for Protestants whom they killed in the most brutal fashion, while the Protestants of the north did nothing to help anyone.

It is hardly surprising that in the middle of all this stress, the ministers responsible and the Viceroy of Ireland had no time to consider the needs of an impecunious and not very influential colonel of infantry. Colonel Wesley was tireless in his approach to authorities in London and Dublin, beginning his applications with a proposal that he should be appointed Secretary for War and steadily reducing his scale of hope till he ended by begging for something, for almost anything, in the Revenue and Treasury Boards. His brother Richard, now a rising politician and a member of the Board of Control for India, loyally did what he could to help and wrote to Lord Camden about a possible vacancy in the office of the Surveyor-General for Ireland. Camden was polite but not encouraging, and in the autumn Colonel Wesley gave up the attempt and resigned himself to a military career. The 33rd was stationed near Southampton, and he joined it there with cold comfort of a promise from Lord Camden that "I shall be very glad if I can make some arrangement satisfactory to you against your come back, but, if a vacancy should happen in the Revenue Board, I fear that Speaker's son must have the first."

In his letter Lord Camden congratulated Wesley on "your determination to accompany your regiment to the West Indies, as I am convinced that a profession once embraced should not be given up." Colonel Wesley had by now come to the same conclusion. As he could not afford to marry Miss Pakenham, he parted from her with an understanding that on his return he would renew his suit, should his financial position have improved enough to warrant it. He was never anything but a tepid suitor, but he was all that Kitty Pakenham wanted and she promised to wait for him for as long as might be needed.

The 33rd embarked for the voyage to Barbados in November, but after being storm-stayed at sea for six weeks, they were ordered to disembark at Poole (in Dorset), where they stayed till the spring of 1796.

Colonel Wesley was ill during most of that winter, as a legacy from the hardships of the campaign in Holland. The 33rd did not see much of their colonel, who was often in London consulting doctors about his recurrent fever and making such arrangements as he could for paying his more pressing debts. He was a little consoled by his promotion to full colonel but did not recover his health enough to warrant his travelling with the 33rd, now transferred to India. They sailed in the late spring, and he stayed at Portsmouth till the end of June, when he left in a fast frigate and caught up with the slower troopship at the Cape. Halfway through February 1797 Colonel Wesley and his regiment landed at Calcutta. He had never really wanted to be a soldier but there seemed to be nothing else for it. It was his destiny and at last he accepted it.

PART II

1797-1805

VIII

W HEN COLONEL WESLEY sailed for India in 1797, he had no reason
to expect, and probably did not look forward to, anything beyond
the routine work of a regimental officer, possibly enlivened by a minor
campaign, and, in due course, promotion to the command of a brigade
of infantry. His ambition must have run a little beyond this, since he told
someone soon after his arrival, "My highest ambition is to serve His
Majesty as a major-general."

Certainly he had no idea that within the next few years his elder
brother Richard, Earl of Mornington since their father's death, would
follow him out to India, where together they would have a large share in
the work of converting the property of a trading company into an em-
bryo empire. Mornington was already a member of the Board of Control,
the government department which supervised the operation of the Honourable East India Company, who were then and would be for another
century and a half, the legal owners of British India. Not till 1858, after
the Indian Mutiny, would India pass into the direct rule of the Crown
and be transformed by the exuberant and oriental fancy of Disraeli into
the Indian Empire. The British had recently lost one group of colonies,
by their inept dealing with their possessions in America. They were now
about to acquire another in their own casual and empirical fashion. The
way Britain won India is typical of her methods and her people. She can
never be numbered among the great exploring nations of the world as
Spain and Portugal and, to a lesser degree, France had been. The nature

of her people was too matter-of-fact and too little visionary to set out deliberately to plant her flag on a foreign land for the honour of discovery and dominion. She was quite willing to leave that to more visionary peoples and preferred to take away from them what they had already found and proved to be profitable. All her overseas possessions were won by private traders in the pursuit of their business. They came, for the most part, without official support, financed their own ventures, took the responsibility for their own defence and pocketed the proceeds. When their possessions became greater and the proceeds worth the attention of a perpetually hungry government, or the problem of their protection threatened to be too serious for their own amateur fighters, then the soldiers followed to protect the traders; and eventually another territory was added to the piecemeal collection which Britain, the jackdaw of the world, was amassing.

It was only in the second half of the eighteenth century that the concept of India as a responsibility to be shouldered as well as an endless treasure house to be ransacked began to grow in the British political mind, and its development owed almost everything to Hastings, who went out as Governor-General in 1772. The company's trading rights were held under an act of 1744 and were due to expire in 1780. The British government had for a long time been casting envious glances toward a source of revenue far richer than any other that had ever been open to them, but which lay in the hands of a private trading company who had no intention of sharing it. Apart from the question of profit, it was becoming obvious that British India was far too large and too vulnerable a property to be protected and controlled with only such modest resources as John Company could muster. The French in the south were still a potential danger behind which lurked the graver possibility of a deliberate attempt by France to summon enough strength to invade India and to turn out the British. Such an idea indeed lay already in the mind of General Bonaparte, in which fantastic dreams of oriental splendour kept company with a very practical belief that the best way to injure Britain was to strike at her through India—a belief which led him to the venture and disaster of his Egyptian expedition in 1799. "The master of Egypt" must eventually be the master of India, and his instructions from the Directory were to "chase the English from all their possessions in the East that he can reach." If Britain wished to keep India, she would have to provide troops for its defence, money and administrators for its government. The happy days of irresponsible plundering were over, the days when men of no particular ability had made fantastic fortunes in a very short time and had returned to England to spend them with an ostentation and extravagance which earned for them from a half-contemp-tuous, half-envious society at home the nickname of "Nabobs."

Clive's achievement at Plassey had stirred British imagination, and India's prosperity under Hastings suggested that a new British dominion in the East might more than compensate for the loss of the Thirteen Colonies in the West. In any case there would have to be some decision taken before the company's privileges expired in 1780. There were plenty of leading men in both political parties who thought that they knew how India should be administered, and within a few years both Fox and Pitt were to introduce Indian bills into Parliament. The Regulat-ing Act of 1774 was really an interim measure to tide over the date of expiry of the company's rights and to provide a system pending a per-manent settlement. It had all the demerits of a compromise, as well as some of the merits, and it still left the respective spheres of rights and duties of the company and the government ill-defined, but it did assert the government's right to interfere in Indian affairs and put a check on irresponsible acts and assumption of power by the company's servants. Its main organ of regulation was a government body, called the Board of Control, which did not supersede the court of the company but exer-cised some control over it at home and also in India by the newly-ap-pointed council, whose chief duty was to advise and control the Governor-General. The first connection between the Wesley family and India was Lord Mornington's appointment to membership of the board, which was to lead a few years later to his selection as Governor-General. But, for the moment, the two men who had most effect on Indian policy and on the fortunes of the Governor-General were Edmund Burke at home and Philip Francis in India, where he was a member of the council.

History has never satisfactorily accounted for the extraordinary venom which was Francis' almost sole distinction. He was a man of little breed-ing or education and of only the most moderate ability, whose employ-ment as a War Office clerk had only been remarkable for his abominable manner toward anyone of whom he was not afraid. He represents the ideal example of what the British rail at as the "bureaucrat" or "Jack in Office," but he was more. He was not simply boorish or a snob, though he was both. He seems to have been one of those fortunately few men who love viciousness for its own sake or for the appeasement of some deep inner need or wound in themselves. He is now generally accepted as having been the author of the famous "Letters of Junius," those polit-ical diatribes of the eighteenth century which are as blasting and as merciless as anything in the history of anonymous stabbing. What inner devil tore him no one knew or can now guess. He lived all his life like a wounded beast striking out at anything or anyone that came near him.

The reason for Francis' selection as a councillor in India has not yet been discovered, though undoubtedly Burke's mistaken fancy for him helped his advancement. Nothing in his previous history suggested that he was fit to keep the insignificant job that he had, far less to deserve promotion to one of vast responsibility and at a salary of £10,000 a year. Yet promoted he was and it was he, more than any other man, who ruined Hastings—ruined him deliberately, of set purpose, without reason and without any attempt at understanding. It would almost seem that he had determined on this course before he ever set foot in India, and of India he knew nothing except that it was governed by the class of rich and successful men to which he knew he could never belong. If he had any other ideas at all, they were the ill-digested remnants of a superficial study of a few of the recently published works of metaphysics which gave him some hazy feelings about the rights of the people.

Perhaps Tragedy revolted at the paltry figure of Francis as the agent of the Gods or more simply the fault lay in the chance that while the principals were word perfect, the chorus had been inadequately rehearsed. Whatever the reason—perhaps Mr. Sheridan appreciated the dramatic rightness of it—there was a farce to be played as a curtain raiser before the main piece, and the curtain raiser was to last for three years.

In April 1782 Dundas rose in the House to move the recall of Hastings to England, and the House agreed to the motion a fortnight later. But the House had reckoned without the court of John Company and without the tortuous ingenuities of their own Regulating Act. They found that they had no power to recall a Governor-General. All that they could do was to request the court in Leadenhall Street to petition the Crown at Windsor to allow Parliament at Westminster to recall Hastings from Calcutta. This the court flatly refused to do, having every reason to be grateful for the wealth which Hastings had earned for them and caring little about the methods by which he had won it. Between June, when they first defied Parliament, and October, when they grudgingly gave way, they held eleven meetings to discuss the position. When, at last, they gave way, they were promptly set right themselves by the Court of Proprietors—the equivalent of the modern general meeting of shareholders—who reversed, as they had power to do, the decision of the Court of Directors.

Hastings remained in India and India remained one of the main preoccupations of Parliament. General policy, for a time, thrust the Governor-General into the background until Parliament could decide between the rival policies submitted to them by Whigs and Tories, in Fox's and Pitt's Indian bills. And there was a diversion and a flurry of excitement in home affairs when the King made one of his last attempts to interfere with parliamentary government by sending to his faithful Commons a message: "Those who vote for Mr. Fox's India bill will not be considered friends of the King."

By now it was December 1783. The Commons voted that it was a breach of privilege to report any opinion of His Majesty to Parliament in session. His Majesty, having failed to get his way by indirect methods, defied the House and dismissed the government. The coalition, which had lasted for eight months, was out. The Tories were in. The case of Hastings took on a new urgency and importance as a counter-attack against the new administration.

Hastings himself saved his enemies from any further trouble in recalling him by offering his resignation. He had studied the new Indian Bill and seen that the old autocratic rule of the Governor-General was over. He had no mind to become one official among many. The actors began to gather for the tragedy. Mr. Burke's preparations for playing the lead were hampered by the unwelcome necessity of appearing in another court to defend himself on a charge of sodomy—a charge of which he was in fact guiltless but which was given some suggestion of probability because of the violence with which he had defended the general cause of those accused of that vice. For that or some reason, he was below his histrionic best when he appeared in the House to speak on India and was warned that if he continued to insult the House, his extravagance would no longer be tolerated.

Burke was howled down in the House in July 1784 when he moved for papers relative to the conduct of Hastings in a characteristically extravagant speech replete with appeals to Providence and the wrath of Heaven, which he emphasized by swearing a sacred oath on the Report of a Select Committee which had to do duty for a missing Testament. But his demon would not let him rest and Nemesis was still waiting for Hastings, who landed in England on June 13, 1785. A week later, on the twentieth, Burke gave formal notice in the House that he would, in due course, bring in a motion "to enquire into the conduct of a gentleman lately returned from India." There could be no stopping it now and the stage was to be Westminster Hall.

The trial was prolonged for seven years. The court sat for fifty-five days in 1788, seventeen in 1789, fourteen in 1790 and only five days in 1791. Public interest had soon faded and even the managers began to lose heart. Burke, indeed, was indefatigable having, for once, found an ideal subject for his style of oratory and being bent on making a full and public exposition of his theories of colonial government.

In 1792 and again in 1793 the court sat for twenty-two days, but the next year, probably because of dangers from abroad, there were only five sessions. It was in this year that Joseph Farington, the artist, looked in as he was passing the hall and found "not above five and twenty" people there—and not only that, but was shocked to the depth of his artistic soul by the décor and costumes. The trial was no longer a fashion parade and peers came to it—if they came at all—unrobed and without their coronets. The Commons had never had much decorative value and Lady Cherlemont, who sat opposite to them throughout several long dull days, found them "creatures looking so little like gentlemen and so much like hairdressers." But what shocked Mr. Farington most of all was the sight of Charles Grey in the manager's box wearing riding boots and spurs. It was plainly time to put an end to an affair in which nobody took any more interest and Burke made his closing speech in 1795 when he won back the record by speaking for nine days.

Hastings was a free man again but ruined financially and blasted in reputation. The court of the company, who had never been unsympathetic, lent him the money with which to pay his costs, and he had saved just enough for a quiet existence at Daylesford, the old home of his ancestors which, while still a boy and lonely after his parents' death, he had sworn to buy back some day as a home for his own retirement and a permanent possession for his family. Even this he could not have done had not the court of John Company, who were not without gratitude, lent him the money at a low rate of interest. They had never been really opposed to him, for he had enormously increased their wealth and they had found him scrupulously honest in his personal dealings. It may be that they did not choose to inquire too closely into the means used to pay their satisfactory dividends.

On the whole, public sympathy was on Hastings' side and has been ever since. The attack upon him was so venomous and excessive that many people could not help seeing in it some personal vendetta and a trace of political opportunism. Undoubtedly he did a number of things which he ought not to have done and several quite proper things in the wrong way. He was autocratic, almost despotic, but he was governing in a country where only such methods were understood. History has struck a fairer balance between his good deeds and bad and has not failed to mark—as no one did at the time—that he was the first Governor-General of India who took any interest in India's traditional art and literature. He was himself neither artist nor scholar, but he had a respect for learning and he was far ahead of his time in trying to stimulate the native talents of the land which he governed. One somewhat less important habit of his, which distressed the court because they had to pay for it, was his insistence on keeping an establishment of some splendour and his

WELLINGTON

By Sir Thomas Lawrence, Apsley House

NEW GOVERNMENT HOUSE, CALCUTTA

taste for building in the grand style. He argued in correspondence with Leadenhall Street that Oriental peoples did not understand a ruler who showed no visible signs of his power and wealth or who lived in anything but a palace. The argument may or may not be valid, and it is a suspiciously comfortable one for a man whose tastes lie in those directions. Hastings, on the testimony of men who knew him and served under him, had little interest in personal display and was always the most soberly dressed person at any of the grand entertainments which he was expected to give, but, by contrast with his predecessors, he gave an impression of extravagance to the men at home who had to foot the bill.

As soon as he resigned they instituted a campaign of rigorous retrenchment and impressed the necessity of it on the Governors who came after Hastings. Lord Cornwallis was a soldier and had spent so many years in active service that he had grown accustomed to doing with the minimum of personal comfort, and Sir John Shore, who succeeded him, was a man of the most simple tastes, so that the directors congratulated themselves on having killed once and for all the tradition of the Governor-General's magnificent background. If Hastings' trial had shown to the public that a Governor-General was only the company's servant and that condemnation waited for a man who tried to make himself into a royal personage, it would, they felt, be a very long time before any holder of the office would again try such methods. They proposed to appoint Lord Mornington who was a member of the Board of Control and so must know all about the need for economy and the shamefulness of personal display at the company's expense.

They must have suffered a severe shock before he had been very long in India, for, though his public actions were more circumspect than Hastings', his estimate of the state necessary for his household was infinitely greater than Hastings had ever thought of. The whole of his period of office in India was to have a running accompaniment of acrimonious correspondence about living expenses, his determination to increase the dignity of his office by enlarging old buildings and adding new ones and by increasing the size of his personal escort and the number of his servants, and most of all, his prudent habit of putting work in hand before telling the court that he contemplated it. Hastings may, as they thought, have had delusions of grandeur, but there were no delusions about Lord Mornington's. Hastings' trial may seem today a trivial happening hardly worthy of remembrance but it had great historical importance. It was the beginning of Britain's awareness of her dominions in India as something more than a source of wealth and something which needed constant governmental vigilance and control. Though India did

C

not become a British possession until 1858, the idea was recognized as a distant possibility before Mornington landed at Calcutta.

Clive fought Plassey and established the British Raj, in a rudimentary form, in 1757. The Hindoos prophesied that in a hundred years the British would be driven out of India. The Indian mutiny in 1857 came near to fulfilling the prophecy, but when it was all over, the prophets revised their estimate, blandly explaining that they had meant not one but two hundred years. This time they were right but for the matter of a few years. In 1954 the flag which had flown above the Residency of Lucknow ever since the siege in 1857 was struck by the British themselves. The sound of their bands died away down the great trunk roads, and India was at last a free country, or, taking into account the division with Pakistan, two free countries. The prophets had been nearly right this time, but they had made one more mistake. Britain was not driven out but went of her own free will and because she thought that it was right. If she took—as she did—much from India, she gave much back. If any critic of the British rule will compare the condition of India when the British came with the condition when they left, he will be hard put to it to maintain that her rule was not merciful and her care for the people of India genuine.

IX

THEIR NAME was Wellesley now. Colonel Wesley adopted the new style within a few days of landing in India in February 1797. It can hardly have been arranged without previous consultation with Richard, newly created Marquis of Wellesley and head of the family. The name of Wellesley had been in their ancestry as far back as the fourteenth century before its less dignified form of Wesley had crept in. A certain Waleran de Wellesley had owned land at Wellesley in Somerset—or, as some traditions said, at Wellington in the same country—before going to Ireland as Justice Itinerary. So the name had good authority behind it as well as being more euphonious than the "Wesley," with its faint flavour of religious irregularity. Lord Wellesley, as John Company was soon to find to its cost, was a man of large ideas in matters both public and private. It was not a name which had any earlier connection with India, nor was it to have a later one, after the few years when it blazed across the history of the British Raj. Even when Colonel Wellesley adopted it, he had no idea that his brother was soon to follow him to Calcutta, though Lord Mornington, as a member of the Board of Control, must have entertained hopes.

It was not by any means a light task to hold on to present gains, as the Wellesley brothers were soon to find out. The defence of India against foreign aggression—quite apart from the ever-present danger of native uprising—was to be a source of perpetual anxiety to British statesmen almost until the day when the British themselves left the country. The reports and correspondence of almost every Governor-General and Viceroy speak of threats from one or another foreign power, which in later years crystallized into the fear of Russia striking through Persia and Afghanistan.

The danger was real and pressing at the end of the eighteenth century, and it came, or threatened to come, from France, the enemy of half the world. Clive had destroyed Dupleix's rule in the south of India and had driven the French from the country, but he had never removed their influence over the native rulers or their determination through these to strike back at British possessions and power.

Great Indian powers like Mysore, under Tippoo Sultan, and like the Mahrattas, the most formidable fighting men in India, maintained enormous standing armies; and the officers who trained them and who would lead them in war were mostly French. A French garrison lay in Mauritius, a standing menace from which an invasion could be mounted when the time was ripe, for the Directory in Paris still looked covetously eastward toward their lost possessions there. Certainly there lurked in General Bonaparte's head ideas and ambitions no less imperial than any entertained by Hastings or Wellesley. The plan for his Egyptian expedition, which was to lead him on to India, was already being sketched out when Colonel Wellesley left England and was approved in March 1798, only a month before Lord Mornington landed in India.

Eastward of India, too, there was a potential danger from the Dutch who held Batavia and Manila. They were old allies of Britain, largely because of their Protestant ties, but the chances of European policy had brought them under French influence and might turn them into active enemies. They controlled a vast amount of the Eastern trade in spices which Britain felt would be more suitably held in her own hands. The danger of their staging a full-scale invasion was remote. The Dutch, though stout in defence, were not by nature aggressors, but should French pressure develop from the west they could be a nuisance, and perhaps worse, in rear of the defenders of India by raiding the coast or even by nothing more than snapping up trade or attacking convoys which the British might be too hard pressed to be able to protect. At the very least their harbours would be a refuge and their stores a stand-by for hunted French privateers or for assembling French squadrons in support of a French stroke from the west. Even Sir John Shore, least aggressive of Governors, was looking suspiciously toward the Dutch colonies to the eastward and asking himself whether a preventive attack on them might not be a shrewd defensive move. One of the first duties which awaited Colonel Wellesley on arrival was the preparation of an appreciation and plan for such a stroke in the near future.

He was still commanding the 33rd but his reputation as a potential staff officer had preceded him, and Shore detached him from regimental duty to direct the planning of operations. Shore was no soldier himself— Wellesley was his choice not only as planner but as commander of the force for the expedition. (His promotion to full colonel was gazetted in May of that year.)

Colonel Wellesley had not wasted the long and tedious weeks at sea. It was not the custom of serving officers, then or at any time, to devote much time to the theoretical study of their profession, but he had pro- vided himself for the voyage with a formidable library of technical works, including a large number of geographical books about India and its sur- rounding lands. He was able to reply to Shore's demand in a very short time with a long and extremely detailed report, which included the siting of batteries in Batavia and the suitability of the anchorage in Manila Bay, with a wealth of information about the conditions which might be ex- pected in the time of the monsoons. He was of the opinion that the op- eration was feasible, though with a courage and honesty unusual in such documents, he questioned the propriety of attacking Batavia unless there should be some earlier aggression by the Dutch.

Shore was satisfied with the report and had made the offer of com- mand to Wellesley, not realizing in his ignorance of military procedure that no officer could be appointed if there were another anywhere near who was senior in service by years, however decrepit and incompetent he might be. Wellesley had already experienced the working of this strange but inviolable law during the campaign in the Low Countries and was to see it in operation more than once before attaining a rank which delivered him from its futility. He wrote to the Deputy Governor, Mr. Speke, calling his attention to the existence of Colonel Doyle, who was his senior by a few years. He was still a little diffident about his own lack of experience in command and added, "If anything should prevent Doyle from accepting it, in case they offer it to him, and they should afterwards offer it to me, I intend to accept of it; taking the chance that the large force they intend to send, the known pusillanimity of the en- emy, and my exertions will compensate in some degree for my want of experience."

Such honesty deserved a better fate than it found. Before either he or Doyle was selected, Wellesley was annoyed to learn that the Governor had remembered an even older officer who was already a general, Gen- eral St. Leger, whom Wellesley had known in Holland and whom he now described as "an officer who knows his own incapacity."

"Shore is mistaken," he wrote to Mornington on May 20, "if he sup- poses that a good high-spirited army can be kept in order by other

means than by the abilities and firmness of the Commander-in-Chief."
He had apparently held no great opinion of St. Leger while in Holland,
as either a soldier or a man, and having met him again since landing in
India, saw no reason to change his estimation of him. In another letter
to his brother, he remarked a little sourly that the General was "a professed judge of every circumstance connected with good living" and,
further and with even darker implication, that he had "damaged himself
in health and fortune in the service of H.R.H. the Prince Regent." The
chief damage had been to General St. Leger's liver, and indeed he died
of apoplexy within a few months of his selection to command the expedition.

Wellesley had good reason to know all about it. He had renewed his
acquaintance with the General at one of those appalling drinking parties
which were the fashion among a certain, by no means small, section of
Indian society. Wellesley had not been in India for long before being introduced to a form of hospitality which was as lethal as any battery defending Batavia. It is obvious from his correspondence, especially from
his letters to his brother in England, that the Indian hospitality was a
shock to him, and one which disgusted him with its opulence and sheer
gluttony. It was not an abstemious age, nor were serving officers, during
their long periods of inactivity, the most sober of men, but Wellesley
had never had and never acquired a taste for dissipation of any sort. His
upbringing had been fastidious. He was used to the frugality of his own
home, to the good taste of the aristocratic French officers in Belgium
with whom he had lived and dined in his earlier years, to the hospitality
of the friends of his own family, where breeding counted for more than
money and, lately, to the decent ways of the mess of the 33rd, which had
naturally taken its tone from him. He found in Calcutta and Madras a
society such as he had never before encountered—a society of men who
had made a lot of money, made it very quickly and not always too honestly, and who had no idea of spending it in any other way than gross
excess in food and drink.

He soon met Mr. William Hickey, an attorney with a good practice in
Calcutta, whose published memoirs give a full and shameless description of the way in which he and his many friends spent their time and
their money. Hickey was a lover of claret, but a lover of the type who
reckoned his enjoyment by the number of bottles rather than the quality
of the wine. He chronicles every party, almost every meal with its at-
tendant claret, brandy and champagne, and never ceases to complain of
the persistent ill-health which he did everything possible to encourage
and intensify. He writes once happily of a dinner in Calcutta where "instead of drinking a glass of wine with a gentleman it was usual to throw

a chicken at his head, while the ladies pelted each other with sweetmeats and pastry"; of another in Bombay after which he was unable to rise from his bed for forty-eight hours, a really monumental orgy, where he sat with "eight as strong-headed fellows as could be found in Hindostan" and drank "two and twenty bumpers in glasses of considerable magnitude" (this being, of course, what they consumed after dinner and on top of the claret and champagne which accompanied the meal).

Colonel Wellesley happened to be a guest at this dinner and also at a memorable afternoon at the races when the company refreshed themselves with "turtle soup, a fat deer, with claret, champagne, hock and madeira." Hickey explained a custom, of which he highly approved, by which after the ritual drinkings of health in bumpers, the host would announce that "everyone might fill according to his discretion." "So discreet," he adds, "were all of the company that we followed his example of drinking nothing short of bumpers until two o'clock in the morning, at which hour every person staggered to his carriage or palankeen."

The 33rd mess, according to Mr. Hickey, soon fell into the convivial customs of the country, living, as he noted, "inimitable well and always sending their guests away with a liberal quantity of the best claret"—and Hickey's idea of a "liberal quantity" was a generous one. But this was due more to their second-in-command, Lieutenant-Colonel Sherbrake, than to their commanding officer, who necessarily spent some time away from his regiment while preparing his reports and carrying out various other staff duties. He cannot have enjoyed the raffish company and drunken life, for several times he wrote home expressing his dislike of India—"a miserable country to live in, and I now begin to think that a man deserves some of the wealth which is sometimes brought home for having spent his life here." He soon recorded his resolution to keep his own health by abstaining almost completely from wine while serving in India. He had seen the devastating effects of hospitality like Hickey's on junior officers, not only physically but financially. Most regiments serving abroad, unlike those at home in those days, had among their officers a large proportion who, like himself, had little or no private income to supplement their pay and so ran into debt. There were swarms of Indian moneylenders who infested garrison towns and, charging exorbitant rates of interest to needy subalterns, easily passed from servile willingness to lend to insolent and overbearing manners when it was time to demand repayment. Wellesley had had his own experience of running into debt a few years earlier when in Ireland. He had been sorely put to it to clear himself before going abroad and was determined never again to land himself in the same unhappy position.

Soon he began to find that life in India, once he had adopted his own sensible routine, was tolerable and even that he felt fitter than he had for many years. He decided that the hair powder which was regulation for all ranks was "very prejudicial to health as impeding perspiration" and continued to defy dress regulations by wearing his hair cropped.

He grew to tolerate the country, but for its native population he never lost the contempt which was his first reaction to them. A few weeks after his arrival he wrote, "The natives, as far as I have observed, are much misrepresented. They are the most mischievous, deceitful race of people I have ever seen or read of. I have not yet met with a Hindoo who had one good quality, even for the state of society in his own country, and the Mussulmans are worse than they are. Their meekness and mildness do not exist."

As long as he served in India he never saw reason to modify this opinion, which applied equally to Rajahs and native bearers. All Indian allies were unreliable—"They think that when once they have put their seal to a treaty with us, they have nothing to do but amuse themselves and sleep"—so he wrote in 1803. All of them, without exception, were corrupt and greedy, equally ready to give or demand bribes, and the more highly placed the native the less scruples did he appear to have. "In respect to the bribe," he wrote to a British officer in the same year, "offered to you and myself by the Rajah (of Kittoor) I am surprised that any man in the character of a British officer should not have given the Rajah to understand that the offer would be considered an insult." It was his first experience of the unreliability of allies, and it stood him in good stead later when he discovered in the Spanish a lack of honesty and an utter inability to keep a promise which put the less pleasing attributes of the Indians altogether in the shade.

Sir John Shore had decided to send the expedition to the Eastern Islands, and Wellesley resigned himself to the knowledge that he was to go in no higher position than in command of the 33rd. He was annoyed but, just before the time for sailing, he received the good and quite unexpected news that his brother had been appointed as Governor-General of India and would be arriving as soon as his ship could make the passage. Arthur wrote at once to congratulate him, offering "my service to your Government" and adding, very properly, though not perhaps altogether unhopefully, "I can't expect to derive any advantage from it which I should not obtain if any other person were Governor-General."

He had reason to expect that he would, at any rate, gain all the advantage to which his ability—of which he rightly thought very highly— entitled him; and Richard, as it was soon evident, had every intention of making use of an officer whom he knew to be able, determined and trustworthy. He was not one of those men who refuse to make use of a valuable friend or connection for fear of being accused of nepotism or favouritism. Sir John Fortescue, the historian of the British Army, writes, "One of the characteristics of Richard Wellesley's rule in India was his almost unerring gift of choosing able subordinates. Not until Lord Dalhousie came out in 1848 was there so brilliant a Governor-General of India."

The relations between the two brothers had always been good, though the younger had inevitably felt his dependence on the favour of the elder. It had always been to the brilliant Richard that the family had looked to advance the prospects of the somewhat ordinary younger brother who was "food for powder and nothing more". The next few years would do much to redress the balance and make each a sharer in the work and success of both. It was a balance which later years were to reverse until the day came when Richard was the less prominent partner and was able —and with a readiness which did him infinite credit—to act in a subordinate role and to help his brother to the heights of success. During the next few years the name of Wellesley was to be written indelibly on the roll of men who have served British India with honour.

X

History, on the whole, confirms Sir John Fortescue's estimate of the Marquis of Wellesley. The contemporary Court of Directors of John Company were far from enthusiastic. They had felt enormous confidence in him when they had sent him out to India. He had been a member of the Board of Control and knew all about the company's affairs as well as the whole truth about Hastings' activities. He knew that the court asked only one thing of Cornwallis and Shore, to cut down the cost and to increase dividends. He must surely realize that imperial ideas were out of place and that Hastings' downfall had disposed of them for a time if not forever. The directors felt that a man with his experience would confine himself to following their policy and would attempt no startling ventures of his own.

It was not long before they began to find out how completely mistaken they had been. Wellesley had no interest whatever in business or in the company's dividends—his aristocracy was of the old-fashioned type which looks down on trade as on something unclean. On the other hand, he had even bigger ideas of territorial expansion than Hastings' and infinitely bigger of what his own dignity required in the way of personal grandeur and expenditure. His first reaction on entering the Governor-General's residence was that it was totally unsuitable for its purpose. He immediately authorized a vast scheme of rebuilding in Calcutta and of erecting a country residence a few miles away at Barrackpur. Being fully aware that it would be at least six or nine months before the court

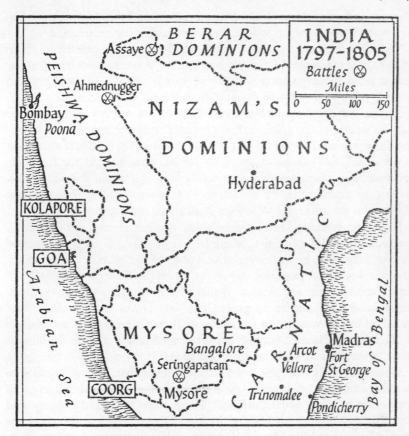

in London could approve (or more probably disapprove) his plan, he put the work in hand as soon as he had decided on it.

Even that was not the worst of Wellesley. His public ideas marched with those of his private establishment, and his first and openly avowed object was the increase of the company's territory and the firm establishment of British dominion in India. He had barely settled down to his new task when he began to look round for an objective and very soon discovered just what he wanted in Tippoo, Sultan of Mysore. The Sultan was a wealthy man and ruled a large and prosperous country. He was patently disloyal to the British and well-disposed toward the French, and he maintained a standing army which was large and well-trained enough (by French officers) to be a threat to British possessions. Soon Wellesley received a copy of a proclamation issued by the French Governor of Mauritius, urging men to volunteer for service in the Army of

Mysore, and was informed that French envoys had recently been seen to arrive at Tippoo's palace, where they were still being entertained.

Wellesley needed no further incitement but, knowing himself to be no soldier, had the sense to consult his brother Arthur, who had just returned from the expedition which was meant to take Batavia but had actually got no further than Penang, from where it was recalled.

Arthur was far from encouraging and did not temper his words. He was, he wrote, of the opinion that Tippoo's reinforcements from Mauritius did not exceed 150 in all and that the most which he could ever hope to get was 3,000 French troops. The British were not "in the fortunate circumstances which are desirable before we enter a war." And, in conclusion, he advised that "if we are to have a war at all, it must be one of our own creating; one which we shall think necessary."

If Arthur Wellesley had ever held his brother in awe, he did so no longer, and in military affairs, where he knew what was right and trusted his own judgment, he was never reluctant to speak his mind to any man, however senior or powerful he might be. The Governor-General accepted the caution, and Arthur Wellesley left Bengal to go to Madras, where Lord Clive, son of the great Clive, was Governor. The 33rd went with him but he was not to see much of them as he was to act, though unofficially, as Chief-of-Staff to the forces in Madras and, as he himself said, "to keep Lord Clive on the right road."

It was not a difficult task, for Clive was amenable. Arthur found him "a mild, moderate man, remarkably reserved, having a bad delivery and apparently a heavy understanding." There were men in the Army and government who did not hesitate to assert that Clive was the stupidest man in India, but after some experience of him, Arthur found him manageable and reported, "I doubt whether he is so dull as he appears or as people imagine he is." Like many other men, he probably suffered from being the son of a famous father and being unduly doubtful of his own capacity. He had had thoughts of attacking Tippoo with the Madras troops but was easily dissuaded when he was shown how unready they were and how powerful was Tippoo's army.

The Governor-General's ardour for war was a little cooled by his brother's common-sense advice and though he believed it to be the inevitable and only solution of the trouble with Tippoo, he resolutely spent the whole autumn of 1798 and half the winter of 1799 in trying, by correspondence, to reach a peaceful settlement and to persuade Tippoo to dismiss his French officers and to send the lately arrived French diplomats about their business.

Tippoo was determined to have his own way, though he had all the Oriental's relish for prolonged argument and futile negotiations. As long as the Governor-General would play with him at that game, he would keep it up and never tire. It was the Governor-General who tired, when he began to perceive—what his brother Arthur could have told him—that Tippoo would and could correspond with him to all eternity without the least intention of coming to an agreement, and that if he came to one he would not keep it. So, before the coming of Christmas, 1798, Wellesley gave orders for a force to assemble at Vellore, which was 180 miles from Seringapatam, Tippoo's capital and the final objective. Vellore was about a thousand miles from Madras. The force which was to be under the command of General Harris was to consist of two brigades, one each from the Bombay and Madras commands, with the usual attached troops.

Lord Clive's understanding was not so heavy as to prevent him from appreciating Colonel Wellesley's help in "keeping him on the right road." He asked that the 33rd and their colonel might be retained to form part of the Madras Brigade. Colonel Wellesley in fact was virtually in command of it throughout the winter, while he was carrying out the duties of Chief-of-Staff, Quartermaster-General and Adjutant-General of the Madras Brigade. His correspondence during these winter months is an unceasing round of indents, requests and what a later British Army knew as "hasteners" about bullocks, rice, ammunition, "beef, biscuits and arrack, . . . doll, sweetmeats, ghee, oil, betel-nuts, tobacco, bhangarah, massaulah and greens."

The reason for this monstrous accumulation was one with which every commander in India was familiar. No British army could take the field without hordes of native hangers-on, camp followers, bullock drivers, cooks, bearers, butchers, mahouts and, in many cases, their wives and womenfolk as well. The force which assembled at and finally marched from Vellore consisted of 36,000 fighting troops accompanied by what Fortescue justly calls "an enormous and bizarre convoy of about 200,000 camp followers, 120,000 bullocks, vast numbers of horses, donkeys and elephants, carrying the supplies with ponderous and noisy slowness, amid ceaseless trumpeting, braying, bellowing and whinneying."

Colonel Wellesley himself most strongly objected to this most cumbrous procedure, calling it "that monstrous equipment" and "that ponderous machine" and describing the regulations which required it as "a parcel of absurd, impracticable, shop-keeping regulations . . . under which no great undertaking could ever prosper," and urging his superiors to leave behind at Vellore "many stores . . . absolutely useless except as lumber". When at last they left Vellore in February 1799 they must have been an astonishing sight, for they marched in a hollow square, three miles by seven, protected by a few squadrons of cavalry and capable at best of no more than ten miles a day on the march.

Colonel Wellesley continued to observe this colossal circus with gloom, and before they marched had already told his brother that "affairs have been in some degree mismanaged," adding gloomily, "I am glad you are prepared for a failure. It is better to see and to communicate the difficulties and dangers of the enterprise and to endeavour to overcome them than to be blind to everything but success till the moment of difficulty comes and then to despond." (It is easy to understand why, six years later, Pitt should have said that he preferred General Wellesley to any other officer of his rank because, when told to undertake a task, he at once stated the difficulties of it and then proceeded to overcome them.)

The whole of the administrative turmoil and confusion during those last months of 1798, however harassing and depressing they may have been to the man who had charge of them, gave Colonel Wellesley a wealth of experience and taught him a multitude of expedients which came to his help a few years later in the Peninsula. He learned what must accompany an army in the way of stores and transport and what could safely be left behind; and, above all, how to pay for all these things and at the same time to pay his troops without any money. John Company was no readier a payer in India than the Treasury was to prove in Spain, and more than once in both countries, Wellesley was driven to use his own capital and to borrow on his own security to pay even some of the arrears which were due to his troops. In February 1799 he wrote from Vellore to Calcutta, "The want of money in my own camp was so great that I was obliged to borrow from the officers and to sell my own horses to find money to send off two detachments." Three months later he wrote, "I assure you that since December I have in some months spent five times, in others four times more than I received."

The Low Countries had, as he had admitted, taught him how not to do things. India taught him, above all, to see and do things for himself. In the Peninsula he never had an official Chief-of-Staff, as Napoleon had Berthier, because he never needed one. Where Napoleon would decide on the strategic and tactical plan and turn it over to Berthier saying, "Write the orders for that," Wellington nearly always made his plan and wrote, or at least dictated, his own orders for it. It was not an example to be unwisely followed for it needed not only an exceptionally clear-headed general but also a force of limited size. Napoleon might—though he did not—have written the orders for Waterloo, but he could never have controlled an army of the size of those at Wagram or Friedland without a competent staff to relieve him of the details. Wellington was always operating with small forces compared to the Grande Armée at its greatest and so was never compelled to rely on anyone else for carrying out his plans. While he was there the method worked well, but it left a dreadful legacy after his death in an army which neglected staff work and, for many years, made no effort to train officers for such duties. Much of the chaos of the Crimean War in 1857 must be attributed to this tradition of neglect and to the mistaken belief that a method which was good enough for Wellington was good enough for any successor.

The India Office files contain a voluminous correspondence between India and London which becomes more acrimonious as the full extent of the Governor-General's extravagance is revealed. By the time that the court had heard about it, considered it and finally disowned it, that particular piece of work was probably nearing completion and the next begun. Wellesley, like so many eighteenth-century aristocrats, had almost a mania for building, but while some of them had ruined themselves by indulging it, he was in the happy position of spending the company's money.

Not all of it went on buildings. Wellesley's estimate of the necessary staff and servants was on the same scale. Hastings had not stinted himself. In fact, Francis had inveighed against the horde of servants who worked at Government House. Francis himself, with a household of only four, kept over a hundred indoor servants, which he considered a very modest number. The new Governor-General employed a still larger multitude of them, and even that did not satisfy him. He must have a stronger military escort with a full military band, so he more than trebled the Governor's guard, which Hastings had instituted, lavishly redressed and mounted them and provided them with a band of musicians taken from wherever he could find them. Some of them came from the 33rd, which had a well-known regimental band. Hickey remarked that Wellesley did not rest till he had persuaded them all to transfer to his personal service. It was perhaps fortunate for him that his brother Arthur was so constantly away from his regiment and employed on staff duties, leaving the 33rd to the casual care of Colonel Sherbrake whose whole mind was absorbed by the pursuit of luxurious living.

Colonel Wellesley cannot have entertained any hopes of going on campaign as anything more than a regimental commander, though he had commanded a brigade in Holland with some success. But he was, after all, only thirty years old and a recently promoted colonel, and he knew enough of the Army to accept the fact that age and not efficiency was the qualification for higher command. There was a certain justice in the selection of General Baird for an attack on Seringapatam, where he had lately suffered a period of imprisonment as Tippoo's captive. It was Tippoo's habit to chain his officer prisoners together in pairs, and Baird had endured this cruelty, though he may have suffered less than the unfortunate officer who was chained to him. His mother, on hearing at her Scottish home what her son was undergoing, had commented with some feeling, "God help the man wha's chained to our Davy."

Baird was a competent soldier and his experience guaranteed that there would be no undue delay in taking Seringapatam nor any excess of mercy when it was taken. Wellesley did not resent Baird's arrival to claim the credit for the work which he had himself done, but he did most strongly resent the next plan for command of the expedition when the Governor-General announced his intention of joining the Army, and not only joining but taking command. The military status of the Governor-General had never been clearly defined, and there was precedent for the suggestion in Clive's success at Plassey, though he was only a junior at the time, and in Cornwallis' recent assumption of command. That could be tolerated, since Cornwallis was a soldier by profession, but all Colonel Wellesley's military instincts and training revolted at the impertinence of his brother, a mere civilian who had never worn a sword or drilled a half company. Neither respect for his office nor affection for his person was able to restrain the Colonel's horrified protest.

"I am entirely ignorant," he wrote at once, "of the object which you may have in view in coming, which may certainly counterbalance the objection I have to the measure; but it appears to me that your presence in camp, instead of giving confidence to the General, would in fact deprive him of the command of the army. All I can say on the subject is, that if I were in General Harris' situation, and you joined the army, I should quit it."

"All that the Colonel could say" was enough. The Governor-General gave up his dream of military glory and stayed in Calcutta. The army marched under General Harris, with Baird commanding the Madras Brigade and Wellesley the 33rd Foot. But it temporarily estranged the two brothers, and the letters addressed cordially to "My dear Mornington" gave way for a time to more formal dispatches, coolly beginning, "Your Excellency." It was only a temporary breach of good feeling but it was to recur before they both left India. Several times—and especially when Colonel Wellesley failed to get his own way—"My dear Mornington" becomes frozen into "Your Excellency."

XI

GENERAL HARRIS' "ponderous machine" ground slowly forward and, on March 5, 1799, crossed the Mysore border and headed for Tippoo's capital, Seringapatam. Colonel Wellesley was in command of a composite division of British and native troops, including his own 33rd. He had also an enormous horde of native cavalry, variously estimated, in the absence of parade states or nominal rolls, at a strength somewhere between 10,000 and 25,000. It was his first experience of commanding cavalry and he cautiously assessed them as "some good and some bad," which was at any rate more charitable than most of his expressed opinions of cavalry in later campaigns. They had a brush with the enemy at Malavelly but easily swept them aside and camped before Seringapatam on April 5. The city was strongly fortified and garrisoned and was protected by numerous outworks and strong points, which had to be cleared away before the assault could go in.

One of the strongest was a sacred grove known as the Sultan Pettah Tope, and on the night of their arrival, Harris detailed Wellesley with the 33rd and a native battalion to take it and open the approach on that side.

It was to be Wellesley's second lesson in the art of making war. In the Low Countries he had learned what not to do and resolved to avoid other men's mistakes. Now he began to make his own and to learn "what not to do" not as an observer but as a commander. He decided to approach and assault the position under cover of darkness, but neither he nor his troops had had much experience in night operations and the attempt was a complete failure. There had been no reconnaissance, and the column soon lost its direction and then its formation. They stumbled into a little wood where they became more hopelessly bunched than ever and came under a heavy fire from the Tope, which they tried to return, with the result that they found that they were firing on each other.

Wellesley was struck on the knee by a spent bullet and, having by this time lost his troops as well as his way, limped back to camp to report his failure. He retrieved it quite brilliantly in the daylight of the next morning and carried the position, but the night of confusion and impending disaster had bitten into his memory so deeply that long after his triumphs in the Peninsula and at Waterloo, he could still draw from memory an accurate sketch map of the action.

He was always a man to profit by experience and to store up from any memorable day its lessons for the future. The lesson learned before Seringapatam was summed up in his letter to Mornington—"never to suffer an attack to be made by night upon an enemy who is prepared and strongly posted, and whose posts have not been reconnoitred by daylight."

Reconnaissance was a duty which the British Army of that day (and for many years afterward) was inclined to take very lightly, but Wellesley made it his guiding rule never to neglect an opportunity of seeing for himself the ground over which he had to fight and as much as possible of the dispositions of the enemy. As he often used to say, he liked to know what was going on "on the other side of the hill." Within two years of his first lesson, he was confirmed in his resolve before the bloody fight of Assaye.

He spent those two years as Governor of Seringapatam. His appointment caused him a moment of embarrassment with General Baird, his senior officer. Baird, having previously suffered as a prisoner in Seringapatam and having led the successful assault on it, had, without other authority, assumed the right to govern it and was surprised one morning at breakfast with his staff in the palace by the arrival of Wellesley, bearing General Harris' letter of appointment of himself as Governor. The two men disliked each other. Wellesley, while he admired Baird's courage, complained of his lack of "talent and tact" and his "strong prejudices against the natives" which, in his opinion, disqualified Baird "from his manner, habits, etc., and, it was supposed, his temper from the management of them."

Baird gave strong proof of his temper when Wellesley interrupted his breakfast with the blunt announcement, "General Baird, I am appointed to the command of Seringapatam, and here is the order of General

Harris." Baird was furious and made much display of collecting his staff and leaving the palace at once, since they were no longer wanted there. It was an unpleasant situation for a newly-appointed officer who was supplanting a man many years his senior, but incidents which would have covered most men with embarrassment had small impact on Colonel Wellesley's self-possession. He did not argue with Baird or try to appease him, contenting himself with an invitation to him to finish his breakfast before going.

In 1800, Wellesley had his next experience in active service, this time in the role of commander of a flying column. It was not an affair of importance, being only a punitive expedition sent to destroy an ex-trooper of the Mahrattas named Dhoondiah, who had set up in business for himself as a marauder and was terrifying and robbing a wide stretch of the territory of Bednur. Wellesley's column made a rapid march of 150 miles, drew Dhoondiah into a neatly-set trap and cut his company to pieces in a few hours' fighting during which Wellesley, for the first and last time in his life, led a charge of cavalry. His next operation came two years later, in 1802 and, shortly before it, he was promoted to major-general, the rank which he had regarded as the summit of his ambition. Again his enemy was a Mahratta, but this was a chief, and no stray bandit, Dowlut Rao Scindia, whose territory included Delhi and Angria and the surrounding district.

Scindia had allies of his own race and, between them, they commanded a total strength of 40,000 cavalry, 14,000 infantry and 250 guns. Wellesley could muster only 9,000 European and 5,000 native troops, and with these he advanced to the attack. He knew more nowadays about the rules of Indian warfare, one of the chief of which among British commanders was to ignore any possible superiority of numbers when dealing with a native enemy. He had read his history and knew that at Plassey in 1757, Clive, with only 1,000 Europeans, 2,100 Sepoys and 10 guns, had routed Surajud Dowlah's enormous horde, consisting of 35,000 infantry, 18,000 cavalry and some 50 guns, as well as innumerable elephants. Scindia's troops had been trained by French officers and would no doubt be first-class fighting men, as far as they went, but they would not account for the bulk of his numbers. Most of his cavalry would be auxiliaries, almost untrained and wholly undisciplined, equally capable of a decisive charge or a devastating panic and quite likely, in their panic, to gallop through and over their own infantry. In addition there would be the usual horde of noncombatants and camp followers, including their womenfolk, who could be fairly relied on to get in the way of their fighting men, while the more elephants that a native commander could bring into the field the better his British opponent liked it. They

were useful beasts of burden but more likely even than the camp followers to cause confusion and panic.

Major-General Wellesley, since he was in sole command of his force,
marched without incumbrances; and his troops, both European and
native, were fully aware of their general's ideas of discipline. In any
case, a British commander in India expected to be outnumbered by anything from twice to ten times his own strength. If British strategy had
taken numbers into account, there would never have been a British Raj
in India. In 1857 during the mutiny, General Havelock relieved Cawn-
pore and reached Lucknow with the strength of less than a normal
brigade.

In later years, Wellington acquired such a reputation as a master of
the defensive that his talents in the attack have been unfairly overshadowed. In the Peninsula he was, for a long time, confined to the defensive
because he was always facing superior numbers, not of native levies but
of troops as well-trained and well-officered as his own. When he had the
chance to attack he grasped it, as he did when he chased Soult out of
Portugal in 1809 and hunted him through the Pyrenees four years later.
He had already shown against Dhoondiah that he could move with astonishing speed and deliver a fierce attack at the end of it. His long chase
of Scindia till he came up with him at Assaye showed that he had committed to memory every lesson which India had so far taught him. It was
on September 23, 1803, a little more than three months from his setting
out, that he brought Scindia to battle before Assaye on the banks of
the river Kaitna.

The Kaitna, deep, wide and swift-running, lay between his force and
the position which Scindia had taken up. Scindia had seized or destroyed
every available boat and was strongly covering the only ford practicable
for troops. Wellesley's native guides swore that no other ford existed
and that it was impossible to cross the river anywhere else. But Wellesley was experienced now in the ways and limitations of native guides
and informers, and his first failure at Seringapatam had convinced him
that only personal reconnaissance could bring results. He rode out with
a small escort to the banks of the Kaitna and, before long, selected a
spot where he felt certain that there was a ford, though the guides
vehemently denied it. Wellesley ignored them. At the point on the river
which he had noted there was, on either bank, a tiny village, no more
than a cluster of huts. But they were huts and men lived in them and he
drew the common-sense conclusion. "I fought and won the battle," he
said later, "the bloodiest for the number engaged that ever I saw; and
this was all from the common sense of guessing that men did not build
villages on opposite sides of a stream without some means of commu-

nication between them." If, as is often said, war is the art of the possible, then the common sense which was so marked a characteristic of his make-up was ideal equipment for his task.

Wellington often spoke afterward of Assaye, taking its terrible casualty list as a standard by which to judge the severity of a battle. Seven years later, after the slaughter of Talavera, his assessment was that, though the fire there was more intense, the loss of life at Assaye was greater in comparison with the troops involved.

Scindia had had 50,000 troops, strongly posted and entrenched in a prepared position behind a river. In less than three hours, Wellesley's 14,000, of whom only 1,000 were British, put them to utter rout. They fled leaving 1,200 dead on the field, thousands of wounded there and in nearby villages, 98 guns and all their ammunition, stores and baggage. Such a victory could only be won at a heavy cost to the victors and Wellesley's casualty returns showed 22 officers and 386 men killed, 57 officers and 526 men wounded. "Worse than Assaye"—it was always to be his phrase for a murderous battle.

It took him two more months to finish the campaign and to drive the last remaining forces of Scindia out of the field. He ended with a brilliant little action when he stormed the rock-based fortress of Gawilghur, after a march across mountains and gorges where his men had to make roads as they went and to manhandle guns up steep rock faces and across gaping chasms. So difficult was the country that they made no more than thirty miles in the last six days, but they dragged up the heavy guns and carried the fortress by assault on December 15, after a two days' bombardment. (He remembered that, too, in front of Badajoz, ten years later.)

Gawilghur was the last engagement of the war which, as Wellesley said, "left the British Government in a most glorious situation, as the sovereigns of a great part of India; the protectors of the principal powers and the mediators, by treaty, of the disputes of all." It left Wellesley with an established reputation, the Knighthood of the Bath, the thanks of both Houses of Parliament and a gold vase and sword of honour presented by his officers and by the citizens of Calcutta. Unfortunately it left him, too, with impaired health, the result of fatigue and repeated attacks of dysentery.

He stayed for a short time longer to recover his health, and then, in 1804, he applied for leave to return to England. He had served India well and he needed to recuperate in a milder climate.

He did not sail for England till March 1805. By that time, Europe was threatened by dangers of which no one had dreamed when he had left home eight years earlier. Already the colours of the French regiments were emblazoned with the golden names of Arcola, Rivoli, Castiglione and Marengo. The long rows of their tents stretched for miles along the cliffs near Boulogne and England was arming for home defence. The coup d'état of Brumaire was over in Paris, and the man who had worked these miracles had become in quick succession Consul, First Consul, then Consul for Life. Now he sat on an imperial throne. If an artillery subaltern could achieve so much, perhaps the rank of major-general need not be the ultimate ambition of a British officer who was still only thirty-six years old—the same age as the newly-crowned Emperor of France.

There were other ties which bound him to England and which were now pulling at him, ties of family and home. A man could not always be thinking of his career or a soldier of his duty. There was his elder brother, Mornington, left behind in India to face a steadily growing stream of complaints and threats from John Company's directors about the lighthearted way in which he was dissipating their resources. There had even been a threat of impeachment, and Mornington urgently needed a friend at home to look after his interests. No one, surely, would do it as well as his younger brother, Arthur, whom he had so often helped in the past and who was now in a position to be able to return old favours. (Richard had been created Marquis of Wellesley in 1799 but to the family he was always Mornington.) Their mother was still alive and there were the younger children who needed a guiding hand. And— there was Kitty Pakenham.

Sir Arthur was never in the habit of revealing his inmost feelings, and we can only guess at the extent of his longing to see Kitty again. It had not, so far, been a passionate courtship, but they had an understanding that they would marry when he returned from India. It was an under- standing which amounted, on his side at least, to a promise, and a gentle- man must keep his promise. Besides, his memory of her was a little dim, so much had happened since—she was charming, and she was waiting for him at home. He was, of course, longing to be with her again, longing as keenly as she was—or almost as keenly.

XII

Seven years in India had changed Colonel Wesley of the 33rd Foot into Major-General Sir Arthur Wellesley, K.C.B., and had added Assaye and Seringapatam to the growing list of his battle honours. He had once announced that his highest ambition was to serve His Majesty as a major-general and there seemed to be no reason why he might not achieve a higher rank still. Sir Arthur had perhaps benefited by his relationship to the Governor-General of India, but he was shrewd enough to know that that would count for very little at home, especially since Richard had made himself so unpopular with the Board of Control and the directors of John Company that there was talk in England of recalling him or even of impeaching him. Indeed, one of the tasks with which Sir Arthur was charged on his return home was to try to remove the prejudice against his elder brother and to bring to bear in his favour any influence which he could command.

For all his success and his growing reputation as a soldier, that influence was not yet very powerful, and he was uncertain about even his own prospects at home. England and France were at war again after the short peace which followed the Treaty of Amiens—the peace which the Whigs had christened "The Peace of God" because, they said, it passed all understanding. Pitt had retired from the Premiership in 1801 and had been succeeded by Addington, who was generally called "The Doctor" because his father had been one of the Royal physicians. Of him Canning had written, "Pitt is to Addington as London is to Paddington."

That had been in the year 1801, while Wellesley was still in India, the year in which the last battalions of the French army which General Bonaparte had led to Egypt and abandoned there surrendered to the British; the year in which Nelson had fought and won at Copenhagen, and which, at home, had seen the Act of Union between Ireland and Great Britain. The Treaty of Amiens lasted for no more than two years. In 1803 Britain and France were at war again. It was the year of Wellesley's victory at Assaye, and in the following year Pitt came back to the Treasury. Addington had achieved a futile and fleeting peace, and there was no reason to expect that he would do any better as a war minister. The country clamoured for the return of Pitt, least warlike and aggressive of men, whose genius lay in finance and administration and whom an irony of fate condemned to serve in time of war. Even wartime, when Pitt was premier, was not likely to yield many opportunities of promotion to Wellesley and his fellows.

Pitt was not the man to commit British troops to action on the Continent if he could hire other nations to do the fighting. He took up the threads of his earlier diplomacy, seeking always allies in Europe against France and offering generous subsidies to make and keep the alliances in being and the allied troops in the field. So there were many senior officers at home, kicking their heels on half-pay or besieging the Horse Guards for employment. Sir Arthur had had a good run of luck, and now it was his turn to wait. Those seven years which had raised him to a decent dignity had sent his great rival and contemporary rocketing into such power as only one man ever reaches in many generations. The year which brought to Wellesley his K.C.B. saw Napoleon Bonaparte crowned as Emperor of the French.

The year 1805 brought England nearer to the danger of invasion than she had been since the Norman Conquest or would be again till 1940. The Grande Armée was encamped on the cliffs of Normandy round Dunkirk and Wimereux, while in every French port, workmen were building the flat-bottomed boats which the Emperor had ordered by the thousand to carry his troops across the channel as soon as Admiral Villeneuve had cleared the way for him. The grand strategy was for Villeneuve to slip past Nelson's watching cordon and sail for the West Indies, luring Nelson after him. He was then to elude Nelson and double back, making contact with the Spanish fleet off Cadiz, after which the combined fleets would be strong enough to hold the Channel till Napoleon could establish a bridgehead in southern England and transport the main body of his troops to security and to march on London.

That army had begun to assemble in the Boulogne area in 1803, and for the next two years England was never to be free from the threat of invasion. The danger grew nearer and receded with the season of the year, with the tides and the moons, but, unlike the threats which existed in 1940, there never seemed to come a time when it could be written off as improbable. When its full strength was mustered, from 1804 onward, the French army at Boulogne consisted of six army corps of nearly 200,000 men, all of them highly trained and superbly fit soldiers with every equipment, every weapon that a force could possibly need. Their cavalry and artillery were on a scale far greater than those of any other Continental army and were commanded by men who had already proved their worth in the field and whose names were soon to be familiar throughout Europe.

The old Royal Army of France had had their marshals, some of them old, a few of them unskilled in arms. When Napoleon took for himself the dignity of Emperor he lost no time in setting up a royal establishment and a court in which the titles of princes and dukes sometimes sat oddly on men who had little to boast of in the way of birth, breeding, education or possessions. The older courts of Europe might laugh contemptuously at M. le Duc or even le Prince whose mother had been a pastry cook or whose father had tilled the soil of Brittany, but there was little cause for hostile laughter in the men whom Napoleon selected as the first marshals of France under the new regime. Among them were all the corps commanders of the army which lay at Boulogne.

The six corps were commanded by Bernadotte, Marmont, Davout, Soult, Lannes, and Ney. Murat had the cavalry reserve. Napoleon himself was with them as often as his other duties allowed and occupied a villa near Boulogne. There he had built a tall wooden structure from which, on a clear day, he could see the white cliffs of England and, occasionally, a sloop or a frigate from the British Fleet which kept its unending watch in the Channel. During those two years, nothing stood between Britain and destruction but the Fleet, which stretched in a great arc round the European coast from Holland to the Mediterranean.

In that Fleet, were names which were soon to be as well known as those of marshals of France. Admiral Keith was watching the Texel against a possible danger from the remains of the Dutch Fleet which had been so roughly handled at Camperdown and at the Helder. Cornwallis was blockading Brest, L'Orient and Rochefort with Collingwood as his second in command. Cochrane (later Pellew) lay off the coast of Spain, "five hundred miles from their base at Berehaven and Plymouth," Sir Arthur Bryant writes, "and the stormiest seashore in Europe."

South of them, with the most difficult task of all, as he was the most certain to fulfil it, was Nelson, watching Toulon and the Mediterranean. For him it was a time of unceasing anxiety, since unlike most of the others, he had a multiplicity of dangers to guard against. The squadrons in the Channel and the Atlantic had to face all the rough conditions and hardships in remaining constantly afloat and alert in all weathers at all seasons, without shelter of a harbour or even the protection afforded by a quiet bay or the windbreak of a headland. They were at action stations not for weeks but for months at a time. On very rare occasions a ship or two could put into Plymouth or Portsmouth to refit or revictual or even to give their men a brief hour of liberty ashore, but these were few and desperately short intervals. Cornwallis stood over to England on the last day of 1801 for an hour's shelter so that his carpenters might tackle only the most urgent repairs such as could not be botched up at sea, but next day he put to sea again and resumed his former station. A month later and after two severe gales, he put in for a few more hours and returned to duty as soon as the work was done.

It was England's seamen who saved her from her greatest danger and, in saving her, saved Europe and freedom in Europe. Their lives were hard, comfortless, without rest or leisure. They spent months at a time without seeing land; they were vilely fed so that they developed scurvy and ulcers; and even their drinking water was so filthy that no thirst could induce them to swallow a mouthful of it—"O! for a draught of fresh water I cry out," Midshipman Bernard Coleridge wrote to his mother, "for our water stinks enough to poison a person." They lived always in danger, from the enemy, from wind and sea and, not seldom, from the sheer unseaworthiness of their ships, since many of them had had no serious repairs and no overhaul for years. Collingwood wrote of his own flagship, which surely might have been expected to be in as good condition as any, "We have been sailing for the last six months with only a sheet of copper between us and eternity."

All these things the seamen endured for the sake of one chance of a fight with the French and for their duty. It is commonly thought that most of them were pressed men, so much prominence has been given in fiction and drama to the work of the press gangs, but the fact is that for every pressed man in the Fleet during those years there were twelve volunteers.

All these hardships were the lot of Nelson's men and ships, apart from what comfort they could get from the sheltered waters of the Mediterranean for such of them as lay east of Gibraltar, but in addition their task was even more difficult and exacting. The Channel and the Atlantic squadrons had, for the most part, the comparatively simple task of watching each his own bolt-hole and maintaining communications with the rest of the Fleet. Nelson's task was manifold. He had first to blockade Brest where a French fleet lay in harbour, second to watch the Straits of

Gibraltar and the coastline of North Africa against possible enemy renewal of ventures toward the Middle East and Egypt. Behind him, where
he lay east of Gibraltar, and to his left in the Atlantic lay a possibility
of new danger, should Spain, as seemed only too likely, join France in
making war on England. Even though the Portuguese, England's oldest
allies, were still friendly, they knew that France was watching them and
that, should Spain join her, their existence would be threatened; so that,
though they helped Britain when and where they could, they did it in
fear and within limits. And behind and beyond those dangers lay the
sea routes to the West Indies and to England's wealth and possessions
there. Any French squadron which might manage to break out of harbour
and elude the watching men-of-war would be likely to sail for the West
to damage English prestige and possessions there and to draw off the
ships which guarded English shores.

Almost inevitably any such ships would sail first southward through
the Bay of Biscay and past Cape Trafalgar making for Madeira, there
to turn eastward to get the favouring trade winds, and such a course
would bring them across Nelson's rear. If he was aware of them in time,
he would have to concentrate as much of his strength as he could and
fight them, and should they slip past him, he would have to chase them
across the Atlantic for a thousand miles or more. And—as if all this
were not enough for one man and one fleet—he was charged with a
perpetual watch on Sicily where it was believed that the French intended
a landing. So strong, in fact, was this belief that in 1804 the British
mustered an army with transports—generally known as the "Seacret
Expedition"—which was to forestall the French by landing first in Sicily
and for whose protection during the voyage and support during the landing Nelson would be responsible as soon as they passed into his area and
out of Cornwallis' keeping. It was true that they might, on the whole,
expect rather better weather than the Atlantic squadrons, though they
took their turns in the buffeting west of the Straits and on the coast of
Portugal. On the other hand, if they suffered any damage there was no
friendly port into which they could put for the simplest of repairs, as did
the ships in the Channel; and though they might have been able to supplement their wretched rations by purchase in Sicily, as long as she remained intact, or by bringing fruit and fresh water from Morocco, the
British government made quite sure that they should enjoy no undue
luxury by stinting them of money. Nelson had to spend his private income and involve himself in debt to pay his men some of their wages
and occasionally to buy what little he could of fresh provisions to ward
off their diseases, brought on by an endless diet of fat salt pork, weevily
biscuits and foul water.

Yet it was all those squadrons which stood between England's coast and the man who paced up and down in his lookout post near Boulogne and continually turned his glass seaward in search of the white sails and black and yellow hulls—a hopeless search, for the men-of-war lay always hull-down beyond the horizon and only the busy, flashing frigates and sloops plied up and down the Channel as they carried out their duties as watchers and messengers. Napoleon could, and did, order thousands of flat-bottomed invasion barges to be built in French ports, but the men who had to build them knew that it was not just as easy as making so many wooden boxes, that even such utilitarian craft had to be seaworthy and capable of being steered for a short distance. In the same way he could issue one order after another to Villeneuve or Ganteaume, moving his model ships about on the painted oceans of his maps like chessmen on a board. But he could not realize—he would never realize—that tides and winds were beyond his control; that he could not order an admiral to set out into the teeth of a northwest gale and make the same speed as if he had a favouring wind behind him.

Napoleon never understood the sea. It had always baffled him and in the end was to work his ruin. He had grown up, as did most Corsican boys, among fishermen. Seamen and boats were as familiar to him as ponies to a country-bred child. His first desire had been for the sea and only his mother's stern denial had kept him from taking the Navy as his career. "Madame Mère" had seen too many desolate homes in Corsica after one of the sudden storms which blew up in the Mediterranean. She had stood among the crowds on the quay at Ajaccio through the long hours of darkness, when the howling wind blew the flame and sparks from the torches in a devil's dance of light and shadow and the women waited for the crippled fishing fleet to make harbour. She knew the risks of battle and had shared them with her husband when Paoli and his patriots fought a losing battle with the invading French, even while the child who was to be an Emperor was quickening in her womb. It was right that a man should face those dangers, but no son of hers should go out to meet danger and court it on the high seas.

Napoleon did not give up his dream even while he was at the Royal Military School at Brienne, preparing to enter the Army. Once his parents, coming unexpectedly upon him for the only visit they paid him during his six years there, found him resting in a hammock slung between two trees to accustom himself to that way of sleeping. Madame Mère was a woman of decision and action; when Napoleon was seventeen and wearing the King's uniform, she flogged him for making fun of his grandmother—and Charles Bonaparte was no match for her. There was to be no seagoing life for Napoleon, and perhaps partly for that reason, he always in later life hated and resented the sea and the men who followed it. Intolerable as he could be and often was to his marshals and his courtiers, he never treated them with the harsh unreason which he showed to his admirals.

The sea would always be his danger and his bane. It was Britain's navy which wrecked his dream of an Oriental empire by destroying his fleet by the action at Copenhagen, as it was that fleet which alone stood now between him and the conquest of Britain. It would soon be that fleet which would enable his worst enemies to maintain and supply an army on the Spanish Peninsula, since their lines of communication lay across the sea of which they and never he were masters. It was to be the sea which would be the ruin of his country when his Berlin Decrees shut off Britain from the world's trade only for him to learn from the British Order in Council and from the way in which it was put into force, how much more skilful at that game were his enemies than his own servants and allies. It would be the sea which would enclose his first island prison of Elba and his last loneliness at St. Helena.

XIII

I T IS BOTH tempting and easy to draw the obvious comparison between
Britain in 1804 and in 1940. In both years she was without allies
and faced with the danger of invasion from the French coast. In both,
her power to defend herself had been perilously reduced by insane ideas
of economy in the fighting forces in peacetime, and in both she was hastily recruiting and arming new defenders. In both, the resources of her
Navy were stretched to their utmost limit to keep free her communications by sea and to watch her overseas possessions. In 1804, as in 1940,
the country swarmed with newly raised and wholly amateur soldiers, the
Home Guard, repeating the earlier history of the Fencibles, repeating it,
indeed, even in the detail that when they were clamouring for firearms
they were offered pikes.

In 1804 Lord Mulgrave reported that every village in Yorkshire was
seething with indignation under the insult. "I cannot think without disgust," he wrote, "of the cool confidence with which pikes are pressed
upon masses of untrained, unarmed peasants that they might exercise
their spirit with that weapon against the enemy. No progress of the
French in the first instance could give them so much spirit or operate
so strongly on the minds of the people as the easy conquest they must
gain with musketry, artillery and discipline against a mob of brave fellows with flimsy and unwieldy pikes." (At least one company commander of the Home Guard in 1940 remembers turning out on an alarm
with nothing better than a thick ashplant and a revolver for which he

had not ammunition.) When later the Home Guard were armed with rifles they were bedevilled by instructions from the War Office telling them to stand in defended localities—it was the military cliché of the moment but the reality was often a few overturned farm carts and a few strands of wire—and fight against the invaders as though they were fully trained and equipped regular troops.

In 1804 the same authority proposed to use them much in the same way, to bar the approach to London, though the men of those days were at least luckier in two respects. They were not armed with the fearsome bombards and projectors for which the men of 1940 felt more and better-founded distaste than they did for the Germans. In 1804 there were two senior officers, Moore and Moira, who had enough military intelligence to see that the only possible role for untrained and lightly armed irregulars was the true role of an irregular. Moore was then at Shorncliffe training the regiments who were forming the nucleus of what was later to become famous as the Light Division. Lord Moira had seen during the American War what such men, who knew their countryside and who would be fighting in front of their own homes, could achieve when they were properly handled as guerrillas and as nothing else. In a speech at Leicester he told his volunteers to concentrate on musketry, which with their knowledge of ground would be all that they would need once they learned to obey orders. "Their task," Bryant writes, "should be to operate in small bodies in the enemy's flank and rear, availing themselves of every inequality of ground; to retire when the foe, stung by such gad-fly tactics, moved against them in force, only to advance again when his detachments withdrew to his main body." "You must not," Moira warned them, "think this is unworthy of your courage." Moore argued that "in open battle their untrained enthusiasm could achieve nothing but their own destruction."

There was great likeness too in the way in which the people of England reacted to the threat. In 1804 there were mercifully few press writers to weary men with their clichés about "an island embattled," but their place was taken by writers of ballads and lampoons, generally trite and often drivelling which yet occasionally sounded the real note of danger and watchfulness. They varied in quality from the doggerel of "The Bellman and Little Boney" with such verses as:

> *This little Boney says he'll come*
> *At merry Christmas time*
> *But this, I say, is all a hum*
> *Or I no more will rhyme.*

—from such limping verse to the authentic note of childish terror heard in the verses with which women in Kent and Sussex used to sing their children to sleep:

> Baby, baby, naughty baby,
> Hush you naughty thing, I say,
> Hush your squalling or it may be
> Bonaparte will come this way.
>
> Baby, baby, he's a giant
> Tall and dark as Rouen steeple
> And he'll dine and sup, rely on't,
> Every day on naughty people.
>
> Baby, baby, he will hear you
> As he passes by the house,
> And he limb from limb will tear you
> Just as pussy tears a mouse.

Beneath this froth of ballad and the cheap laughter at the expense of an enemy who was still far away there were then, as later, true courage and genuine determination to fight to the last in defence of home and country.

"We will fight them in the towns and villages, we will fight them in the fields and hills, we will never surrender." The words were Sir Winston Churchill's in 1940. They might well have been those of a Prime Minister of 1804, had he been anyone but the supine Addington, whom Canning impolitely called "Britain's guardian gander" and whose scheme for blocking the mouth of the Thames drew from the same critic the poetical comment:

> If blocks can the nation deliver
> Two places are safe from the French:
> The one is the mouth of the river
> The other the Treasury Bench.

Those political amenities from one colleague to another point to the real and tremendous difference between the dangers of 1804 and 1940. The cause of it, of course, was the absence of air power in the one and its predominance in the other. For the truth was that in 1804 Britain was never in real danger of invasion as long as her Fleet kept watch over the Channel ports and the ports of Spain. Even had an invasion fleet got through the cordon, it would have arrived mangled and exhausted after a cross-Channel journey made in boats with no other power except that

Supplementary Militia, turning out for Twenty Days Amusement. — 'The French Invade us, hay?' — damme, where, where are they?

Loyal Souls, or — a peep into the Mess Room at St James's

'SUPPLEMENTARY MILITIA' AND 'LOYAL SOULS'

By Gillray

'WATCHING THE COAST'

By *Thomas Rowlandson*

of oars. Napoleon had ordered that no barge should hoist sail during the crossing for the sake of invisibility. When such a force had landed, if any of it ever did, it would be without heavy guns and with its horses and transports disorganized. And it would have been completely cut off by sea, for the ships which it had eluded would swarm into the Channel preventing reinforcements from landing and cutting off supplies of ammunition and other necessaries.

Unless some great and almost miraculous change had come about, the British coast in the early nineteenth century was virtually inviolable, and her people knew it. They jeered or ranted or were grimly silent according to their various natures, but perhaps not one in ten believed in the possibility of the French crossing the Channel when the Royal Navy guarded it. In 1940-1941, all through those summer months, there were few men in England who did not realize that invasion was a possibility and, for a short time, even more. And yet, Field Marshal Lord Alanbrooke, who was then Chief of the Imperial General Staff and knew the truth if anyone did, noted in his diary that, in spite of everything, he could never wholly get himself to believe that it would happen.

In 1804 a large part of England's people did not even try to believe it. Their Fleet was incomparable, invincible; their Army, of which it is true they never before thought highly, was ready on the coast. They themselves were marching through country lanes or drilling in city squares wearing an astonishing variety of gaudy uniforms—a thing which, no doubt, many of them had since childhood longed to do had it not involved the disagreeable duties and discomforts attaching to real soldiering.

The only zone of danger, they felt, was the southern coast and the route from there to London. Even should the invaders land, they would all be mopped up before they could penetrate as far north as St. Albans or as far west as Slough. The rest of Britain, naturally enough, took up arms, when they could get them, and put on uniforms, which somehow they never failed to get—they would have been shocked and disgusted by the Local Defence Volunteers armbands of June 1940 and the later issue of denims.

Sir Walter Scott with a Border regiment of Yeomanry galloped over the sands of Musselburgh, slashing at turnips on poles, and once rode from home to his headquarters, a distance of a hundred miles, on an alarm. Even William Wordsworth twice walked over the fells from Grasmere to enlist in the local infantry volunteers though—whether it was their fault or his own is unknown—he never actually achieved his object. Behind and besides all this preparation the peaceful life of England went on untroubled. There was still racing at Newmarket and Ascot and

D

Doncaster, hunting in the shires, cricket on Broadhalfpenny Down and at the Marylebone Club, Dorset Square, in London. A great Whig lady complained that no one in London could talk of anything but the debut of "Master Batty the Infant Roscius" at Drury Lane, while the Lyceum was installing its first system of gaslighting. The Adelphi Theatre was going up; Kemble was managing Drury Lane (and the Infant Roscius); there were concerts at Sadler's Wells and equestrian performances at Astleys. The Game Chicken was offering to fight all comers, and the Marquis of Queensberry, the infamous "Old Q," had still a few years of his disreputable life to run, while Lord Byron at Harrow was on the verge of the cricket XI.

Above all, the greatest enjoyment of the leisured classes in London, which was party politics, went on undisturbed and unabated. The modern understanding between parties, by which they sink their differences and combine against a national danger, finds no precedent in the early nineteenth century. Whig or Tory, whoever happened to be in power, had to contend with not only the common enemy but the equally hostile Tory or Whig opposition, and it was thought no disgrace to try to turn out the government when the French were knocking at the gates.

In 1804 Addington was still in power but no one knew how much longer he would be able to hold on to it. Pitt, who was always ready to put country before party, did nothing to harass him and must have found no little relief from the cares of office in commanding a battalion of volunteers at Dover. Indeed, he had time for relaxation in an occasional convivial dinner, at one of which, at Walmer, he proposed the toast, "A speedy meeting with the enemy on our own shores," a sentiment which was strongly resented by the Admiralty who had no intention of letting the French get so far. Early in 1804 even Pitt began to feel that the country had had enough of the Doctor's medicine and needed a stronger dose. Addington's own Tory supporters, though they voted with him, made no pretence of holding him in anything but contempt. George Canning especially took every opportunity of sharpening his cruel wit on his leader both in speech and in writing, till the rest of his party began to feel that he was exceeding even the very wide limits of permissible party warfare. The result was that he was marked down for years afterward as a man who would sacrifice anyone or anything for the sake of a sneer. It was said of him that he never made a speech without making an enemy, for his wit had brilliance but neither justice nor mercy. Had he been able to restrain himself he could hardly have failed to reach the Premiership many years before he did. He was perhaps the ablest man in the party, but nothing is more damaging in politics than a reputation for unsoundness. Canning had yet to serve weary years of expiation before he was fully trusted, even by his friends.

In the same way, Lord Castlereagh, another man of real ability, was looked on with some suspicion. His frozen manner and his aloofness alienated men who respected his ability, and he still bore, not altogether justly, a reputation for the cruelty with which he had enforced the laws and put down revolt in Ireland. He was to incur more than his share of reproach for the government's repressive measures in England because, as Leader of the House, it fell to him to introduce many of them, though his true strength and his main employment were in foreign affairs. His unpopularity was perpetuated later by Byron, who wrote:

I met with Murder on the way,
He wore a mask like Castlereagh.

Yet it was clear that in any future Tory administration these two able men must carry great weight, perhaps the greatest. Addington was a laughing-stock and his days were numbered. The only alternative to a change of administration, for which the Whigs were not ready, lay in Pitt's return, and Pitt was a sick man. He had never been strong. The weight of office, the burden of his great name in comparison with the memory of his father and, it may be, the enormous amount of port which he drank by his doctor's orders, were sapping the remnant of his strength.

Worse, perhaps, was the compulsion to carry on a foreign war. All Pitt's instincts and desires were for peace. To enforce repression at home, when at heart he was a reformer, preyed on his spirit, nor had he the consolation of many friends, though he had many admirers. His cold and haughty manner had been assumed years before to support the dignity which he sorely needed as Prime Minister in his early twenties, but it had become a habit and, except to a very few who knew him well, as did Dundas, he was as repellent as Castlereagh.

Ironically it was Henry Dundas, later Lord Melville and his closest friend, who was unwittingly to do him the worst possible harm and come near to effecting his ruin. Late in 1804, when Melville was at the Admiralty, strange stories began to spread about him. It was said that he was keeping company too often for discretion with certain bankers in the city, and from there it was only a step to the insinuation that he was gambling in the funds and not with his own money.

By the end of 1804 there was a strong impression that Pitt was a party to this iniquity and might possibly have been sharing the profits. There was talk—which turned out to be accurate—of a deficit of over £20,000 in the Admiralty accounts. Pitt was known to be as poor as he

was believed to be honest. He had, unlike nearly all his colleagues, stead-
fastly refused to take any of the sinecures and their salaries which
abounded in those days and were looked upon as the legitimate per-
quisites of the party in control. In the early days of his power an office
called the Clerkship of the Pells fell open, and Whig and Tory alike
expected Pitt to assume it for himself. Nor, to do them justice, would
they have thought any less of him had he done so, since few of them
would have hesitated had they had the offer.

Pitt would have none of it. He lived and died a poor man, even refusing a loan or a gift from the King's privy purse, which George III
pressed on him. (After his death it was found that his debts amounted
to over £60,000, and it was thought a great credit to him that they
were owing to no one more important than a few tradesmen.)

Pitt, if he were well enough, was the obvious replacement for Britain's
"Guardian Gander," but there was still one obstacle to his return, and it
was the obstacle which had caused him to stumble while in office and
in the end to resign.

In everything but one thing he and the King were of the same mind,
but they differed violently on the question of religious toleration. George
was a rabid opponent of toleration, especially of the Roman Catholics,
because he believed that to grant it would be a violation of his coronation
oath. Few men could be as obstinate as he when his mind was made up,
and this had for a long time been a cause of dissension between him
and Pitt, who, whether he personally favoured toleration or not, was wise
enough to know that it could no longer be denied or postponed. He
would always be too intelligent and fair-minded to become the type of
Tory represented a few years later by Lord Eldon and the Duke of Wellington, to whom the mere fact that a measure or an idea was new was
enough to damn it eternally.

Pitt was in an awkward position. He himself was probably willing to
grant emancipation to both Catholics and Dissenters. The King would
never agree to it, and what made it worse was the realization that it was
one of the subjects which was most likely to bring on a recurrence of his
madness, which had already twice shown itself. He had betrayed the
first symptoms as far back as 1765; they had been slight but alarming.
Happily he recovered quickly and seemed perfectly sane until 1788 when
he had a far worse attack—so bad that he had to be restrained for a
time at Windsor after the disastrous attempt of his doctors to treat what
they had diagnosed as biliousness with a course of the Cheltenham waters. As these only made him worse, the doctors altered their diagnosis
to what they described as "a surfeit of Cheltenham waters," but soon

even they were forced to admit that the trouble was mental. For a time it seemed probable that he might be permanently disabled, and serious debates arose about a regency.

The prospect alarmed the country, who felt that on the whole even a mad George III would be preferable to a sane Prince Regent. The King unexpectedly recovered, in spite of his medical advisers, in 1789, but those who were about him understood how careful they must be to avoid certain subjects of conversation which would threaten his mental balance, and the most dangerous of these was toleration.

Pitt was understood to have given the King his word in private that, as long as he reigned, he would never again raise the proposal. Now his goodhearted care for his sovereign was putting him in a great difficulty. It was probable, so tired was the country of Addington, that if Pitt chose to exert himself, he could return to power. But he held himself to be still bound by his promise. Should he return, he knew that, sooner or later, he would have to propose toleration, if for no other reason than that the affairs of Ireland would have demanded it. His Irish policy had resulted in the Act of Union in 1801, which had removed the absurd sight of a predominantly Catholic country under a wholly Protestant Parliament. Now Irish members sat in the House at Westminster, whose debates they were to bedevil for the next hundred years and more. Some measure of religious toleration had been implicit, if tacit, in the bargaining which brought about the Act of Union. There was also the growing realization that, in time of war, it was ridiculous to deny commissions simply on the grounds of their religion to men who would be first-rate officers.

Pitt knew it, but his hands were tied. If he returned to power he would be faced with a choice of breaking his word and possibly of driving his King mad or else of perpetrating a policy in which he did not believe and which was obsolete and, at the moment, actively harmful.

While he was hesitating he was saved from the agony of a decision by one of the very alternatives which he dreaded.

George the III, when about to open Parliament, was heard rehearsing his speech with the somewhat novel opening, "My Lords and Peacocks." He was prevented from this innovation and managed to get through the ceremony without causing alarm to any but a few who really knew the danger, but shortly afterward, his symptoms became so alarming that his doctors were called in again. This time, having learned from experience, they were right in their diagnosis and at once hustled the poor, sick man away to his palace of Kew, where they proceeded to apply brutal methods of restraint and treatment which were then common, including a straight waistcoat and a prolific use of cold douches.

Mad as the King undoubtedly was, he showed some lingering strains of sanity when dealing with his doctors. One of them was a parson, and the King remonstrated with him for undertaking an employment so little in keeping with his holy office. The doctor somewhat pompously replied that his Master, Jesus Christ, had gone about healing the sick, to which his royal patient answered, with a flash of his old spirit, "That may well be so, sir, but he did not go about charging them 600 guineas for it."

Not only Pitt but the whole of both parties faced a new and delicate situation. They did not know how long the King's illness might last, or whether he would ever be fit for business again. The Whigs, for purely selfish reasons, had always supported the Prince of Wales, who on his side gave them every encouragement for the future, partly out of his loathing of his father, which, and for somewhat better reasons, his father cordially returned. In fact, the vagaries of the King's sons were to be the bane of successive administrations for some time to come. It was not without good reason that Wellington later described them comprehensively as "the damndest millstone that were ever hung round the neck of a government."

PART III

1805-1809

XIV

IN THE MIDSUMMER of the year 1805, the *Trident* with Sir Arthur
Wellesley aboard and homeward bound put in at Jamestown, the
port of St. Helena, and Sir Arthur went ashore for a stay of three weeks.
He had been ill during his last few months in India, and though the
voyage had done him some good, he suffered badly from seasickness
and was glad of a turn ashore. The rest and the climate of the island did
much to restore him, and he ever afterward remembered the weather as
"charming." (Some ten years later he revived the recollection when an
even more distinguished visitor to the island was noisily complaining of
the unhealthiness of his enforced residence.) Sir Arthur was also to recall that the house in which he stayed, the Briars, was a pleasant place,
lying in its own grounds in a deep valley through which ran a road that
soon began to rise steeply to one of the highest points of the island. Since
he was recuperating and had no official duties, he spent much of his
time on horseback, exploring the not very exciting resources of St.
Helena. One day, in idle curiosity he rode up the hill from the Briars,
characteristically noting that in several fields beside it there were admirable sites for shore batteries which could command the harbour and its
approaches. But there did not seem to be any reason why an enemy
should ever want to attack St. Helena, or why any guns should ever be
sited there—certainly he could not foresee the day when every commanding site by the roadside would bristle with guns, when the green fields
would be white with soldiers' tents and when infantry bugles would usher

in every morning and lay to rest every night. There was a good view
from the high point but nothing of interest on the ground—only a derelict farm called Longwood. Yet, ten years later, and for another six
thereafter, the eyes of half the world would be turning apprehensively toward that farm, which had been hastily prepared as a residence for the
man who would live and die there—the man whom the world could never
forget and whom it still feared. Sir Arthur soon tired of the scanty interest of St. Helena—it was after all only a "Little Island," a description
which, according to the tradition which is too good not to be true, had
been the last words written in an unfinished "Geographical Register of
the World," begun by Lieutenant Bonaparte of the Artillery Regiment
of La Fer somewhere about the year 1790.

Sir Arthur could not foresee the future. Indeed, so isolated from the
world was a traveller by sea in those days that when he resumed his voyage to England he had not the least idea of what was going on in Europe
and on the very sea across which the *Trident* was beating to northward.
She sailed in convoy with "about forty sail of Indiamen and Chinamen,"
while hundreds of miles to the west of her course Admiral Nelson was
hunting Villeneuve's fleet toward the West Indies and beginning, with
sinking heart, to believe that he had lost touch with them—that, while
he sought for and eventually found them but never came up with them,
his departure from home waters, essential though it was, had torn a
gap in the wall of ships which kept ceaseless watch round England and
left her naked and vulnerable to a thrust from Brest or Cadiz or both.

The *Trident* sailed on northward, passing a long way west of Cape
Trafalgar. Since it was high summer and the days were clear and the
sun bright, Sir Arthur caught a glimpse in the far eastern distance of the
Portuguese hills near Torres Vedras and of the barren mountains of
Spain where they towered above Corunna. The *Trident* had an easy
passage of the Bay of Biscay and he saw Ushant in the distance, standing
up out of the sea. (Ten years later H.M.S. *Bellerophon,* sailing south-
westward, would pass it a little further out, so that her chief passenger,
who came scrambling up on deck when they told him, had to stand
straining his eyes for the last glimpse which he would ever get of France.)
Sensibly enough, *Trident* stood well away from the more northerly coast
of France, and no one aboard could see the streets of Boulogne or the
dunes about Wimereux and Étaples, Montreuil and the Canche River.
They could not know that, almost at the same time that Nelson turned
eastward again and took up the stern chase of Villeneuve's squadrons,
the Grande Armée, through all its cantonments on the coast of Normandy, was astir and that it, too, was turning to the east. Had they
known they could hardly have believed it any more than the people of

the south coast of England believed it when at last the news filtered across the Channel. The threat had hung over England's head so long that her people, being what they were, had almost come to accept it as an inherited but unpleasant part of their daily existence, not unlike their climate. Like their successors of 1940 they never really believed that the enemy would get across, and, again like their successors, they felt almost aggrieved when he abandoned the attempt.

It is always rash to insist too far upon historical parallels. The men and women who lived in the England of 1805 knew nothing of the death that comes from the skies, nor had any reason to think that their own cities and fields would ever be anything but inviolate. Total war, though it was one of the Emperor Napoleon's more dubious legacies to mankind, had not yet sunk into the consciousness of England's people or dimmed England's traditional merriment. In many counties it was still a disgrace to "list for a sojer."

Behind the sure protection of England's ships and seamen, the Hambledon heroes played against "All England" on Broadhalfpenny Down, and the Marylebone Club was considering a move to Mr. William Lord's new ground in St. John's Wood. In a London untroubled by "blackout" the Lyceum Theatre was experimenting with Winsor's new system of gaslighting, and *Leonore* was in rehearsal at Covent Garden. Racing went on unabated, without even the excuse which later generations were to make, in the words of Mr. John Jorrocks, M.F.H., "It improved the breed of cavalry 'oss and so enabled us to lick the world." Fashionable London sniggered at the latest scandal about the Prince of Wales and his intolerable brothers, and preparations had already begun for that least delicate of proceedings known as "The Delicate Investigation." This was yet another manoeuvre of the Prince, made in the vain hope of concentrating attention on his wife's follies in the hope of distracting it from his own indecencies. Its final result would be seen many years later in the Bill of Pains and Penalties, commonly miscalled the "Trial of Queen Caroline" and more accurately described by Mr. Creevey as "a Bill to declare the Queen a whore and to settle her on the King for life."

England did not yet know it but this year of 1805 was the year of her deliverance. It was not to be a deliverance like that of the years which followed 1940, with the steady diminution of a threat. The deliverance of 1805 came suddenly and before anyone was aware of the lifting of the threat. One week the Grande Armée crouched menacingly on the cliffs at Boulogne. The next week they had turned their backs on the French coast and the English venture and were swinging east and northward along the dusty lanes which led to the frontiers and were to lead eventually to the bloody fields of Austerlitz and Ulm and Jena. Murat, jewelled, feathered and furred, rode ahead of the cavalry reserve. The Imperial Guard, anticipating the mechanized infantry of a later century, travelled in commandeered farm carts. The ordinary infantry of the line marched for mile after mile after weary mile behind their corps commanders.

For a few days Berthier was in command but, as the army had nothing to do except to march and as he had already drawn up the march tables, there was little mischief that he could do. He would no longer be in command when they met the enemy. A few days after the divisions had turned northward, a fast carriage drove out of Paris, with an escort of the green-clad Lancers of the Imperial Guard. Its occupant was a little man, wearing the same green uniform, a cocked hat across his brow and, on his white waistcoat, the scarlet ribbon of the newly-formed Légion d'Honneur. The carriage rattled on through all the days and much of the nights, with frequent changes of horses; and when the nights began to grow cold, the passenger would pull on his grey overcoat—all Europe was soon to know and fear the "petite redingote grise." He overtook them long before they reached the frontier, and though he still travelled in his berline most of the time, there were days when he would send it to the rear and mount his white Arab, Marengo, which had carried him in the Italian campaigns and which would carry him at Austerlitz, Jena, Wagram, Friedland, Eylau, Borodino and on the dreary trail back from Moscow; in the years of departing fortune at Lützen and Bautzen, Dresden and Leipzig, and in the hour of defeat as he ran for his life away from the field of Waterloo. He had been to France a deliverer from the evil men of the Revolution and the "Mountain," and he was soon to become her greatest danger and ultimately her destroyer. To the rest of Europe he was first a pest, then a destruction and finally a malign growth which to save life must at all costs be cut out and destroyed. To the British, always irreverent about their enemies, he was all these but also "Bonaparte the Corsican Banditto, led in chains by a British Tar," or "Little Boney" who would—but they knew he would not—come down, "and march his men on London Town." So, a hundred and more years later, Adolf Hitler, the enemy of the world, would be to England's Prime Minister, "this blood-thirsty guttersnipe," and to his fellow Englishmen not only that but also an unsuccessful and ridiculous parody of Charlie Chaplin.

To all Europe—to nearly all the world—Napoleon would become the legend whom the French poets remembered and which they used to keep alive Bonapartism in the hearts of the French, till an Emperor should come to his own again. "Napoleon," Philip Guedalla wrote, "be-

came a name for all the fine freedom and brave endeavour of the past . . .
the cold figure of Caesar came alive and stepped down from his niche,
and the conqueror of the world became the people's friend." Beranger
tells of the old Frenchwoman, recalling her memories of him for the
benefit of her grandchildren who ask:

> "Parlez-nous de lui, grand-meré,
> Parlez-nous de lui."

"Mes enfants," she says, "dans ce village,
> Suivi des rois, il passa. . . .

> . . . . . .

> "Il avait petit chapeau
> Avec redingote grise,
> Presque de lui Je me troublai,
> Il me dit: 'Bonjour, ma chère.'"

And her children cry out as to one who has seen a great vision and
heard a divine voice:

> "Bonjour, ma chère!
> Il vous a parlé grand-meré,
> Il vous a parlé!"

The Emperor had made his decision and that decision delivered England. He distrusted Villeneuve as he distrusted all his admirals, and he
knew that none of them had any heart for the invasion of England. But
above all, he distrusted and hated the sea. Perhaps that distrust was a
legacy from the boy who had wanted to serve the sea and had been
denied his desire. Perhaps it sprang even more from the conviction of
the mature man that here was an element over which he had less authority than had the islanders whom he hated and yet, in some queer
way, respected and almost loved.

Hitler is said to have felt something of the same ambivalence for
Britain, something of the same conviction that, when all else was
reckoned up and accounted, there were only two European nations of
stature, his own and Great Britain. Years later, at St. Helena, Napoleon
admitted it more than once, saying, "After all, there are only two nations
who count, France and England," and explicitly to the British Admiral
Malcolm, "There are only you and our people. No one else matters."
His history had always moved from one island to another and would to
the end of his days—Corsica, England, Elba, St. Helena, they were all
his enemies or his prisons and the sea was his destruction.

Yet neither at the height of his power nor in the day of his humiliation does he appear to have mentioned or even to have recognized the

existence of the sea's greatest servant, who was also one of the greatest causes of his downfall. As he cursed Villeneuve and turned eastward, Nelson, also cursing Villeneuve—but never the sea—was racing westward with a fervent prayer in his heart and on his lips that he might not come too late to save England.

August was the month of crisis and decision. In the middle of June, Nelson, then at Antigua, learned at last that beyond a shadow of doubt Villeneuve had turned for home and was several days' sailing ahead of him, but even then he was not altogether certain of his information. It was not impossible, it was not even unlikely, that Villeneuve, though he had undoubtedly sailed, might have headed for Jamaica where he would threaten, and might do worse than threaten, one of England's richest colonies. If that were so and Nelson allowed himself to be hoodwinked, England would suffer a grievous loss by his fault, although if he came up with the French off Jamaica, he could save the island and destroy the fleet in the same battle. But, if his information were true and the French were really sailing eastward, every ship, every gun and man, would be needed in the western approaches, in the Channel or off Cadiz, where the Spanish Fleet was ready to join Villeneuve as soon as he gave the order. The blow might fall directly on the south and west coast of England or, no less probably, might round Land's End and strike at Ireland. Nelson knew only that he must be close at hand to wherever it was to fall. With all the strength that he could muster and in touch with Collingwood and Calder and all the others whose guard in the Atlantic had never slackened through the long months and the rough seas and blasting winds, he had to make his decision with imperfect knowledge and without help. Being what he was, he made it in a moment because he knew what his duty was.

He had been on the Mediterranean station when he left to chase Villeneuve, and failing different orders, his duty was to return there even if by so doing he should not be just at the point where he was needed. He would at least be where the Admiralty's fast frigates could find him, whereas now he was, and during his Atlantic crossing would be, out of reach of messages or orders. On June 12 he made up his mind that the French were sailing for Europe and took his decision. "I am going towards the Mediterranean," he wrote to Lord Barham at the Admiralty, "after Gravina and Villeneuve, and hope to catch them." He had covered the 3,200 miles which separate the Straits of Gibraltar from Barbados in little more than three weeks, an average pace of 135 miles a day. He and every man in his fleet set themselves to beat what was almost a record for so long a voyage and to make landfall in Europe under the three weeks which the outward voyage had taken. He said nothing of his intention to his officers and men. There was no need; they all knew him and knew where his heart was.

England had no lack of great seamen in that age. She had Collingwood, Cornwallis, Bickerton, Home Popham, Calder—no less great for being unlucky—and immediately below them such captains as Blackwood, Berry, Hardy, Codrington. She had only one Nelson—a little frail man, always in poor health, invariably and dismally seasick on every commission and every voyage, with a lion's courage and a woman's gentleness; who had or made time, whatever else was happening, to look after the raw and puzzled new midshipmen and to protect them from the hell of cruelty and the abyss of ignorance which had been their lot in his own younger days; who kept perfect discipline aboard his ships and throughout his fleets without ever flogging a man, as indeed did Collingwood, though few other commanders in those days; who had always about him a touch of that showmanship which is no hindrance but rather an asset to any commander who is so perfect in his duties and so absolute in his valour that he can afford a few eccentricities and can render them endearing; who above all was a man whose trust in and reliance on his God were so complete and so unquestioning that they spread without words spoken outward from him and downward to every half-naked gunner and blackened powder monkey who, often drunk and generally blaspheming, and perhaps devoid of any personal faith, yet did not question that the Lord of Hosts was on his commander's side.

Nelson loved the courtesy and hospitality of the sea and always had his captains to dinner on the eve of battle. He loved his own uniform and decorations so deeply that he was always the most smartly dressed officer in the Fleet when the guns sounded and the drums beat to quarters for action—so much so that Sir John Moore, himself well-decorated and smartly uniformed, complained that Nelson always looked more like "a Prince in an opera" than a seaman on the verge of action. England had decided—and England was coming to know—that she had but the one Nelson and would never have another. And now it was August 1805; England would have him for no more than another two months.

Greatly as Nelson fretted on the return voyage and anxiously as he awaited news of the situation nearer to home, the reality was little less perilous and disaster not less possible than in his most distracted imaginings. The squadrons near the English coast and the western approaches were stretched to the utmost to keep their watch, and there was no reserve to spare for additional dangers. Cornwallis, known and loved by his men as "Old Billy Go-tight," was blockading Ganteaume's twenty-one battleships in Brest with twenty-two of his own. Stirling's five ships were holding Missiesay's equal number in Rochefort, while Calder, with twelve sail of the line, held fourteen combined French and Spanish ships in Ferrol. Thirteen sail were in the West Indies or on their way there, and one lay on guard off Naples. In the Channel there were seven in reserve; and Collingwood off Gibraltar, with only five of the line, was watching the Straits and Cadiz, in which port lay ready for sea two Spanish first-rates and two lesser battleships together with an unknown number, any or all of whom would soon have finished their refitting and be ready to put to sea.

Nelson's ten sail were hundreds of miles away to the west and, even should they catch up with Villeneuve, would be faced with his ten battleships. If he should miss them, these ten would be added to the strength to match them. The position was made even worse by the imminence of one of Pitt's less judicious ventures, for a large convoy of transports carrying Sir John Craig and some 8,000 soldiers lay in Portsmouth harbor, ready to sail on "a foreign expedition, going no one knew whither," so wrote Ensign Boothby of the Royal Engineers who was a member of it. They were in fact destined for a grandiose scheme of combining with a Russian force, which should, but might not, meet them off Corfu for the liberation of the Neapolitan mainland and the defence of Sicily. It was an ambitious, if not wildcat scheme, for the Russians were notoriously unreliable and the Neapolitans reliable only in their unwillingness to help themselves. Nelson himself had said of a recent attempt of theirs, "They lost not much honour by it, for God knows they had not much to lose; but they lost what they had." Perhaps the worst thing about the venture was the strain which escorting it would put upon a British Fleet which already had its hands full and more than full. Fortunately it never sailed.

On July 7 Villeneuve's ships were reported in sight, and Barham from the Admiralty moved every available squadron to intercept him before he could make Cadiz. Sir Robert Calder met him on the twenty-second and fought an inconclusive action in which he captured two Spanish ships but, possibly through no fault and certainly through no failure of courage of his own, allowed the rest to put safely into Cadiz. Villeneuve naturally claimed it as a victory, but England, with something less than justice, called it a defeat and prepared to wreak on Calder such a vengeance as they had meted out to Admiral Byng, "pour encourager les autres."

Nelson's *Victory* for all her efforts failed to beat the record time for her outward voyage, and the pace as they beat to eastward against headwind after headwind must have seemed to them intolerably slow. The Fleet itself, from too much hard service and too little time for repairs and maintenance, was below its best sailing form and was much hampered by the lagging of one or two ships whose bottoms were hopelessly foul and by one, the old *Superb,* which should have been scrapped or converted long before—the "lame duck lagging, lagging all the way" of Newbolt's ballad. It had been "Eastward-ho for Trinidad," now it was "Westward-ho for Spain," and though it was "ship ahoy a hundred times a day" there was never a glimpse of Villeneuve's topsails. It was a captured frigate, the *Curieux,* which had seen them and raced for Plymouth Sound to carry the news which set Barham at the Admiralty to issuing rapid orders and sent Calder to Teneriffe and to the ruin of an honourable career.

Nelson and his men first heard of them when they landed at Gibraltar on July 20, 1805. It was the first time that Nelson had set foot ashore since June 16, 1803, two years earlier. Three days later, having waited for orders which never came, he was at sea again, making for Ushant, for Collingwood and for the Channel Fleet. The stay at Gibraltar had allowed the lame ducks to catch up, and when Nelson met Collingwood, he handed over twelve sail of the line, ten of which had served under him for the last two years. Their names are like a chime of remembered bells or the chorus of a familiar sea shanty—*Victory, Canopus, Superb, Spencer, Tiger* (once *Tigre*), *Swiftsure, Belleisle, Conqueror, Leviathan,* and *Donegal,* with two others, *Royal Sovereign* and *Spartiate.*

Two ships only left for England. Nelson sailed in *Victory* and dropped anchor off Spithead on August 18, 1805. She had still before her an honourable and battle-scarred career before the fate of the seas brought her ashore to lie, as she lies still, in Portsmouth Harbour. For Vice-Admiral the Viscount Nelson and Bronte there remained exactly two months and three days of life before Trafalgar and death.

XV

IN NOVEMBER 1805, Pitt returned thanks to the Lord Mayor's banquet in London, in what must surely have been the shortest and perhaps the most felicitous speech ever made by a Prime Minister at that function. The Lord Mayor had referred to him as the "Saviour of Britain," and Pitt answered, "My Lord Mayor, I return you thanks for the honour which you have paid me, but Britain is not to be saved by any one man. She will, I trust, save herself by her efforts and Europe by her example."

That was only a month after Trafalgar had been fought. If two months earlier an inquirer had asked almost anyone in England for the name of the man who would save her, it is almost certain that there would have been only one answer, "Nelson." Ten years later, had the same question been put, the answer would probably have been "Wellington," but they never loved him as they did Nelson. In the summer of this year these two men, who did not know each other even by sight, were to have their first and last meeting.

It seems unlikely that, had they been able to know each other longer and better, they would ever have become friends. Their characters were too fundamentally different for that. They were alike in their devotion to duty, their courage and their skill as fighting men, but in nearly every other way they were as unlike as two men can be. There was in Wellesley nothing of Nelson's flamboyance and showmanship. It is not surprising that when they met in "the little waiting room on the right hand" in the old Colonial Office in Downing Street, Sir Arthur's first impression should have been one of shock and distaste. Strange as it must seem to us today, who know their greatness, both of them were calling by appointment on Lord Castlereagh, who did not trouble himself to send for Nelson for the best part of an hour and kept Sir Arthur waiting until he had finished his first interview.

Nelson had no idea who the other man was but Wellesley recognized Nelson at once, "from his likeness to his pictures," as he later told Croker, "and the loss of an arm." One can imagine that Wellesley would have been satisfied with a civil exchange of greeting followed by a silent period of waiting, but Nelson began to talk at once. Wellington told the story of their meeting to J. W. Croker nineteen years later. "Nelson," he said, "entered at once into conversation with me, if I can call it conversation, for it was almost all on his side and all about himself and in, really, a style so vain and so silly as to surprise and almost disgust me." There is nothing surprising in this, for Nelson's nerves must have been as taut as violin strings, after his long and agonizing chase of Villeneuve and his constant seasickness. Keyed up for the tremendous fighting which he knew must come in a matter of days or weeks, he was confident in his country, his ships, his God and in himself. He would not have been the human man that he was if he had not been deeply moved by the overwhelming expressions of love which had greeted him on his landing at Portsmouth and had followed him wherever he went (except perhaps into the old Colonial Office in Downing Street). Many men will know from their own experience of the nervousness which precedes even such a tiny ordeal as going in to bat in an important match or lining up at the start of a big race how the overcharged nerves find release in a torrent of often quite trivial chatter. There is little evidence that Sir Arthur Wellesley ever experienced such tremors, and he was intolerant of any display of feeling or evidence of self-absorption.

It may be—it would not be at all unlike him—that he showed his boredom and irritation, for in a few minutes Nelson left the room to ask, Sir Arthur suspected, the identity of his companion. When he returned he spoke in a very different way. "He talked of the state of this country and of the aspect and probabilities of affairs on the Continent with a good sense and a knowledge of subjects both at home and abroad that surprised me equally and more agreeably than the first part of our interview had done; in fact he talked like an officer and a statesman. I don't know that I ever had a conversation that interested me more." Wellesley added the comment, "If the Secretary of State had been punctual and admitted Lord Nelson in the first quarter of an hour, I should have had the same impression of a light and trivial character that other people have had, but luckily I saw enough to be satisfied that he was really a very superior man; but a more sudden and complete metamorphosis I never saw." They never met again, but at least Nelson went to his death and apotheosis knowing that owing to Lord Castlereagh's unpunctuality, Sir Arthur had revised his earlier opinion ("charlatan" was the word which he used to Croker) and considered him a "very superior man." In which opinion Sir Arthur found himself for once in agreement with the great heart of England's people.

Nelson was at his country house at Merton when his orders came, brought by another seafaring friend, Captain Blackwood, a frigate commander. It was about five o'clock in the morning of a lovely day of late summer. The apples were red and heavy on the trees in the orchard, and the long herbaceous border was full of the season's flowers—crimson, pink and white phlox, purple asters, red-brown hellenium, scarlet geum and golden elecampane. The air was full of the scent of the dew-drenched herb garden—thyme, mint, wormwood, lovage, dittany—and above all of the pungency of trodden chamomile on the paths and the lawn. Sleepy grooms were around to change the horses of the carriage which had brought Blackwood, and soon it was running through the Surrey fields and the villages where the first threads of smoke were beginning to rise from the cottage chimneys. But it was not to be his last sight of Merton, nor his departure from England. There was much to do in the way of making plans and refitting *Victory* for the coming fight.

At the Admiralty, Lord Barham gave Nelson a virtually free hand in every way, but when he handed to him the Navy List and asked him to choose his officers, Nelson gave it back saying, "Do you choose, my Lord. The same spirit actuates the whole profession; you cannot choose wrong." The conference in London took several days, but he was not to sail until after the fifteenth of September, so that he was granted one more time of happiness in Merton and with his Emma. On the thirteenth, Lord Minto went there to wish him Godspeed and found Lady Hamilton "in tears all day yesterday, could not eat and hardly drink, and near swooning, and all at table."

On the fourteenth, all was ready and the carriage ordered for ten o'clock at night. "At half-past ten," Nelson wrote in his diary, "drove from dear, dear Merton, where I left all which I hold dear in this world, to go to serve my King and Country. May the great God, whom I adore, enable me to fulfil the expectations of my country. If it is His good Providence to cut short my days on earth, I bow with the greatest submission."

It was dark when the carriage ran through the Surrey lanes and over the county border into Hampshire. There were dim lights in the windows of the farm labourers' cottages and an occasional glimpse of fully lighted buildings—some great house stood among elms or oaks, in the middle of silent pastures where sleeping cattle lay. It was nearly full light when they turned due south to take the Portsmouth road through Petersfield and the fringes of the Southwick Forest. (Their way lay very near to Hambledon and Broadhalfpenny Down—did any Hambledon hero, one wonders, turn restlessly in his bed or wake at the sound of the hooves and wheels, not knowing that part of England's greatness was passing by?)

It was just before six in the morning when the carriage came into Portsmouth. The people were astir in the streets, where apprentices were taking down the shutters from before the shops and sprinkling the pavements—when there were any—with fresh water. In the cavalry barracks the trumpets sounded reveille, and occasionally the carriage had to slow down because of long lines of horses going out to exercise, each half-dressed and lounging trooper leading three horses beside the one on which he rode. Out in the bay the great ships, in their black and yellow stripes, swung gently at their anchors, and so still was the morning that the notes of the boatswains' pipes came clearly across the water as hands were piped to breakfast. At the foot of the harbour steps the Admiral's barge waited with its crew of bronzed and pigtailed seamen in their straw hats and striped jerseys, under the command of a junior officer in blue and gold.

The streets were crowded and every person in them seemed to be making for the harbour. They had come dressed in their best, as though for a fair, the girls in their prints and sprig muslins, the men in home-spun coats and woollen stockings or leather gaiters, with bunches of ribbons in their caps—yet not without a wary glance around and behind in case the hated Press Gang should be watching. The ale houses were already open, and here and there could be seen a recruiting sergeant in cavalry blue or in the scarlet of the line, his shako or helmet gay with red, white and blue ribbons, standing a last mug of ale to the wretched rustic boys who had signed on the night before and were now facing the realization presented by sore heads and the consciousness that they had "listed for a sojer." (Somehow the sergeant seemed less genial than he had a few hours ago in the bar, when he had regaled them with beer and wonderful stories of the luxury in which the Fusiliers or Dragoons lived and of the probability of every recruit becoming at least a colonel within the month.)

The crowd was thickest near the steps which led from the quay to the waiting barge, and the soldiers who were responsible for keeping the way clear were hard put to it to avoid using violence. (One foolish or inexperienced subaltern went so far as to order his men to use their bayonets, but the men were slow to obey and the crowd became so threatening that he thought better of it.) All England seemed to have come to wish their hero Godspeed, as indeed all England did in their hearts. The oars of the boat's crew went upright in salute as the Admiral stepped aboard, and a few minutes later the barge was crossing the harbour to carry Nelson to his flagship, *Victory*.

"The reception I met on joining the Fleet," Nelson wrote, "caused the sweetest sensation of my life." Collingwood's twenty-nine sail of the line lay off Cadiz, and *Victory* joined them on the eve of Nelson's forty-seventh birthday. There was, by his orders, to be no official sign of his arrival, neither by dressing ship nor by hoisting flag nor by the sound of gun. He was too keenly alive to the danger of any unusual bustle or display in the Fleet being observed by a French frigate or a fishing vessel which might pass on the news. The welcome was informal in the rows of grinning faces aboard every ship and the cheers which rang out from ship to ship as the Admiral's barge brought him home to them. Officers then serving remarked afterward of the lightening of hearts throughout the Fleet when they knew that their Admiral had taken command of them. The men respected Collingwood, for his courage and fairness, but he did not inspire them with his dour North Country ways as Nelson did. The officers, who also respected and liked Collingwood, had been complaining of a lack of that social life throughout the Fleet, so unlike the gaiety which Nelson encouraged because he knew how sorely needed was any distraction for men who lived hard and seldom set foot ashore. It had always been his pleasant custom to invite all his officers to dinner in his flagship, and it was that generous heart of his which no one could fail to recognize. Collingwood was a good sailor and, like his superior, a disciplinarian who hated cruelty and used mercy. He had, his officers admitted, all the virtues, but he was admittedly a dull dog. He disliked either giving or attending parties and his principal hobby, when he had time for one, was trying to accustom his dog "Bounce" who accompanied him on all his voyages to the sound of gunfire. Collingwood's heart was always in his own Northumberland and among the oaks and ash trees on his estate. He was a typical example of the men who provided many of Britain's fighting leaders, a countryman and a sportsman, such a man as the officers in Wellington's Peninsular army who shot "red-legged partridges" and followed the hounds which had been sent out from the Shires for their relaxation. It must have seemed intolerable to Collingwood that Bounce should be so obstinately cannon-shy. Nelson knew what was in their minds. His easy hospitality had done much to weld them into what they were, "Nelson's Band of Brothers."

His birthday gave him the opportunity of entertaining them on a large scale. And since, birthday or no, time was pressing and they might have to fight any day, he would combine it with a conference on his plan. It was the plan which he had evolved against this day and which he had discussed with Barham at the Admiralty. No battle plan can be laid down in advance without the probability that some unforeseen happening will interfere with it, but the basic principle of it can survive much that is unforeseen as long as the plan itself is sound. It was this plan to which Nelson casually referred as the "Nelson Touch" and it had the great merits of simplicity and boldness.

He expounded it to them on that evening of his birthday in his cabin. The table had been cleared of all except the bowls of fruit, the wide-bottomed ship's decanters and the glasses. The light of the candles struck fire from the ruby heart of the wine and was thrown back in splinters of flame from the braid and decorations of the naval uniforms. (A few days later the whole cabin would be stripped and guns would be run in and lashed secure, with their muzzles pointing out of the portholes. In British ships the Admiral's and captain's cabins became in action no more than a gun position.) Lanterns hung from the roof which was so low that Captain Hardy, the tallest officer present, could hardly stand upright. Their light shone down on the polished table on which lay the charts over which Nelson leaned as he made his meaning clear, and under which lay Collingwood's Bounce, happily oblivious of the thunderous gunfire which the near future would so surely bring. There was a faint sound of music from the ship's band which was playing somewhere outside the cabin while, further off and inaudible, some of her company were hastily preparing the sets for a play which they had begged to be allowed to present before the officers.

The "Nelson Touch" was simple in its objects and its methods. The main object, he reminded them again and again, was "annihilation"— not simply victory but annihilation. There were to be no more indecisive fights—such fights as he had called "Howe" victories—with an enemy fleet badly mauled but just able to crawl into port. The last of them had been Calder's unhappy affair off Finisterre, and Calder was under orders to leave the Fleet and report to the Admiralty for court-martial. (Characteristically, Nelson insisted that Calder must go home in his own flag-ship, as his right was. It would deprive the Fleet of a capital ship on the eve of action, and it was contrary to standing orders in such circumstances. But it would not be the first time that Admiral Nelson had disobeyed orders, nor the twentieth that he had done some generous act of the sort that made men love him.)

Since "annihilation" was the only object, attack was the only means of accomplishing it. Nelson had laid down the general principle of attack and was willing to leave most of the details to his captains, confident that they would observe his standing instructions that, in the event of orders not being received or signals not being seen in the heat and smoke of battle, "no captain can do very wrong if he lays his ship alongside the nearest enemy to him." He had always been the most daring of commanders, and this new plan of his was based on the abandonment of all previous principles of naval tactics.

It had been the custom for fleets to advance in column formation, in line ahead, until they had made contact with the enemy, who, of course, would be performing the same movements in accordance with the fixed custom of eighteenth-century war. As soon as the fleets made contact each of them would perform complicated manoeuvres to bring the column into line, and that line abreast would be the order of battle. It was all a part of the eighteenth-century formalism which had set the armies of Europe to a stately pavane in the neighbourhood of the nearest fortress, in which manoeuvre was of more importance than fighting and a pitched battle to be avoided at all cost. The Revolutionary armies had torn a hole through the stiff marching and countermarching of Austria and Prussia, and the Emperor was dictating the new art of war as he fought it. Naval tactics were still untroubled by a hint of the new unorthodoxy, till this night in the Admiral's cabin on *Victory*.

Nelson would make no distinction between sailing order and battle order. His ships would advance in two divisions, each in line ahead, and in those positions they would fight. There need be no manoeuvring from one formation to another, since the head of each division would be given a certain point in the enemy's line at which to break through. If they were lucky they might even catch the enemy in their change of formation, since it was certain that the Combined Fleets would follow the old way of advance, manoeuvre and attack. Collingwood with one division would pierce near to one flank and turn inward, rolling the line up toward the centre.

The plan could succeed only if the Combined Fleet were to adopt their usual tactics, but Nelson had every reason to hope that they would do as they had always done. The French and Spanish ships were excellent in battle, being mostly bigger and more heavily gunned than the British. But they were not nearly so fast or so easy to manoeuvre, nor were they manned by sailors with anything like the experience and training of Nelson's men. If they attempted any new and difficult kind of tactics in face of the enemy, it was a fair chance that they would throw themselves into confusion. The risk which Nelson took was calculated and not excessive.

His officers received the "Nelson Touch" with enthusiasm. "Some shed tears," he wrote to Lady Hamilton, "all approved. It was new—it was singular—it was simple," and from admirals downward it was repeated. "It must succeed, if ever they allow us to get at them! You are, my Lord, surrounded by friends whom you inspire with confidence." By an odd contrast the plan which Nelson had made was in one respect very like the tactics which Wellington was to employ in the Peninsular War, and in another the exact opposite of it. Both were based on the knowledge that the enemy would adopt a certain formation and that this was the best way of countering it. The fundamental difference was that whereas Nelson proposed to use column against line, Wellington would use line against column.

Nothing better shows the difference between the two men than their methods of giving orders and their relations with their immediate subordinates. It is impossible to imagine Picton, Crawford, Hill or Uxbridge shedding tears at a tactical novelty, however startling, nor does it appear likely that such a demonstration would have been cordially received by the Commander-in-Chief. His commanders were good soldiers and loyal men, but there was no "Band of Brothers" feeling among them. They were used to curt oral orders or to scribbled notes, which, while economical in words, told them all that they needed to know. It is possible that had they assured him that he was surrounded by friends whom he inspired he would have answered with his favourite rebuke, "Don't be a damned fool, sir."

There was only one Nelson. A scene which might have been ridiculous with any other commander was in his presence as natural and genuine as he himself. It is to be believed that Nelson knew that he would never come out of this battle alive. This is no romance built up after the facts are known, for he spoke words during those few days before action which showed that he expected to find death in it. On the day that he left Portsmouth his youngest sister, Catherine Matcham, came with her husband to see him off, and as they were parting he said to her, "Oh, Katty! that gipsy!" He had had his fortune told many years before in the West Indies by a gipsy, who had told him that he would be at the head of his profession when he was forty. He had asked, "What then?" and she had answered, "I can tell you no more. The book is closed." In the prayers which he confided to his diary, he seemed to contemplate death without fear and with complete acceptance if it were the will of God. Early in the morning of the twenty-first, when the Combined Fleet was in sight, his frigate captains came aboard *Victory* to get their final orders. Among them was Blackwood of the *Euryalus,* an old friend, and to him as he was going overboard to rejoin his ship, Nelson said a friend's good-bye, adding, "I shall never see you again." He wrote to his daughter,

Horatia, and to Lady Hamilton and confided many thoughts of them to his diary. Especially was he worried that, should he die, there would be no money to support Emma unless the country would see to it as repayment of the debt which they would owe him.

He was astir early on the twenty-first of October. The Combined Fleet had been at sea since the day before, and he was all but in contact with them. He stood on deck at five in the morning, wearing his full-dress uniform without his sword (men said afterward that he knew that he would be shot and did not want sword or sword-belt driven into his body). His frigate captains came and went, and still he stood on deck watching through his telescope the distant sails of Villeneuve's fleet.

The morning of October 21, 1805, was fine with a little mist, which soon began to clear, and across the sparkling morning sea, the enemy fleet looked imposing in its array of thirty-seven galleons and three-deckers. He had been afraid till this moment that they might still seek to run from him or turn back into harbour, but now he knew that they were ready to fight. Even at a distance of some miles, he saw that his instincts had not been at fault, and the ships were coming out in a way which made it clear that they were about to move into line abreast. For the moment he could do no more, and he went down to his cabin to break his fast. There he recorded in his diary, "At daylight saw Enemy's Combined Fleet from East to E.S.E. bore away; made the signal for Order of Sailing, and to Prepare for Battle. The enemy with their heads to Southward; at seven the enemy wearing in succession." It was a hurried and scanty meal, for a fatigue party was waiting to strip the cabin and run in the guns. Nelson watched them taking down the pictures and said to the officer, who was handling the portrait of Lady Hamilton, "Take care of my guardian angel." His servant had laid out his white gloves and dress sword. He took the gloves and went back on deck.

Some of the frigate captains were still waiting, and Blackwood begged him to transfer his flag into *Euryalus,* fearing that *Victory* leading the van would become too obvious and doomed a target, but Nelson refused, just as he refused to take off the decorations which would make him so conspicuous. It is almost certain that there had been a concerted move by some of the captains to thrust their ships ahead of *Victory* when she closed on the Combined Fleet to protect her from the worst of the fire, though it may have been that the other ships' companies were eager to come to grips and coveted the honour of firing the first shot. Whatever may have been the reason, Nelson was soon aware of the bows of a ship beginning to draw up on his own quarter ahead of him. As she still crept up alongside, Nelson ran to the side of *Victory* and called across the narrow strip of water, "I'll thank you, Captain Harvey, to keep your proper station." If there were any conspiracy to protect him it is certain that Nelson knew nothing of it.

The story of the action of Trafalgar belongs to naval history and has been told well and often. The story of Nelson's last hours and death has become a part of Britain's tradition. In those hours he showed every side of him, which made him the man that he was—his courage and skill, his devotion to his God, his touch of showmanship. About eleven o'clock in the morning the fleets were only three miles apart, and he went down to his cabin for the last time. The big day-cabin was bare and grim, stripped of all its ornaments and furniture, and half-naked gunners stood to their guns. But his little night-cabin was not needed for battle, and there he wrote in his diary the prayer which was later to become so well known.

"May the great God, whom I worship, grant to my country and for the benefit of Europe in general, a great and glorious Victory; and may no misconduct in any one tarnish it; and may humanity after Victory be the predominant feature in the British Fleet. For myself, individually, I commit my life to Him who made me, and may His blessing light upon my endeavours for serving my country faithfully. To Him I resign myself and the just cause which is entrusted to me to defend. Amen. Amen. Amen." Immediately he had finished he went on deck again and dictated his famous signal to Pasco, his flag lieutenant. It was characteristic of him that he wished to begin it with his own name, "Nelson confides—" but had to substitute "England expects—" owing to the limitations of the signalling code.

It is perhaps inevitable that words which are to pass into history and tradition should be less highly regarded by the men who hear them spoken and who are often too much engaged in other matters and duties to pay great heed to them. Lincoln's immortal speech at Gettysburg seemed an afterthought, an extempore postscript to the main speech of the day, which was delivered at great length by a popular orator and not a word of which has passed into history. Nelson's signal has since become a living part of British naval tradition, but the only recorded comment on it by a contemporary was a testy remark by Collingwood on the *Royal Sovereign*—"I wish Nelson would stop signalling. We know well enough what we have to do." The signal went out at 11:35. Half an hour later the *Royal Sovereign* burst into the enemy line ahead of the lee division—too far ahead, in fact, since the perfect condition of the ship and the captain's eagerness to close brought him to action a quarter of an hour before the next ship of his division had come near enough to open fire. At twenty minutes past midday the French *Bucentaure* fired a ranging shot at *Victory,* a mile and a half away. There were no more entries made in *Victory*'s log until the evening. Then the entry ran— "Partial firing continued until 4:30, when, a victory having been reported to the Right Honourable Lord Viscount Nelson K.C.B., he died of his wound."

XVI

THE COACHES which ran throughout England to carry the news of Trafalgar were decked with laurels for a victory and with black for a death. The nation's sorrow for the loss of Nelson was so sincere and overwhelming that that loss almost overshadowed the immensity of the victory. Men realized that they had won a battle and had lost a hero, but it would be a little time before they came to understand how much more than a battle their hero had won for them. In London the crowds went silently about the streets nor was any window alight in celebration. In the country the bonfires, which had stood ready for lighting in the event of an invasion, did not spring up into flames to acclaim a victory, and more passing bells than chimes of thanksgiving rang out from cathedrals and churches.

What the British could not yet realize—it would have been a miracle if they had—was that there might be sporadic fighting as long as the land war lasted but that the French and Spanish fleets had taken such a thrashing at Trafalgar that their hearts were broken. If they could avoid it they would never put to sea again when a British squadron was anywhere near, nor would Napoleon, powerful as he was and more powerful as he was to become, dare to use sea power as a part of his grand strategy. The vagaries and vacillations of admirals and, even more, the incalculability of wind and wave had thoroughly disgusted him with the sea and with the men who went down to it in ships. Like Hitler after 1940, he still talked grandly of the invasion of Britain which he would accomplish when he could spare the time, but he knew that the time had passed and that it would never come again.

His failure only increased his bitterness against Britain and his determination to conquer her by other means. A victory on land he did not doubt that he could achieve if only the perfidious British would come near enough to him to be smashed. Until that should come he turned his attention to another method of attack by hitting at Britain where she was strongest and therefore most vulnerable, in her financial system and her trade. He could not hope, as later enemies hoped, to starve her into submission, for Britain at the beginning of the nineteenth century was still mainly an agricultural nation and grew enough supplies to feed her population, though so fast was the population growing and so many of them were turning from the countryside to the towns that she could not hope to be for long in that happy position.

Pitt was a financier and no fighting man. He had long had the design of using Britain's wealth as a weapon of war by buying foreign allies to save British lives. During the years before Trafalgar he had been steadily building up an alliance against France, wooing Austria, Russia and Prussia with subsidies and trade concessions to attract their military power and appealing to their spiritual and monarchial principles with the idea of an alliance of ancient monarchies to stand together to resist the usurper Bonaparte. It was a scheme such as only a mind of the greatness of Pitt's could have conceived and partly carried through, but to succeed it needed more time than was available and endless co-ordination between allies. Austria would be loyal to her commitments and, except the French, had the largest and most fully trained army in Europe, but it was also the slowest moving army and possibly the most out-of-date. The white-coated Austrian infantry were first-class fighting material, but they had been trained in the tradition of Frederick the Great's Prussians. Their courage in battle was admirable, their drill and turn-out were superb, but they had not the faintest idea that war had gone beyond the days of the fortress and the march and countermarch. They had learned nothing from the history of the last few years, when a new and highly unorthodox military machine had been started and was running successfully. They would not learn without a dreadful lesson because they still chose their commanders on the double principle of aristocracy and imbecility. The Archduke Charles, a really good and intelligent soldier, was relegated to a watching role in the south of Austria, against the threat through Italy or Switzerland. The Austrian Army, which was to form part of the joint forces of the Grand Alliance to smash Napoleon, was committed to the care of an incompetent called Mack, whom Nelson, who had had previous experience of him in Naples, called "a fool and a coward."

Russia was incalculable as ever. Her Emperor would, no doubt, honour his agreements but in his own good time and in the aura of royal and religious mystery with which he surrounded himself. Of the Russian Army no one knew much except that it was very large and that it was always late for everything.

The Prussians were at least calculable in the sense that they could be bought, but they were greedy and apt to bargain with both sides at once. Their King was a nonentity with a brave and splendid Queen, their army was only a shadow of the formidable force which Frederick had commanded. Though there was a party in the country consisting of patriotic young men, devoted to their Queen and to a vision of a strong and independent Prussia, their movement was only in its infancy; and it was to be several years before, as the Jungbund, they could make their influence felt in arousing resistance to the French. Pitt's Grand Alliance was in mortal danger before it had had time to become a reality.

No one knew this better than Pitt himself, and all through the winter of 1805 he worked to restore the confidence of a Britain which had swung from the triumph of Trafalgar to a gloomy foreboding of events in Europe. Not all that he did was wise; some things were rash to the point of folly, and the most rash were the two military expeditions he sponsored. Craig and his force were at last shipped off to the Mediterranean to see what they could do to help a rather problematical Russian operation against the Neapolitan mainland and, in the hope of forcing Prussia's hand, a mixed force of Hanoverians and a few British battalions were sent to the Elbe.

Meanwhile despondency and rumour were sapping British confidence in Pitt's strategy and in Britain's allies. It became known that a Prussian envoy had been sent to the French headquarters to confer with the Emperor, presumably in the hope of getting better terms than those which Pitt offered. The envoy stayed an unconscionable time there while Prince Talleyrand of Périgord exerted his considerable charm and unlimited resource to carry out Napoleon's orders to him, which were that it did not matter what he told the Prussian as long as he took a long time over telling it. And while he told it the Grande Armée was deploying for the winter's campaign.

In London the rumours multiplied. At first they told of disaster to the Austrians and of Napoleon triumphantly entering Vienna, so that in November the Marquis of Buckingham gloomily gave it as his opinion that Trafalgar had been fought in vain. The next report spoke of the utter collapse of Austria and the almost certain defection of Prussia. These moved Pitt to the dubious expedient of sending fresh troops to reinforce those already uselessly employed on the banks of the Elbe. (Sir Arthur Wellesley was appointed to command a brigade in this force.)

Then, as Christmas drew near, the tone of the rumours changed from despair to reckless optimism and with as little reason. It was said that the Russians, under their Czar, had beaten the French in Moravia, that the Archduke Charles with a huge army was marching up from the south to complete the ruin of the French and, soon afterward, that the French had again been defeated, this time utterly, in Bohemia. Britain, on the whole, enjoyed a prosperous and optimistic Christmas. She was to have a shattering New Year's greeting.

The truth came through in the last days of December. The Prince of Wales had spent his Christmas at the Pavilion at Brighton, and on December 29 was entertaining a number of guests to dinner. In the flush of the time of year or the hour of the day, he announced to his guests that all was over with the French and the war was won. Since he fancied himself as a strategist, with all the assurance of a man who had never seen a battlefield, he sent for his maps and spread them out on the table, inviting the company to gather round to hear his exposition of the victorious Austrian tactics. Before he had got into his stride a servant interrupted him with the news that a messenger had arrived from the Horse Guards with an urgent dispatch. His Highness was absent from the room for a long time, while his guests sat on at the tables, passing wine and talking idly, and the long candles burned lower and lower. The exhausted band outside played and replayed all the available music in their repertoire. The hour grew later, and there was almost complete silence round the table. The Prince had been so long absent, and though it was a time when hopes ran high, there was always the possibility of a sudden reverse.

They were confirmed in their guess, though not yet told the facts; when at last the Prince returned, he showed no disposition to renew his tactical lecture but ordered a servant to take the maps away and excused himself to his guests on the ground of urgent business. Next day the whole country knew that what Pitt had most prayed for, his alliance, had not been granted to them. Indeed, any man who hoped for time as an ally when Napoleon was his enemy had nothing to hope for. The French had marched across Europe at a steady pace of fifteen miles a day, while the Allies were mobilizing and equipping their troops and not very enthusiastically making plans for the campaign. In September the French had struck their first blow at Ulm, where Ney surprised Mack and captured fifty thousand prisoners. Though Britain had before this December day learned of this, it had been reported as an isolated skirmish of no importance, since the bulk of the Austrian Army lay on the

Danube and had made contact with the Russians under Kutusoff. That was true enough, though the deductions which were based on it were fallacious. It was said that Napoleon had only had a brush with a small force of the Austrians and that he would not dare to attack the main Russian and Austrian armies under the direct command of their sovereigns.

It would seem that the Allies did not yet fully understand Napoleon, who had no respect for dynastic sovereigns and less still for the Austrian Army, which he had beaten before and was confident that he could beat again. He knew that they would certainly move too late and probably in the wrong direction and that the Russians, under Kutusoff, would be prudent to the point of inaction. He swept down on them and came face to face with them at the village of Austerlitz. They stood to fight on the first day of December, 1805, which was the eve of the anniversary of Napoleon's coronation. On the second he routed them and sent his cavalry hurtling after them in pursuit all that night and into the next day. Within a fortnight he had imposed his own terms on Austria. The Russians withdrew into their own fastnesses, and he was ready for Prussia.

Britain knew the shock of disaster made all the worse by their previous pipe dreams of victory. Pitt had indulged in no dreams but he recognized disaster, and his strength gave way under this terrible blow. All through that winter he had kept his courage high and reassured his anxious colleagues and country, and all the time he had been failing physically and suffering agonies from gout, trailing from London to Bath for the cure and back again, knowing that for what ailed him there was no cure. He had put his trust in the Grand Alliance, and it had broken at the first shock. Prussia would be the next to fall, and that any time Napoleon cared to take her.

Of all his life work there was nothing left. The thousands of pounds of his country's money which he had poured out were a dead loss. He himself was so bedevilled by debts that he hardly knew where to turn for help, while obstinately refusing the aid of colleagues. He had even known the humiliation of being followed by duns and dreading the sound of a knocking at his door. In his state of mind and health he was unable to realize that all was not over with the Grand Alliance of his making. It had moved slowly and creakingly and had fallen to pieces at the first shock. But—this was the great thing—it had moved. And if it had moved it could surely move again.

The Russians had endless resources in men; their main army was more or less intact and their Emperor so deeply wounded in his pride that he thought more of revenge than retirement from the struggle. Prussia had been of no help, but she had not turned against her friends—Pitt

E

was never to know that she soon did so. If the British forces which he had sent to the Mediterranean and the Elbe were of no use, they had succeeded in remaining intact. The Alliance was not broken beyond mending; the damage which it had suffered was no more than the initial trouble which might happen to any machine driven beyond its strength too soon. If he lived he might yet be the first to put his hand to the task of repairing what he had made.

But he had no reserve of strength and he was in pain and despair as the news worsened with every passing day. Lord Harrowby, who had been sent on an urgent mission to Prussia to try to stiffen her resistance, returned home to report failure. Gower, the British ambassador there, wrote that all idea of resistance to France had vanished. Pitt lay dying in his house at Putney for a little time after the last news from Berlin had come in. Sometimes he seemed to rally but there was no strength in him and he became delirious, crying out for news from Europe, asking for Harrowby, whom he did not recognize when he came, and occasionally breaking out into cries of "hear hear" thinking himself to be back in the House of Commons. He died on January 23, 1806. Britain had had her year of deliverance and had paid a terrible price for it in the loss of two of her best servants and greatest men, Nelson and Pitt, within three months. There had been no hope of deliverance in Pitt's heart when he died, nothing but a consciousness of utter failure, in both public and private life.

Pitt's death shocked the country profoundly. "Now all is void and blank," Lord Aberdeen wrote, "in whom can we put our trust?" while Fox, who had been his lifelong opponent, cried out that something was missing from the world. Lord Sheffield wrote to a friend, "Unless something very extraordinary happens I shall consider the game as lost." There was reason for depression if not for despair. The Treaty of Pressburg which Napoleon had forced on the Austrians after Austerlitz gave Istria and Dalmatia to France and acknowledged the Emperor's right to the throne of Italy and to the disposal of all Germany. The Holy Roman Empire had for some time been little but a name. Austerlitz and Pressburg destroyed even that. Prussia was being drawn into the net, for her envoy had stayed too long at French headquarters and had listened to too much of Prince Talleyrand's charming talk. Having seen at first hand the apparent invincibility of the French Army he committed his country to an alliance with France, gaining in exchange the possession of Hanover, which belonged to Britain, his country's ally. The Czar of Russia had withdrawn to nurse his wounded pride, and no man could guess when next he would take the field.

The immediate need in Britain was for a government to carry on the

work of Pitt in rescuing and strengthening the Grand Alliance. There
was at the moment no man of such stature as to compare with him,
though there was no lack of able men in both parties. The ablest of them
perhaps were Lord Castlereagh and George Canning, but there were reasons why neither of them could command support. Castlereagh was a
very poor speaker, though, as the Congress of Vienna was later to find,
an admirable debater and negotiator. Also he was unpopular, partly because of his rigorous methods in suppressing rebellion in Ireland and
partly because he had all Pitt's chilly hauteur without yet, it would seem,
Pitt's ability to compensate for it. No one could deny Canning's ability
but he was—and he had mostly himself to blame for it—even more unpopular than Castlereagh. He was possessed of a satirical sense of humour
and a mordant wit to which he allowed far too free play in both speech
and writing. In the time of the French Revolution he had been one of
the chief contributors to *Anti-Jacobin*. Both prose and verse can be read
today with as much enjoyment as when they were topical and up to the
minute. Few men then or since have handled satire and parody better
than he or composed a mock-heroic couplet to compare with—

> *The feathered tribe with pinions beat the air,*
> *Not so the turbot and still less the bear.*

That was all very well when it was directed against the French Revolutionaries and their supporters in England, but it became intolerable when
his own countrymen and colleagues became his butt. It was said of him
that he never made a speech without making an enemy, and by this time
he had made so many that his chance of reaching the premiership was
negligible. And even had there been no other objection to him, the obscurity of his origin was enough to deter possible supporters in an assembly of privilege and aristocracy. Charles Grey, later Earl Grey and himself a Prime Minister, once went so far as to exclaim in public, "God
forbid that the son of an actress should ever become Prime Minister,"
an intolerable remark and one which earned for Grey Canning's undying
enmity.

British political genius in a difficulty runs easily to compromise, and
Pitt's cousin Grenville formed an administration which was called "The
Government of All the Talents," rather on the principle of a travelling
theatrical company without a star which will advertise an "All Star
Cast." But in this assembly of mediocrities there was one undoubted
star, Charles Fox, who, in spite of the King's violent opposition, was
brought in as Foreign Secretary. The King had sworn that never again
would he have Fox as a minister. Grenville swore that he would not try
to form a government without him, and the King yielded. To do him

justice, once he had yielded he did his best to accept the position with grace and to persuade his Queen, who hated Fox even more than he did, to receive him. So successful was he that Fox remarked to a friend, "The Queen's civility to me today was quite marked, especially as it is the first time she spoke to me since 1788."

The new government, lacking Pitt's authority, lacked also his resolution, and there was a marked feeling among them that peace with France was perhaps attainable and should at any rate be attempted. It was the stronger for the presence of Fox, who had always been a passionate lover of and believer in peace and whom, because of his attitude toward France during the Revolution, France might find acceptable as a negotiator. Nothing at the moment could have pleased the Emperor better. He was not remotely interested in peace for its own sake but he needed time. He had to consolidate his gains in Europe and to train recruits for his Army to fill the gaps left by the casualties of Ulm and Austerlitz. In the diplomatic world he was glad of an opportunity to cement his arrangement with Prussia, and he was not without hope of being able to win the Czar of Russia over to his side and away from the Alliance.

Diplomacy was less to Napoleon's taste than the simplicities of war, nor, since he equated the word with dishonesty, was it his strongest asset. His one object was to gain time for preparation for further conquests, and he was quite shameless in his methods. Lord Lauderdale went from England to Paris as a special envoy to discuss terms of peace and found Napoleon not unco-operative. The French would be glad to agree to a treaty on the basis of "uti possidetis," and Napoleon, to guarantee it, as he imagined in good faith, made a secret offer to restore Hanover to Britain, ignoring the promise which he had publicly made, to give it to Prussia. Lauderdale found, as other emissaries to the Emperor had found, that the days and weeks went by and Talleyrand was unfailingly charming but that nothing solid came any nearer nor could anyone give him a definite answer about anything.

Lauderdale remained in Paris, while in the regimental depots and riding schools the new army of France was being forged, and in the shipyards the new fleet was being built. Every time that he saw Talleyrand or had an interview with the Emperor, he found to his disgust that France's terms had become more onerous and less reasonable. Napoleon spoke enthusiastically about peace in Europe, guaranteed by France, Britain and Russia, but he refused to take part in any joint negotiations, insisting on speaking alone and in secret to each power. Lauderdale easily recognized the well-worn device of trying to play off two allies against each other and grew suspicious of Napoleon's good faith. His suspicions grew as, with monotonous regularity, Napoleon explained that he had not meant what he was thought to have meant by "uti possidetis." His interpretation now was the basis that each power should keep what she now held except for any possessions which France wanted to add to her own share. He demanded the return of Sicily and of Malta.

He did not deceive Lauderdale. Still less did he deceive Fox, who was too true a lover of peace to believe that it could be bought by bargaining as in a market. When Napoleon asserted, "I want nothing on the Continent," Fox no more believed him than Mr. Churchill later believed Hitler's rodomontade about coveting no more possessions in Europe. In August of 1806 he told Lauderdale that it was obvious that no good could come of further negotiations and ordered him to leave Paris.

Only a month later Fox died, leaving a memory of a great orator, a devoted friend, a man of goodwill and clemency. It must have been a great happiness to learn in his last days that Parliament had passed the bill to abolish the slave trade. It was a cause to which, through all his life, he had given the best of his strength and of that loving kindness which was always overflowing for all desolate and oppressed, all prisoners and captives. With him died what little chance of peace in Europe remained. He perhaps could not have achieved it. No other man would have again attempted it or come anywhere near to a distant view of it.

The Emperor Napoleon did not want peace. His depots were sending a steady stream of trained men and horses to the fighting units, his forges and furnaces poured out guns and muskets. His diplomacy was never anything but an interlude in his warmaking. Now he was ready and it was Prussia's turn. Steadily the blue-clad infantry and gleaming cuirassiers marched north and west toward the frontier, and once more the carriage with its escort of Lancers of the Guard clattered through the towns and villages of France. He had made a treaty with Prussia only a year earlier, but that was not going to save her and—as if he needed a pretext for war—the King of Prussia lost first his nerve and then his senses and in trying to save his country ensured its destruction. He had been promised Hanover as a gift or a bribe, and he had only lately learned that Napoleon had subsequently promised it to Britain. His Queen and his people were naturally indignant and no less ashamed of the supineness which had allowed him to make the bargain with France in the panic which followed Austerlitz.

The King opened what were meant to be secret negotiations with Russia for an alliance against France—the first real sign of the resuscitation of Pitt's Grand Alliance—but his diplomacy was neither successful nor secret enough to escape the vigilance of Napoleon.

Prussia, with the precipitancy of desperation, gave France an ultimatum on September 26. The French advance guards had crossed into

Germany, and the Prussians demanded their immediate withdrawal. The ultimatum was sent on September 26. On October 14, 1806, Napoleon answered it by destroying the Prussian Army at the joint battles of Jena and Auerstädt. In November he was in Berlin as a conqueror.

XVII

WHEN SUCH great matters were engaging the attention of ministers, it was hardly to be expected that they would have time to spare for the immediate needs of a major-general, even for one with a good record of service in India. Sir Arthur was given a brigade of three infantry battalions, stationed at Hastings, with which, for a short time, he had one more experience of active service on the Continent.

His brigade was one of those who were sent to reinforce the troops on the river Elbe, though, fortunately for him, not long before the whole force was withdrawn, having accomplished nothing—hardly surprising as they never saw the enemy whom they were supposed to fight. They returned to Hastings with no greater experience than the usual one of bad weather and the invariable incompetence of all who were responsible for British supplies and medical services.

Wellesley did not see much of his three battalions once he and they were home again. One of the duties which he had set himself was the purely family one of watching the interests of his brother Richard, who was on his way back from India and expecting to meet with a hostile reception from the Board of John Company and from Parliament. There was even talk of impeaching him for his extravagance, his autocratic ways and his openly shown contempt for the Board of the Company. The movement was headed by a small group in the Commons led by an Anglo-Indian member called Paull. Had Pitt still lived it would probably have ended in talk and threats, since Pitt was a friend and admirer of Richard and, even had he not been, had the greatness of mind to distinguish between the solid work which a man had done and the irritating way in which he had done it. But, even after Pitt's death, the prospect of impeaching Richard did not seem very hopeful. Fox was against it, and his opinion carried great weight among "All the Talents." He was now in the government and perhaps not unnaturally took a less enthusiastic view of Indian impeachments than he had when in opposition, in the days of the trial of Hastings. Mr. Paull showed some pertinacity in introducing his motion in the Commons but he was unhappy in his moment. Honourable members had not forgotten the waste of time and the inconclusive end of the Hastings trial and were not inclined to stage another. In any case, they were all too much preoccupied with Europe to spare many thoughts for India. One effect of Paull's efforts was to bring Sir Arthur into politics, as member of Parliament for Rye. Since the attack would be opened in the Commons, he had decided to be there to meet it, and there was not much difficulty in finding a seat in those days of close boroughs for any man who could pay for one. In the Commons he proved himself to be more than a match for Mr. Paull, and after a few months, the attack on his brother ceased to interest even the few who had taken it up in the beginning.

Sir Arthur soon began to grow impatient with parliamentary life and to long for more active employment, but there did not seem to be any great prospect of it as long as Pitt's policy of not committing British troops on the Continent survived its author. Grenville had inherited Pitt's distaste for risking an army, though unfortunately he had also inherited the taste for sending small detachments on useless missions, to perish of cold and hunger rather than in battle. Sir John Moore was in Sicily with one such enterprise. But for the present Sir Arthur's brigade lay at Hastings, no one having thought of another destination for a small expedition. In some disgust with the military world, Wellesley's thoughts turned again to employment in a government office, preferably in connection with Ireland where he already had experience. He was better off financially now than he had been when last he had been home, but he was by no means rich and he needed money, since he had not forgotten his gentleman's agreement to marry Kitty Pakenham.

In March 1807 he became Chief Secretary for Ireland. It was a satisfactory arrangement, giving him a position and an income which enabled him to marry and keep his wife in comfort and dignity. Moreover, it gave him work which he understood and liked, although he never looked on it as anything more than a temporary post. He might be bored with soldiering and disgusted with the obsolete ways of the Horse Guards but there could be no other life for him as long as Britain was at war. Before accepting the Irish position he had besieged the Horse Guards and the Prime Minister and anyone who he thought might help him to a command because, as he wrote to Richard, "It is such an object with me to serve with some of the European armies that I have written to Lord Grenville on the subject, and I hope that he will speak to the Duke of York."

For the moment there was no prospect, yet active service on the Continent lay in the nearer future than he or anyone else imagined, and when it came it would be in a part of Europe to which only one man at that date had given serious military thought. The Emperor Napoleon was in Berlin, victorious and apparently unbeatable, with Austria and Prussia at his feet. Russia was at least temporarily repulsed and Poland was falling to Murat's invasion. The Emperor, who saw most things clearly, knew that his most dangerous enemy was Britain, from whose invasion he had turned away. Britain had the sea power to restrain him, the finance to support his adversaries and the foreign trade which France needed but could not win as long as the British fleet ruled the seaways. He could strike at the roots of her prosperity, her overseas and carrying trade, by denying her entrance to the ports of Europe; and he now had control of the coasts of France, the Low Countries, Germany, Italy and Sicily. In effect he controlled every European port of consequence except those of Spain and Portugal. On November 21, six weeks after the battle of Jena, he published the Berlin Decrees which forbade all commerce or correspondence with Britain to as much of Europe as France controlled and declared forfeit all ships and goods hailing from her shores or from those of her colonies. French seamen might be too supine or too cowardly, the sea too unruly, to allow his destroying the British merchantmen, but it would be of little use to Britain to send her ships freely over the seaways if they could find no harbour or port to take the goods which they carried.

Napoleon knew that to make the Decrees fully effective he must control not the greater part but the whole of Europe. To that end he began to lay his long-term plans. Russia, he believed, he could beat on land, and this was to be the first objective. He had met them at Austerlitz and had no great opinion of them as soldiers. He was hopeful of reaching an agreement with the Czar for some sort of alliance between their countries, a hope which he mostly based on his own confidence of his ability to dominate the Czar's mind if negotiations could be opened. The Czar was a strange mixture of autocrat and visionary, liable at any time to seize a strip of someone else's property without warning, if he happened to fancy it, liable at others to see himself as a person half-divine, the possessor of prophetic gifts and Heaven's arbiter among the nations of

Europe. Napoleon hoped, not without reason, to appeal to both his cupidity and his visions, to bring him into the ring of prohibited coasts which was to strangle Britain. It would, no doubt, be easier to accomplish this when the Russian Army had been decisively beaten in the field, and Russia thus frightened into making an agreement with France.

The idea began to grow in his mind that, once the middle of Europe had been made secure, the Spanish Peninsula must be his next objective. Portugal was Britain's oldest ally, and her trade with Britain in wine alone was considerable. Spain was his own ally, though after the debacle of Trafalgar she was noticeably less cordial and he hesitated to rely on her. It was a situation which he would have to clear up if he was to make his blockade of Britain fully effective, and if Spain would not co-operate as an ally she could be forced to submit. Then he would hold the coastline of Europe from Riga round the Cape of Gibraltar to the Adriatic, and Britain must surely be ruined. It was perhaps only a distant vision but it was the logical conclusion of the Berlin Decrees, and it was to give Sir Arthur Wellesley his command on the Continent and to set his feet on the road which led from Portugal, by way of Talavera and Busaco, Vimeiro and Salamanca, Ciudad Rodrigo and Badajoz, into the heart of France.

The Berlin Decrees were a deliberate attempt to strangle Britain's strength by gripping her most vital spot, her overseas trade. Britain, seeing it for what it was and conscious of her own ability to dominate the seaways, met it with instant defiance. In the first week of January 1807 the government issued a series of Orders in Council which forbade neutral vessels to trade between any ports which were closed to British ships. It was a bold move but one which was well within Britain's capability to enforce. The Orders in Council gave to the Navy powers to stop and search any neutral ship and to seize her if she were carrying goods to any of the closed ports, but the Cabinet, wisely, decided not to press those powers too far. There was a large and growing trade between Britain and the United States and a lesser but still important one between Britain and Denmark. Britain had no wish to embroil herself with either, and her ships' captains had orders not to interfere with any American or Danish ship so long as she was not carrying contraband and was plying directly between her own ports and those of France and her allies. If the ship carried goods between one French controlled harbour and another she was to be seized.

It was a reasonable and moderate method of applying the Orders but it was to prove better in theory than in action. In fact, while Britain genuinely tried to make the application of the Orders as little harmful to neutrals as possible, it was almost impossible for her ships to respect neutral rights, as far as stopping and searching them went. In no other way could they satisfy themselves that the neutral vessels were not carrying contraband or be assured of the ports to which they were sailing. The Danish side of the question soon solved itself when Britain, from sheer necessity, immobilized the Danish Fleet in the harbour at Copenhagen, after which Denmark could no longer be called a neutral. The difficulty with the United States was of far more importance and was to lead a few years later to the American War of 1812, along with its repercussions in Canada. The United States was a young, prospering and proud nation and naturally resented any claim by another nation to the right to interfere with her trade. She resented it the more from Britain because time had not yet erased the feeling which had caused the War of Independence. The Americans still regarded the British as exploiting colonizers who cared for no interests but their own, while they kept a warm esteem for the French who had helped them in their struggle for independence. The name of Lafayette was still a powerful memory in Washington, and the Day of Independence was a day of genuine thanksgiving throughout the States for delivery from Britain's tyranny. It is perhaps fair to add that America, being a young nation, was abnormally sensitive about her dignity and ready to resent or even to discover slights on the smallest provocation. The British captains honestly tried to carry out their duties in a moderate way, but it was not easy.

It was made more difficult before long by the Royal Navy's incessant need for men. It was caused partly by the need to replace war casualties and partly by the feeling of relief which followed Trafalgar, after which, it seemed to many men, the command of the seas was fully assured to Britain and could be held with a normal Navy. The Army at home was constantly demanding further drafts as its strength was steadily frittered away in comparatively small and often useless ventures on the fringes of the Continent and in the West Indies. It was common knowledge in the Navy that deserters were often taken into American ships, and after Trafalgar the number of these desertions was increasing. The conditions aboard a ship of the line were such as some men would only endure in a time of the country's danger, when there was active work to be done with the chance of a fight and of prize money from a captured ship. Trafalgar had been fought and won, the French and Spanish fleets had been beaten from off the seas, but the long and tedious work of patrol and protection went on. There were no relaxation of discipline, no increase in comfort; pay was often overdue, sometimes by as much as two years; shore-leave was so scarce as to be a miracle. The sailors in American ships were better paid, better fed and better cared for. They had regular voyages and ports of call and knew more or less when they could expect to see their homes and families again. Undoubtedly there was a steady drain of men from the British to the American ships, and there was a very natural temptation to British captains, when they stopped an American ship for search, to run over her crew in the hope of finding a deserter. Among the American captains there was a no less natural disposition to resent this and to refuse to hand over the men whom the British claimed. At first this was only a minor irritation, but it was steadily to grow as the British became more demanding and the Americans more defiant. Yet it is hard to see how it could have been avoided if the Orders in Council were properly to be carried out.

The Danish episode is not one which any Briton can look back on with pride, and only the sheer necessity of the pressure by France can excuse, though barely justify, it. Britain and Denmark were not at war with each other, but Denmark was being drawn into the ring of unfriendly countries which Napoleon was building up by his Berlin Decrees. She had a strong and efficient fleet, most of which was in 1807 concentrated in the harbour of Copenhagen. Britain could not risk the addition of the Danish ships to the enemy's strength at sea, but had no possible right to harm or seize them. She solved her difficulty by an abrupt demand to Denmark to surrender her fleet to Britain, giving her word as "a sacred pledge" to hold the ships in her own harbours as long as the war at sea went on. The Danish were a proud people with a long tradition of seafaring, and they refused the demand. Britain could hardly give way, and her only other choice was to enforce it, which she did by sending a portion of her own fleet supported by a military force in which Sir Arthur Wellesley commanded the reserve brigade. The troops surrounded Copenhagen and, with some reluctance and after waiting as long as they dared, bombarded it. After a few weeks in the autumn of 1807 the Danes capitulated. The expedition returned bringing with it the Danish ships and without any feeling other than that of a disagreeable task accomplished.

They had done what they had to do, but it was a shabby business. It was made to seem the shabbier by the connection between Copenhagen and their own Nelson on a day when no one could hold in question the honour of the Royal Navy. It was to be some time thereafter before men could hear with their usual contempt Napoleon's sneers against "Perfide Albion." At the moment when Britain was mounting this enterprise the Emperor had his hands too full on the Continent to jeer at Britain or even to think of her. He was caught up in the necessity of breaking the Russian military power and, by so doing, bringing her into the blockading ring against Britain. His first attempt was in February of 1807 after a dreary stay in winter quarters in Poland. The Russians moved first, and there was a scrambling, inconclusive affair at Pultusk just after Christmas of 1806.

In the following February the two armies came face to face at Eylau on a dreadful day of high wind and driving snow, on a battlefield broken up by frozen pools. Napoleon had given his orders for a movement of encirclement such as had been successful against the Prussians at Jena, but, by pure mischance, only one messenger was sent with them to Bernadotte, who had the encircling role, and the messenger was captured. The result was a battle fought without tactical shape, a murderous hand-to-hand fight, in which more than a quarter of the strength of each side became casualties.

The events of the coming years were implicit in the bloody stalemate of Eylau, and the Emperor was bound to the course which in the end was to defeat him. He would have to fight the Russians again and, at whatever cost, to defeat them—as, indeed, he did at Friedland in June 1807. Failing that, he could never bring them into his blockading ring to play their part in his stranglehold on Britain.

Even when he had done that, it would not be enough as long as the ports of Spain and Portugal lay open. After Eylau, he may have known —as later Hitler knew—that he could never feel safe in western Europe with an undefeated Russia at his back, so that he was to be driven on not only to Friedland but to Borodino and Moscow and the horrors of the retreat in the campaign of 1812.

He was to be driven, at the other extreme of his territory, to the attack on Spain and the war which he himself later called the "Spanish Ulcer." He had set himself to dominate Europe and was to learn that, unless he could dominate every square mile of it, his grand strategy must eventually fail. He was to learn, too, that no man—not even he— can direct campaigns at a distance of thousands of miles as though he were giving orders to an army on one field of battle and that subordinates who have been sternly taught to obey orders are often at a loss when those orders are delayed or do not come at all. Alexander the Great, whom Napoleon believed that he resembled, is said to have wept because there were no new worlds to conquer. Napoleon was to find the opposite—that he had conquered a Continent with the exception of one small island. That exception made all the difference between victory and disaster.

XVIII

SIR ARTHUR WELLESLEY was a man of his word and when he landed in England had by no means forgotten his understanding with Miss Kitty Pakenham. He was also, by this time, an experienced tactician and liked to reconnoitre a position before assaulting it. He knew as little about Kitty as a man can well know about his intended bride, and one thing that he did not know was whether she had already been captured by someone else. If so, he was freed from his understanding. After his manner, he reconnoitred unobtrusively by inquiry among mutual friends and, while on a visit to Bath, learned that she was indeed free and waiting.

Kitty, with all her shortcomings, was a woman of constancy and was not only waiting but eager for the man whose image, with small encouragement, it must be admitted, she had faithfully guarded in her heart for eight weary years. He went to find her, was rapturously received, and they were married in 1806. Soon after the wedding he took Kitty to court, where the Queen made much of them, and said to her, "I am happy to see you at my court, so bright an example of constancy. If anybody in this world deserves to be happy, you do. But did you *never* write *one* letter to Sir Arthur Wellesley during his long absence?" Kitty answered, "No, never, Madam." In reply to the Queen's next question, "And did you never think of him?" she said, "Yes, Madam, very often." It was perhaps as well that Her Majesty had the tact to refrain from asking the same questions of Sir Arthur, who was notoriously truthful. He had not written a word to Kitty since last they had seen each other, and it may be doubted whether she had been in his thoughts as constantly as he had been in hers.

No doubt Kitty deserved to be happy and no doubt she was not happy for very long. She was an affectionate creature and really loved him, but they had nothing in common and soon shared the misery which is the lot of two uncongenial people who are thrust into constant and intimate contact. Kitty kept her own counsel and hid her own growing unhappiness, but her husband was less patient and, for him, somewhat less discreet. He early complained to his brother of the ravages which small-pox had made of her skin. Soon, with even more questionable taste, he began to criticize her to other women, notably to his friend Mrs. Arbuthnot. "Is it not the most extraordinary thing you ever heard of?" he lamented. "Would you have believed that anyone could have been such a damned fool?"

As a husband should, he tried to share his own interests with her, while, as many husbands do, he ignored any of hers, which, to be sure, were few and trivial enough. He tried to talk to her of the affairs of the country and the world, but her brain was not equal to grappling with great matters of state or the doings of foreign nations. He reported angrily that talking politics or important subjects to her was like asking her to understand Hebrew. It was not long before he began to find fault with her in little ways and increasingly with her poor gifts as a hostess.

She did her best; God knows how she must have dreaded the entertaining which she found to be expected of her. She was shy and awkward in company, alternating long silences with the silliest of remarks, and no doubt she grew more tongue-tied and incoherent under the cold glance of those disapproving eyes. She had no dress sense, and wore for choice a constantly shapeless hat which she had made herself and which perched precariously on the back of her head. At formal gatherings, when the other women wore formal dress and their jewels, she would appear in plain white muslin without any other adornment and would sit, silent and adoring, following her husband with her eyes as he moved among the guests and tried to make up for her gaucherie. At times he even began to wonder whether she were in her right mind.

It was a sad beginning to their married life, and they were denied even the chance of a few peaceful years together during which they might have come to understand each other better. But Sir Arthur was devoted to his duty and to his career. A man whose home life is unhappy needs little encouragement to busy himself with outside matters and to be often absent from his home. Within a few days of their wedding, he left her to pay a visit to his constituency, assigning to one of his younger brothers the duty of escorting her to London and installing her in their new house.

Thereafter he was often absent on parliamentary or military business and intent all the time on securing for himself—and, of course, for her—some new and more lucrative appointment at home or, preferably, a new and reasonably senior command abroad.

With the world in its troubled state, he had not long to wait. In two years from their marriage, the summons came for him and he made ready to leave her. They parted in 1808 and he was not to see her again for years, except for a short time in the following year, and then he was moody and preoccupied with the business of the Convention of Cintra and the Court of Inquiry. In 1809 he left England again, and thereafter they did not meet until 1814 when he came back almost a stranger and a very alarming one. Now he was a duke and a field-marshal, revered by the nation, deferred to by the government, courted by the Prince Regent; a stern man with grey hair and abrupt speech; a very great man to be sure and bound to be greater still—everyone said so. While she—she was still nothing but poor, silly Kitty, who loved him.

On June 14, 1808, Sir Arthur and Lady Wellesley were entertaining Mr. Croker of the Admiralty to dinner in their London house in Harley Street. It was something more than an evening of ordinary hospitality, for earlier in that day the King had signed a commission appointing Sir Arthur to command a British force "employed on a particular service." The "particular service" was the command of British troops in Portugal and, it was hoped, later in Spain. He was still Chief Secretary for Ireland, and as this mission was intended to be only a temporary diversion there was no reason why he should not return to his duties in a few months. In the meantime Mr. Croker would look after Irish affairs for him.

It was past the power of any of them to guess that this temporary mission would last for seven years and that, when the Duke of Wellington returned, the Irish Office would have ceased to interest him.

Napoleon had moved against Spain to forge the last link in his chain of encirclement of England in the winter of 1807, with a diplomatic move which exceeded in treachery and blatancy any of his previous negotiations, none of which had been remarkable for scruple. In 1807, Spain was still his ally, though a most unwilling one. If he had ever had any regard for her the character and actions of her rulers had now completely abrogated it, and if there could be any excuse for Napoleon's scoundrelly behaviour it lay in those.

Charles IV, King of Spain, was a senile cripple; Ferdinand, the heir-apparent, was a nonentity who hated his father; and the Queen was completely dominated by Godoy, the Chief Minister, whose mistress she was. Ferdinand was plotting against his father; the Queen and Godoy were intriguing to prevent Ferdinand from succeeding to the throne. The Emperor of the French was not the man to be shocked by family disagreements, however scandalous, but he had been seriously annoyed by an indiscretion of Godoy's in the previous year. Godoy, who was known in Spain by the somewhat presumptuous name of "The Prince of Peace," had badly miscalculated the power of France after Trafalgar and had judged it time to withdraw from alliance with her. He had further mistaken the abandonment of the invasion of Britain and the move of the French Army toward the Rhine and the Danube for an admission of failure. He had decided that the time had come when it would be safe to cut the connection between his own country and France and had made his decision public.

It is possible that his desire for peace was genuine and his sobriquet not as absurd as it appears, but his timing was atrocious. The announcement of Spain's wish to withdraw from the French Alliance coincided with the victory of Jena, which showed how far France was from defeat. Godoy tried to retrieve his position by publishing a denial of his announcement, but few people believed him and the Emperor Napoleon was not one of them. From that moment Spain's fate was certain, and Godoy had every reason to fear that his own fate would be as unpleasant.

For the time being it suited Napoleon to overlook this slight and to appear to be on friendly terms with Spain, since there was no profit in fighting her if he could get his way by cheating her. He invited Spain to join with him in the partition of Portugal, which, being Britain's oldest ally, was the enemy of Spain as well as of France. All that he required from Spain was free passage through her territories for the troops who were to overrun Portugal, though he was willing for a Spanish force to co-operate if Spain wished it. The share which Napoleon offered to Spain in the partition of Portugal was a most generous one. He had no need to restrict himself in an offer which he had not the slightest intention of keeping. With a touch of cynical humour he added that it was his intention to give to the King of Spain the title of "Emperor of the Two Americas."

In accordance with the terms of the agreement Junot, with 25,000 men, entered Spain and marched through the country into Portugal, but at that point Napoleon's observance of the terms ended. On the heels of Junot's rearguard came the cavalry of a new French army under Murat which, as it advanced, occupied one after another of the cities of Spain until, in the spring of 1808, Murat himself rode ahead of his squadrons into Madrid. Junot, in Portugal, announced that "The House of Bra-

ganza has ceased to reign." The Emperor, who had by then arrived at
Bayonne and had summoned the Spanish royal family to meet him there,
informed them with as little equivocation that the House of Bourbon
had ceased to rule in Spain.

By way of enforcing his point, he announced that his brother Joseph
had been chosen as King of Spain by the general desire of the Spanish
people, though the desire found expression only within the narrow limits
which were directly in line of fire of Murat's guns. The announcement,
which shocked Europe as much as it dismayed the Spanish royal family,
gave pleasure to nobody but the Emperor of the French. Joseph, who
had not been previously consulted, did not want to be a king of anywhere, least of all of Spain, and had only been chosen because another
brother, Louis, who had already had experience of being King of Holland, refused to consider the translation to the throne of Spain which
was offered to him.

If Napoleon had most of the failings inherent in his Corsican birth he
had all Corsican virtues, not least among them gratitude for past kindness and a memory as long and retentive for that as for revenge. In the
same way as he rewarded his old nurse with money, his schoolmasters
with rich benefices, he heaped honours, riches and power—or perhaps it
would be more accurate to say the appearance of it—on his slightly dazed
and not altogether grateful family. His marshals and his diplomatists
became princes and dukes, but crowns and thrones were reserved for
the Bonaparte family and for those who married them. Family loyalty
and affection were an integral part of his Corsican character, and his
kin had to bear the insignia of his greatness. It did not trouble him at all
that most of them would gladly have forgone it and that hardly any of
them were capable of sustaining it. They were his family and it was his
duty to provide for them.

Nor was he moved by any consideration for the kingdoms on whom
he bestowed the doubtful blessing of a Bonaparte ruler. It was his will
that Joseph should be King of Spain whether Spain liked it or not. He
was soon to learn with a shock of surprise that Spain did not like it at
all and, because of that shock, to make one of his rare but also one of
his most serious miscalculations. In any case, he considered, the Spaniards were a worthless lot. They had failed him badly at sea and their
reputation as fighters on land was of old standing and had not lately
been given much chance of confirmation. The Spanish Army was—and
in this he was right, as Sir Arthur would agree—an army "pour rire." If
it put up any show of resistance a few of Murat's squadrons would soon
disperse it.

The Emperor was seldom at fault in his judgment of an army. Sir

Arthur himself remarked as soon as he made the acquaintance of the Spanish Army that its chief tactical accomplishment was its habit of "dispersing as soon as the first shot was fired and of assembling again later in a state of nature." "I don't know," he said on a later occasion, "what effect they may have on the enemy, but, by God, they frighten me!" The fatal mistake which Napoleon made was to fail to distinguish between the Spanish Army and the Spanish people. He had seldom troubled himself to study the characters of the peoples whom he conquered, contenting himself with his knowledge of their armies; and, for the most part, he did not go far astray, since most European armies were an epitome of their nations. Spain was a different problem, which he did not even try to understand and which did more than most other enemies to ruin him.

The Spanish Army, where it existed at all cxccpt in the form of ceremonial troops in Madrid, was an almost useless body. It was ill-armed, ill-equipped, ill-trained, seldom paid and commanded for the most part by senile aristocrats without knowledge of warfare or even of soldiering. Throughout the whole war in the Peninsula it accomplished very little and consumed enormous quantities of supplies of every sort. Yet it was a mistake to write it off, as the Emperor did, as wholly useless, since it was capable of extraordinary and unforeseen feats of valour as complete as its more frequent displays of cowardice. The first severe check to the French army in the Peninsular War came in the summer of 1808, when a Spanish army—though it is true that it was commanded by a Swiss general—surrounded a French force under General Dupont and compelled its surrender. The news was one of the first pieces of intelligence which greeted Wellesley when he stepped ashore at Corunna. (The Emperor's anger was terrific, and he kept the unhappy Dupont in prison without trial for several years. Yet Dupont had his revenge. He was to be the Minister of War under the first Bourbon Restoration in 1814 and, in that capacity, to sign the order committing his late master to his island prison of Elba.)

The Spanish people were not the best possible material for formal soldiering but they proved to be magnificent guerrillas. Everything in their nature that resented regimentation and corporate discipline came to its flowering when they operated singly or in small bands. Intense pride— pride in his nation, his province, his city and most of all in himself—is the truest and most consistent quality of a Spaniard—that *pundonor* which disdained the carrying of a musket in ordered ranks and forbade the obeying of orders sustained the courage, cunning and cruelty of a wolf when a man of the country fought alone or with a few of his fellows.

The Emperor was soon to find that it was useless to send one messenger or two or half a dozen for even a short distance in Spain. The message nearly always failed to arrive, and a few days later the mangled body of its bearer would be found naked on the hillsides. By the end of 1811 or the early part of 1812, it was considered necessary to send an escort of not less than a cavalry squadron with any courier who had to travel more than a few miles.

In the field the French could nearly always prevail but at the expense of constantly harried lines of communication, ambushed supply trains, massacred vedettes and messengers. The French in Spain were always to be short of supplies and ammunition and always taut-nerved because of the enemy who struck in the night and vanished before dawn. They were soon to learn that whereas a man can be hardened to face the loss of friends and fellows in open battle, he can be utterly undone by waking from sleep to find his comrade who lay down beside him still lying there in the morning with his throat severed or his heart transfixed. The Emperor did not yet know of this peril which walked in the darkness and destroyed in the noonday.

Sir Arthur Wellesley, on this last night in England when Mr. Croker was his guest, knew as little—knew, in fact, hardly anything—about European warfare. His experience on the Continent had been limited to two miserable campaigns in which starvation and disease were more dangerous than enemy guns. All his other experience had been gained in the East. This was a notorious fact and would have prevented his selection for a command in the Peninsula had it not been for Castlereagh's recommendation. As it was, the Horse Guards accepted him with a very ill grace and covered themselves by appointing a senior general to replace him and one yet more senior to replace the second, while, at the same time, sending for Sir John Moore to replace all of them. Wellesley, Moore noted, was "so young a Lieutenant-General that the King and the Duke of York objected to him." So Wellesley sailed for Portugal with the disturbing knowledge that he might at any moment be succeeded by first Sir Hew Dalrymple and second by Sir Harry Burrard and, possibly, finally by Sir John Moore.

It must have been all this which was running through his mind when he fell silent after dinner in Harley Street, thereby distressing that indefatigable diarist, Mr. Croker, who felt that his host ought to be providing him with material and pressed him to tell his thoughts. "Why to say the truth," Wellesley said, "I am thinking of the French whom I am going to fight. I have not seen them since the campaign in Flanders when they were capital soldiers, and a dozen years of victory under Bonaparte must have made them better still. 'Tis enough to make one thoughtful." He explained that his thoughts were running on the new

French tactics of the attack in column, which had been so successful against the most famous soldiers in Europe. He was thinking of it, after his manner, carefully and without fear, "because I am not afraid of them as everyone else seems to be; and, secondly, because I think it a false one against steady troops. I suspect all the continental armies were more than half beaten before the battle was begun. I, at least, will not be frightened beforehand."

Indeed, as he soon found out he had more reason to fear his allies than the enemy. When the French advance guards crossed the Pyrenees, a situation arose which was to be roughly paralleled when the Germans invaded Russia in 1941. Russia, it is true, was not then at war with Britain but she was certainly not friendly. As soon as the Germans entered her territory Mr. Churchill, Britain's Prime Minister, proclaimed that Russia's enemies were Britain's and that Britain would give her aid and support in every possible way, on sea, on land and in the air, till the Nazis were destroyed. In the same way, Britain in 1808 instantly forgot her quarrel with Spain and moved to her support against the world's enemy, France. Spain asked for help and Britain gave it unsparingly, though never quite in the scale which the Spaniards demanded as the minimum. (The Junta of Oporto, for instance, with a force of 4,000 men demanded arms, supplies and ammunition for ten times that number.) There was, under the Bourbon monarchy, a central government in Spain but it was little more than a name. The country was administered, as far as it was administered at all, by the provincial councils, the juntas, who were entirely self-sufficient and mutually exclusive, if not antagonistic. As a gesture of defiance to the invaders, the provincial juntas elected a central junta to co-ordinate their efforts. The central junta, for a time, met regularly, but, once they had settled the amount of their salaries and had created new and resounding titles for themselves, they lost interest in the war and were seldom heard of thereafter, so that the provincial juntas were left to fend for themselves, a task to which, to do them justice, they were quite equal.

"There is a way of conferring a favour," Napier writes in his *History of the Peninsular War*, "which appears like accepting one; and this secret being discovered by the English Cabinet, the Spaniards soon demanded as a right what they had at first solicited as a boon." In the first twelve months after the French invasion, Britain sent to Spain £2,000,000 in gold, 150 field guns, 200,000 muskets, 15,000 barrels of gunpowder, 10,000 sets of camp equipment, 40,000 tents, 92,000 uniforms, 356 sets of equipment and various other supplies. It was a tax on Britain's exchequer, already strained by years of war, but it could have been cheerfully borne had more than a very small part of these supplies reached the fighting line. Napier, who fought in the war as well as writing its history, asserts that "from first to last an English musket was seldom seen in the hands of a Spanish soldier." What made it even worse was that not a few of them were seen in the hands of captured French soldiers. The Spaniards and the Portuguese ate the food, sold the weapons and ammunition, and left the rest of the supplies to rot in their depots.

Wellesley had a speedy and enlightening introduction to these administrative methods as soon as he arrived in Portugal. He had set out alone, in front of his expedition, and travelled in a fast frigate to call first at Corunna for a reconnaissance, going on thence to Lisbon. There he was met by an archbishop, as representative of the local junta, who haughtily informed him that Portugal needed no help in men since she had enough, and those men of singular valour. On the other hand, she needed arms, powder, horses, food, wine, tobacco and above all gold and then more gold. Since Sir Arthur's men were on the way nothing could presumably be done to stop them. But in the meanwhile there were assembled a large force of Portuguese—men of valour, all of them—and the British commander must at once take them over for pay and rations. Sir Arthur was not too much staggered to refuse in his most incisive manner, and he never forgot his introduction to the Peninsula and to Iberian business methods. As he said later, "I have fished many times in troubled waters; but in Spanish waters I will never fish again."

XIX

WELLESLEY'S first campaign in the Peninsular War was short and eventful. His troops disembarked on August 1, 1808, and less than two months later he was on his way back to England with two victories behind him and, through no fault of his own, with a court of inquiry and possibly a court-martial in front of him. He was the victim of the Horse Guards' eccentric theories of command. When he arrived in Portugal he commanded some 12,000 men to whom should have been added 5,000 Portuguese troops. But Freire, their commander, had taken offence at Wellesley's refusal to pay his men and had withdrawn them and himself from the war area, though he had gone so far as to accept 5,000 stand of arms to equip them.

Wellesley spared no regret for the loss of this detachment and may even have been glad to see the last of it. He knew that Junot was at Oporto with 25,000 men and believed that they would move at once to attack him before his troops were ready to fight. He decided not to wait for Junot but to attack and so to deny to the French the choice of ground. He was in sole command of the British force, and he knew that it was too good a state of affairs to last long. Sir Harry Burrard was on his way to the Peninsula with Sir Hew Dalrymple only a few days behind him. Moore was also believed to be coming, though where he was or when he would arrive no one—the Horse Guards least of all—knew. Wellesley had no intention of waiting for his supplanters but moved against Junot by a road parallel to the coast which allowed him to keep in touch with his lines of communication through the Navy. On August 11 there was a skirmish—hardly more than a scuffle—when two British battalions surprised the French pickets, attacked them and, pressing their attack too rashly, suffered some casualties. The name of the village was Obidos but the affair does not merit inclusion in the long line of British victories. It is only memorable because it produced the first of those cold and stately rebukes with which Wellington's officers were to become so familiar. "The affair," he said, "was unpleasant, because it was quite useless and was occasioned contrary to orders, solely by the imprudence of the officers and the dash and eagerness of the men." But it served to show him that his men were good fighting material and needed only discipline from their regimental officers, who must first learn to discipline themselves.

The first serious engagement of the campaign came on the seventeenth of August at Roliça. Not more than a few battalions and batteries on either side were engaged, but for its size the battle was bloody, the British losing in killed and wounded 500 men, the French 600—in each case something like a quarter of the number engaged. The British came off better, and Wellesley decided to advance straight on Lisbon to attack Junot. He was stopped by the news of the arrival of a British convoy carrying stores and ammunition, a brigade of infantry and Sir Harry Burrard, who at once assumed command and signified it by cancelling Wellesley's orders for the advance. Wellesley, who had not yet learned the futility of arguing with a senile and senior officer, pleaded with him to let the movement go on, but Sir Harry was obstinate as well as senile and, in any case, was expecting to be superseded at any moment. So the initiative passed to Junot, who set out from Lisbon to find and attack the British where they lay at Vimeiro. They fought there through all the next day—a bitter infantry battle with musket and bayonet with Burrard commanding and Wellesley giving the orders. Late in the day the French, who had suffered much heavier casualties than the British, began to withdraw. Wellesley was giving the orders for the pursuit which would turn the retreat into a rout and cut the French off from their base at Lisbon, when Burrard came to life and countermanded the order. It was his sole contribution to the victory and proved to be the last order that he would give, since Dalrymple arrived late in the evening and assumed command. It was natural that Wellesley should feel disgust even if he showed something less than the standard of personal discipline which he exacted from his juniors. When Burrard countermanded the order for the pursuit, Wellesley, after pleading unavailingly for its continuance, flung away in disgust, saying audibly: "Well, then there's nothing for us soldiers to do but to go and shoot red-legged partridges." (One may

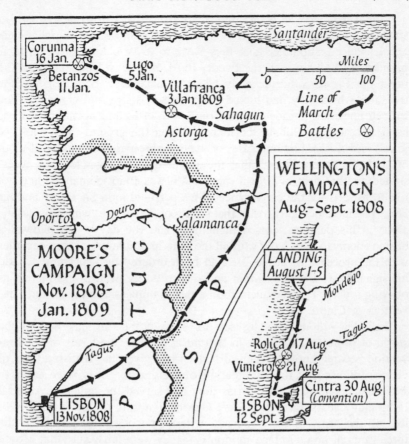

wonder how he would have reacted to similar behaviour by an officer junior to him.)

The next day, Wellesley renewed his entreaties for a forward movement, and all day, while the shattered French Army drew nearer to safety, Burrard and Dalrymple debated the advisability of an offensive move, and even went so far as to make tentative arrangements for one on the following day. It was August 23 and the British were nearly ready to move at midday when they were astonished to see General Kellermann approaching with a flag of truce and a request for an armistice pending arrangements for a French evacuation to Portugal. Wellesley, knowing the advantage to be gained from pressing a beaten enemy, argued hotly against any pause in the action, but his two seniors were happy to have won a victory at such small cost and accepted the French terms without arguing about them.

The French were to evacuate Portugal, which was good. It was not so good that they were to be granted free passage back to France in British ships and allowed to take with them their arms,colours and supplies. One article, indeed, stipulated that they were to leave behind them all their plunder, and all through the twenty-third of August and long into the night the French officers vainly tried to make their men disgorge the treasures which they had looted from houses, shops and churches. The French lines and parade grounds rang with cries and agonized protests as slowly and unwillingly the men piled on the ground their booty of jewels and clocks, furs and cases of wine, embroidered chasubles of cloth of gold. To have taken all that they wanted to take would have necessitated another fleet of British ships. As it was Junot demanded and got five transports for the conveyance of his personal loot. Sir Harry and Sir Hew presided benignly over the scene of departure while Wellesley, alone in his quarters, cursed them both and the day which allowed a beaten enemy to march out with all the arms and honours of war, together with the proceeds of crime. He had been ordered by Dalrymple to add his signature to the convention and did so under protest and merely as obeying orders. The document soon attained unpleasant fame as the Convention of Cintra.

Wellesley—though not his seniors—was not at all surprised at the storm of protest which arose in Britain as soon as the terms of the convention became known. Admiral Nelson had given the British a taste of victory followed by the annihilation of the enemy. They were eager to serve the signatories of Cintra as they had served the unhappy Admiral Byng many years ago. The Horse Guards, ignoring the inadvisability of leaving the army in the Peninsula without a commander, ordered the three generals home to face an inquiry—they were fairly sure that Moore must be somewhere near at this time, and he could take over when he arrived.

The Court of Inquiry, consisting of six generals, sat in Chelsea for six weeks to hear evidence from Burrard, Dalrymple and Wellesley, who restricted his to the statement that he had been ordered to sign the convention and therefore had signed it, but did not approve of it and took no responsibility for it. The court completely absolved him from any blame but commented severely on "the extraordinary circumstances under which two new commanding generals arrived from the ocean and joined the army, the one during and the other immediately after a battle, superseding each other and both the original commander within the space of 24 hours." The evidence was long and detailed and the court's report took so long to prepare that it was many weeks before their verdict became public enough to clear Wellesley's name, and he found himself, to his disgust, unpopular and suspect. He intended to go to court to pay his respect to the King but was plainly warned by a friend that he would not be welcome and was advised to stay away from court for the time being. To this well-meant counsel, his characteristic reply was, "I shall go to court today or I shall never go there again." It is satisfactory to know that the King, who was not an ungrateful master, received him with marked graciousness and spent some time in conversation with him. If there were others who felt less kindly about him they had the sense to keep it to themselves. There was something very chilling about the reserve of this young lieutenant-general which discouraged both familiarity and criticism. A cynical postscript was added to the affair by the Emperor Napoleon who remarked that he had been going to court-martial Junot but the British had saved him the trouble by putting their own generals on trial.

There was to be no more military employment for Burrard and Dalrymple. Wellesley found himself without a command for some time, so that his thoughts began to swing back to the idea of a career in politics, but it was only the irritation of disillusionment. The British still held Portugal, and as long as there was an army there, there was his place. The winter had brought news of Sir John Moore's daring incursion into Spain, his headlong retreat and his fight and death at Corunna. In April 1809, Wellesley resigned his seat in Parliament and his civilian offices. When the messengers came from Spain they brought news, not only of Moore and his army, but of the entry into the country of a new and powerful French army, with vast numbers of guns and cavalry, under the command of the men whose names were by now known throughout Europe—Ney, Soult, Lannes, Mortier, Berthier. The French, dissatisfied with the progress of the Spanish venture, were turning the full power of their war machine into the country. Spanish vedettes and irregulars high up in the mountains of the Pyrenees watched all day, day after day, the seemingly endless stream of men, horses, guns and wagons, which poured through the narrow defiles and down into the open fields of Spain. One day they saw signs that something even more threatening was approaching, when for mile after mile the roads were darkened with the bearskins of the Infantry of the Imperial Guard. In the midst of them, the pennons of the Polish Lancers of the Guard fluttered beside the covered carriage whose postilions wore the imperial livery of green and gold.

At once the tempo of the Spanish war quickened to an allegro as the eight great army corps, a quarter of a million strong in all, debouched from the hills and fanned out in the open ground as they moved to their several objectives. They were the main strength of the Grande Armée, seasoned troops all, many of them victors of Austerlitz and Jena, superbly armed and mounted, fanatically devoted to their Emperor, arrogantly sure of victory. They moved with unquestioning confidence to their tasks in the grand strategy which the genius of Berthier had translated into hundreds of pages of notes and orders. Napoleon himself announced his presence and his intentions with his usual happy freedom from inhibition. "When I shall show myself beyond the Pyrenees," he said, "the Leopard in terror will plunge into the ocean to avoid shame, defeat, and death."

It seemed that he was not overestimating his prospects or his own value as the French armies moved forward and struck at their appointed targets. Soult burst through the centre of the Spanish defence, killing 2,500 of their troops, and captured Bayonne. Victor fell on another force, under Blake, at Espinosa, and sent them reeling down the road to Reinosa with a disordered mob of 7,000 fugitives—"without artillery, without arms, without spirit and without hope," was Napier's graphic description of them. Soult, moving forward, seized Santander while Lefebvre swept into Valladolid. In the first few days of the campaign, the whole of northern Spain passed into French possession, and while the infantry rested and consolidated, the cavalry of France, headed by Lefebvre-Desnoettës's light squadrons, poured into and over the plains of León and Castile, routing Spanish General Castanos with his 45,000 men and hunting him down the roads leading to Madrid. On December 2 the French were at the gates of Madrid, from which the miserable King Joseph had withdrawn thankfully a few months earlier. Two days later Madrid surrendered. In something less than a month the Emperor had destroyed the armed power of Spain and entered as a conqueror yet one more European capital.

The Emperor summoned a council of Spanish nobles to Madrid and announced his intention for the next part of the campaign. "I will drive the English armies from the Peninsula," he boasted. "There is no obstacle capable of resisting the execution of my will." To show his confidence in himself and his power, he then and there bestowed a new constitution on Spain, cancelling all feudal rights, abolishing the Inquisition and reducing the number of convents by a third. He added that if Spain dared to resist him he would find another throne for his brother and crown himself as King of Spain. It is likely that he did not mean half of what he said but the significant thing was that he said it—that he proposed to take away feudal rights from the most fiercely arrogant aristocracy in Europe, to challenge the Catholic Church in her surest stronghold and to inflict himself as sovereign on a people who regarded him as a vulgar little upstart. That he could even say so much publicly showed how completely he was ignorant of and indifferent to the Spanish character and how insolently confident he was in his own inviolability.

He was reaching the turning-point in his career of hitherto almost un-broken success, which had culminated in Austerlitz, Jena and Tilsit. He stood before Europe as the greatest master of war of all time, but he had forgotten the soldier's maxim, "War is the art of the possible." For the rest of the years that remained to him he would fail altogether to dis-tinguish between the possible and the desirable, and would believe that whatever he wished must come to pass. The ancient Athenians would have recognized his state of mind as "hubris," the one sin which the Gods never forgive. He drew up his next operation order with all his old vision and authority but with something less than his old care for pro-vision against the unforeseen. Since the British "Leopard" was about to be thrown into the sea, his strategy treated them as though they had al-ready ceased to resist. He had behind him in Spain some 30,000 men; his lines of communication were secured back to the Pyrenees and through them to France.

He himself, with the main body of his force, would move straight on Portugal and capture Lisbon, while his marshals were overruning Cata-lonia, Andalusia and Valencia. The British were still in Portugal but they could not be in strength, and his columns would easily sweep them away, leaving him master of all Iberia with the whole coastline of Europe closed to British ships. But he had miscalculated. The British were not in Por-tugal. They were in Spain and moving toward a point between Madrid and Bayonne where they could throw their whole force across the French communications and isolate their armies in Spain.

It was a daring, almost crazy scheme, and it was all of Moore's de-vising. He had taken command of the British in Portugal when Wellesley went home, but he had received only the vaguest directive for his future movements. It amounted, in fact, to little more than an order to move into Spain and to see what he could do when he got there, accompanied by the not very reassuring promise of a Spanish supporting army of 100,000 men, not one of whom, of course, put in an appearance. He had only a few squadrons of cavalry and so could do hardly any recon-naissance, for which he had to rely on reports from individual Spanish spies and outposts, who often misled him. They assured him that Madrid would hold out against the French and that Napoleon would be held up in the central plain, presenting an open and unprotected flank to Moore's advance, whereas the truth was the exact opposite. When Moore's col-umns began to move forward across Spain, the Emperor was in undis-puted possession of Madrid and in a position to strike at Moore's right flank as soon as the British came near enough.

It was the sort of venture which a knight errant or a crusading vision-ary might have attempted, but Moore was neither. He was a competent and brave officer, and he knew his weakness in strength and his lack of knowledge of the country and of the enemy's movements. So far was he from being a visionary that his pessimism was a byword in the British Army. Wellesley himself had commented on it. His courage, which was unshakable, had nothing in it of the gaiety of officers like Lefebvre-Desnoettes or Lasalle, the French light-horsemen. It was the typical courage of his country—unspectacular, stubborn in trial or defeat, ready to face any necessary risk but resolute not to look for any. Had he had his choice he would hardly have embarked on so rash an enterprise, but he held himself obliged to strike at least one good blow to maintain the honor of his country and of her army before allies who had appealed to her for help. The nominal strength of his army was 35,000, but sickness had left him with less than 24,000 effectives.

With these and with the strength of his own stout heart, but without hope of a happy outcome, he was marching straight toward a rendezvous with a mythical Spanish force at Burgos, which was already in French hands. In doing so he was laying his flank wide open to an army of ten times the size of his own. He had shrewdly assessed his chance, which he limited to a possibly successful battle with not more than one enemy corps. "If Marshal Soult," he wrote on December 16, "is so agreeable as to approach us, it will be very agreeable to give a wipe to such a corps." But he confided his graver doubts to his diary, writing, "I am making it of the most dangerous kind. I mean to proceed bridle in hand; for if the bubble burst and Madrid falls, we shall have to run for it." Madrid had fallen a fortnight earlier, but so slow were communications in that barren land that Moore did not hear of it until he had begun his march and was well inside Spanish territory. By that time the Emperor himself with an overwhelming force was swinging round to envelop him and destroy him.

Napoleon's mind may have been tinged with megalomania, but nothing had yet marred his tactical sureness and his rapidity of movement. The weather had turned bitterly cold in those days before Christmas, and the Guadarrama hills which the French had to cross were deep in snow and treacherous with ice. In the blizzard-swept plains near Carran, Moore was blindly groping for Soult with an eye over his shoulder for the first sign of the threat which would cause him to abandon the attempt and run for it. Napoleon with 50,000 men was behind and to the east of him, racing to cut his line of retreat and to trap him between his own force and Soult's corps, while Ney's cavalry hurried on the Emperor's left, making a wider sweep to get into position to seal off the last line of retreat. Moore, knowing that he was hard-pressed, but not yet knowing when and from where he would feel the first pressure, had decided on the desperate gamble of a night advance to surprise Soult and was watching the formation of two columns of attack when a dragoon on a sweating and almost foundered horse spurred up to him to give him the news which he dreaded. The dragoon had risked a long and solitary ride in unknown country over snow-covered hills where treacherously hidden crevasses endangered his every step, and he had gained the first definite news of the French that had been brought in for many days. He had crouched on a bare hillside behind a rock, leaving his horse hobbled in a patch of shelter, and he had looked down on a whole army on the move. The long columns of infantry showed like black snakes against the white ground while the squadrons trotted before them seeming to cover the countryside like a cloud of insects. It was not only a whole army, but an army moving as fast as the will of an autocratic commander could drive them. It was no time now for the closed berline and the lancer escort. The Emperor was riding on his white horse, Marengo, ahead of his main body and almost with the advance guard of cavalry and galloper guns. There could be no mistaking that little figure, huddled into a grey "redingote," nor the helmets and cuirasses of the cavalry of the Guard and the plumes and pennons of the Polish Lancers. The Emperor had learned of Moore's whereabouts on December 21 and had started out on the following day. By evening the French were among the foothills of the Guadarrama range where the storm and frozen ground almost brought them to a standstill. Napoleon dismounted and linked arms with Lannes and Duroc, breasted the steep and treacherous slopes with his leading files whom he told to go forward in the same way, with arms linked for support against the tempest and snow.

On the twenty-sixth of December he arrived at Tordesillas with the Guard and two divisions, having made 100 miles in four days, and after a short rest drove his exhausted troops forward to Valderas which lay squarely on Moore's only possible line of retreat, only to find that Moore had beaten him by twenty-four hours and was across the Esla. Moore had called off his attack on Soult and turned to run for safety across the mountains in the direction of Corunna, where British transports would be waiting to take his troops off to safety. He had timed his change of plan with consummate skill, but his position was still desperate. Between him and Corunna lay 150 miles of mountainous and frost-bound country, with no proper roads and few inhabitants or places where a tired battalion might snatch a few hours of sleep out of the storm. Soult was pressing on his rear and threatening the left flank of his retreat. Junot was moving against his right, while Lefebvre came storming up from Salamanca against his line of march with the intention of heading him and driving him back into Soult's arms. And, behind all of them, but coming with all the speed which he could muster, was Napoleon. Their combined strength outnumbered Moore's by more than five to one. There was nothing that he could do but head for the coast as best he might and try to hold off Soult's pressure with his rearguard.

The story of the retreat to Corunna and of the battle there where Moore met his death is a well-known part of military history. The weather and the awful steepness of the route almost destroyed Moore's force and turned them into a mob of flying, terrified refugees, forgetful of discipline, of regimental pride, of everything but the agony of frozen limbs and the misery of abandoned hope. The British commissariat, incompetent at the best of times, had long since given up the attempt to feed the men, and most of what wagons and carts followed the battalions were abandoned on the slopes or overturned into a crevasse, so that the men were unfed, except for any scraps which they could find on the way, with their clothing in tatters and their boots rotted. Many of them marched all but the first few miles in bare feet over which they had wrapped a few bits of rag or cloth. They were eighteen days on the march and during that time they lost over 4,000 men, mostly dead from accident or frostbite and exposure, very few by bullet or cannon ball. Hundreds of them threw away their muskets and ammunition pouches and even, because of the extra weight, their greatcoats, so that at night they shivered and died. Many of them were suffering from snow blindness, or lost limbs by frostbite. Twice they came across small towns, Valderas and Benavente, where there were large stocks of wine maturing in cellars, and they fell on them like wild beasts on flesh, to assuage their misery and to warm their frozen bodies. There were nights of drunken frenzy and their stupor with the inevitable tale of new deaths in the morning and, for those who lived, a more complete hopelessness after the respite and the deceiving warmth and exhilaration. When at last they stumbled over the crests above Corunna and saw the bay empty of the transports which should have awaited them, it must have seemed to them that even God had abandoned them, though the real cause was less exalted, being no more than a chronic incompetence of the staff at the base and in England, who had sent the ships to Vigo.

The army turned to fight with their backs to the sea. It was a marvel that they had the heart not only to fight but to bear themselves so stoutly, yet all through the retreat the only thing that had roused them from their lethargy was a call to turn about and drive back the enemy advance guards. In all the mass of misery and abandonment, there were isolated places where the courage of the soldier shone unconquered, and when the bugles sounded for battle, men who had thrown themselves down to die took heart and joined their fellows in the line. Soult seemed hesitant in pressing his pursuit, and there was always time to form a rearguard

WELLINGTON
By Goya

THE BATTLE OF BADAJOZ

From a contemporary engraving

defence before the French infantry came to the attack. Soult was, by Napoleon's admission, as good a tactician as any of the marshals and better than most, but his genius was more in moving his divisions and bringing them to battle than in the clash of arms. Some of his fellow marshals called him a coward, which he certainly was not, but he suffered from an excess of caution in committing his troops to battle, imagining dangers which a more solid commander would ignore or not think of. His hesitation more than once during the later battles in the Peninsula robbed his skilful tactical moves of the success which they deserved. He hesitated again when he reached the crest of the hills against Corunna and saw the British lines in the valley below him.

The French were nearly as exhausted as the British, and Soult allowed the British three priceless days in which to rest and rearm themselves and to restore something like order and discipline in the battalions. More important still, the pause gave time for the British transports to sail round the coast from Vigo and for Moore to blow up his stores and such guns and ammunition as he could not carry away. The transports reached the bay on January 14, 1809, and Moore began immediately to load them with his sick and wounded and with the few stores that he could accommodate. Finally, he gave the order to shoot all the surviving cavalry and artillery horses rather than let them fall into enemy hands.

Still Soult delayed, and it was not until the sixteenth that he moved to the attack. He had occupied the last two days in setting up a heavy battery of eleven guns on a solitary hill which commanded the right flank of the British. They did much execution during the battle, but Soult might have been better served had he dispensed with them and put in his attack two days earlier, when he might have had the British at a hopeless disadvantage, for, tired as his men were and sorely though they needed rest, the British were, until the fourteenth, in even worse plight. They were disheartened and exhausted, cluttered up with their sick and wounded and with useless horses, nor did they know where their ships were and when they would come. It is hard to think that had Ney or some other French general like him been in Soult's place he would not have called on his men for one last supreme effort and, had he done so, might well have fulfilled Napoleon's promise to drive the Leopard into the sea. Evacuations of beaten armies have been a recurrent feature of British military history up to the latest of her wars, and her command of the sea has always, so far, enabled her to carry them out successfully. Perhaps, too, luck has often been with her and her enemies' mistakes have helped, as Soult's delay did at Corunna and Hitler's failure to follow up his success did at Dunkirk in 1940. But, as Mr. Churchill then remarked, "Wars are not won by evacuations." Britain had suffered a

F

serious setback in losing her foothold in Portugal. The work would have to be done again, probably done against a seacoast defended and entrenched and a force more formidable than Soult's had proved.

The British fought sturdily with their backs to the sea and with the renewed confidence given to them by the waiting transports in the bay. There was one period in the fight, late in the afternoon of the sixteenth, and almost immediately after Moore's death, when a renewed effort by Soult might have prevailed, but once again he held back and waited till morning. When he came again he found the field deserted and only Hill's brigade standing as rearguard in the town of Corunna, covering the last embarkations. Some of the French batteries turned their guns eastward and began to bombard the transports, but an escorting British man-of-war opened on them with her broadsides and the transports drew away from shore and sailed into safety. One of Soult's amiable hobbies was the erecting of monuments in any place where his corps had fought or had camped, and he built one on the field of Corunna. With a rare and creditable chivalry he built it, not as usual in his own honour but to commemorate Moore. It still stands there and bears the simple legend, "John Moore, leader of the English armies, slain in battle, 1809."

The British, as even their detractors must admit, are stubborn in defeat. Historians of the Second World War have recorded how in 1940, after Dunkirk, when Britain was, as it seemed, naked and defenceless before her enemies, Mr. Churchill gave orders for the preparation of schemes for a new invasion of Europe when the time should come for it. Castlereagh, for all his faults of manner and chilly aloofness, knew the temper of the British and was as resolute to carry on the fight as was Mr. Churchill in 1940. He had a unique knowledge of and instinct for foreign politics, and he was certain that before long the Emperor would have to leave Spain and fight for his existence on the Danube. The Austrians were bitterly ashamed of their recent defeats and longed to avenge them. Now they believed that they had found the man to lead them to victory, since they had worked through the list of senior and decrepit generals and had come to the Archduke Charles, by far the ablest soldier in their army, who had not yet been trusted in supreme command. Castlereagh was at Austria's elbow with offers of subsidies and support, while, at the same time, he recognized and encouraged the first signs of a renewal of Prussia's fighting spirit. There were still a few British troops in Portugal under Cradock, and Castlereagh thought less of withdrawing them than of reinforcing them. One of his greatest gifts was the ability to select the right men for the work that was to be done, and he turned to Wellesley for counsel.

This was work which Wellesley understood. Many times in India he had prepared an appreciation for senior officers, and his practical good sense and unique judgment of what was possible helped him to avoid over-optimism and unreality. He submitted his report on March 9 and, in it, concentrated on Portugal, leaving Spain as a separate problem to be dealt with later. That was always his way—to see one step at a time, take it and consolidate his gains, and then consider the next step. Grandiose schemes and visions of glory were not to his fancy, and he knew that they were one of the great weaknesses of the French strategists. As he said himself, about Napoleon's marshals, "They plan their campaigns like a new set of harness. . . . Now I made mine of ropes. If anything went wrong I tied a knot and went on."

He had seen Portugal and fought there, and he knew that he could hold it, since he would have so much in his favour. First, he would have the sea at his back, which would give him, through the predominance of the Navy, a safe and direct line of communications with the ports of Britain. There was no way in which the French or the Spanish could prevent his ammunition, his food and his reinforcements getting through to him. Then, the country favoured him, since he would have to stand on the defensive at first and the hilly and broken ground would be in his favour. There were few open plains, like those round Madrid, where a superior cavalry could manoeuvre against his infantry. He would be fighting in a friendly country where it would be easy to get information and —transport was never far from his thoughts—there would be mules to carry his supplies and muleteers to drive them. As for the Portuguese soldiers, he had very little opinion of them, but, at the worst, they were probably better than the Spanish. Something might even be made of them if they were officered by British officers and, as far as possible, kept in the quieter parts of the line. If they were to prove fit for no more than garrison or lines of communication duties, they would set free British battalions for the fighting line. He estimated that, if this were to prove satisfactory, he would need a permanent strength of 30,000 British troops to hold Portugal.

Beyond that he did not look at the moment. As long as he held Portugal, the French would have corresponding disadvantages to them. Their communications must stretch back for hundreds of miles, across Spain and through the Pyrenees, through a hostile country which swarmed with expert bandits who would prey remorselessly on the rear areas of the army. The preponderance of French cavalry would be robbed of much of its effect if they had no open ground for manoeuvre and for the charge while he kept them, as he meant to, among the hills and rocky slopes at their foot. Where he would hold undivided authority in command, the French would only have the same advantage while Napoleon stayed in Spain, and if Castlereagh was right, he would be more sorely needed on the Danube before long, when not only he but a proportion of his troops, many of them the finest like the Guards and Murat's cavalry, would be withdrawn.

Let them hold Portugal, he told the Cabinet, and be content with that until they saw a further opportunity. Let them resign themselves to a defensive and waiting role which would keep the French communications stretched as taut and as thin as a fiddle-string and would contain them in a hostile country where they might well starve if their communications were threatened and interrupted. He would sweep Portugal bare in his front, and the Portuguese people would give the French nothing that they could keep from them. The first rope in his campaign harness would stretch from the ports of the South Country to Lisbon and the Portuguese coast. It would be time to add the second when he had seen that the first was holding. The Cabinet accepted his appreciation of the situation and asked him to take command and carry out his plan. Now that Castlereagh and Canning, both men of practical good sense and indifferent to military protocol, were in the ascendant there would be no more talk of superseding him with senile nonentities from the Horse Guards. Wellesley accepted their offer and on April 22, 1809, landed once more in the Peninsula, which he was not to leave until the day when his army climbed the passes of the Pyrenees and set foot on French soil.

PART IV

1809-1812

XX

LIEUTENANT-GENERAL SIR ARTHUR WELLESLEY landed at Lisbon to face a situation which might have frightened a less stouthearted man. He was, to begin with, hopelessly outnumbered. His total strength, including the few British who had remained in Portugal, was 26,000 men. Marshal Soult, with more than 20,000, held Oporto, and marching to join him were Ney and Mortier with another 40,000. To the west lay Victor with 24,000 and a force of some 6,000 under Lapisse, encamped round Salamanca, forming a link between the two main armies.

The French troops were flushed with the habit of victory and the knowledge that they had hunted the last British army which had entered Spain across the provinces of León and Galicia and—as Napoleon had promised—into the sea, though it was true that Soult had unaccountably failed to destroy them at Corunna, and their own accursed ships and not the waters of the Bay of Biscay had received them.

Soult had put that unfortunate failure behind him and was already suffering from delusions of grandeur. The Emperor, finding Spain no fit place for a display of his genius, had gone home, and Soult had an incipient vision of himself as an independent King, of Portugal to begin with and afterward—who knew?—perhaps of Spain. By way of endearing himself to his future subjects, he had turned his men loose in Oporto and massacred some 10,000 of its people. Nor had he yet fully learned the lesson that crowns and thrones were reserved by his master for members of the Bonaparte family, however little they wanted them and however incompetent they were to wear and occupy them.

Wellesley's army was of good material but raw, lacking for the most part any experience of battle. They were short of everything that they needed, except allies, without whom they would have been better off. They lacked above all money, not only for their pay—that was always in arrears anyway—but to buy the barest necessities of life, and that in a supposedly friendly country which resented their presence as anything but a possible source of profit. The British in the Peninsula, wrote Napier, the historian of their campaign, were "regarded as galley slaves, needed to drive the ship forward, but hated and feared." Wellesley's previous service in Portugal, short as it was, had warned him of that source of trouble, though he did not yet guess at the spate of it which awaited him in Spain. No one familiar with the history of British expeditionary forces will be surprised to learn that he had no cavalry, only a few guns and practically no transport, nor that these latter arrived in driblets and invariably without their horses, which travelled by another route and might be landed anywhere. The arrangements for supplying the troops, where there were any, were in the incompetent and frequently rascally hands of civilian contractors who were not subject to military discipline and were, it soon appeared, in business mainly for their own profit.

With these resources, Wellesley was charged with the duty of holding Portugal against the enemy, preparatory to driving them through and out of Spain. He had assured the government that Portugal could be held, and beyond that he would not look at the moment.

He had certain advantages on his side. Since the country was, for the most part, broken and hilly, his deficiency in cavalry would not greatly hamper him, while the French, who had large cavalry forces, would find them of little use while they would still have to be supplied and maintained.

The country was friendly, if that could be called an advantage, though Wellesley soon realized that it chiefly meant that he could take nothing without paying cash for it and that he was expected to feed, arm and pay his allies, most of whom looked on mealtimes and pay parades as the utmost of duties required of them.

His greatest assets were his confidence in himself, his determination to do what he had to do and his clear vision of the steps by which he could accomplish it. Once more, war was to be the art of the possible, and he knew that he could hold Portugal.

But that did not mean that he was going to confine himself to passive defense. Nothing was further from his mind than to sit waiting until

Soult came to attack him, still less to allow Soult and Victor to combine to crush him. Each of their armies outnumbered his own, and together they would be overpowering; but he had the interior lines, which meant that he could move against either of them before the other could come up to help.

He moved with a speed and certainty for which he has never been given full credit. On May 2, less than a fortnight after his landing, he had concentrated his force at Coimbra, and on the twelfth he was within a march of Oporto, where Soult was indulging in his visions of future greatness and entirely ignoring the duty of present watchfulness. There was a certain likeness which cannot have escaped Wellesley's notice between the situation before Oporto and the earlier one before Assaye. In both cases the enemy was in a strong position, protected by a practically unfordable river. The key of Soult's position was a large and solid building called the Convent, which stood almost on the bank of the Douro. On its south bank, opposite to the city, was some rising ground called the Serra Rock crowned by another convent, and behind this Wellington collected and hid his assault troops, with his few guns ready to be run into position on the rock.

Soult remained in ignorance of the threat. He had been grossly neglectful about his own protection, and the few patrols which he had sent out had brought him no news of Wellesley's advance. He was suffering, too, from the effect of operating in a hostile country, whose inhabitants would give him no help and bring him no information. After the brutality with which the French had behaved in Oporto, there was hardly a man in Portugal who would be willing or would dare to help him in the smallest degree.

At six o'clock on that morning of May 12, 1809, a rumour of the British approach had reached him, but he must have taken it for a canard for he had sent out no cavalry patrols, and even the sentries in Oporto itself were no more alert than was their slovenly custom. Wellington, as was his habit, had been reconnoitring his line of attack from the time that he had reached Coimbra. In case Soult should be the first to move, he had instructed Major-General Mackenzie to collect every available boat and hold them on the south bank of the Douro. But Soult had already thought of this elementary precaution for his own and had the boats under guard on the north bank. Wellington's patrols had ridden, unobserved, up and down the south bank of the river, seeking for some ford, but not even the Portuguese inhabitants, friendly as they were, knew of any possible crossing-place except that at Oporto itself, which Soult commanded with his guns and troops. There was indeed some sort of a ford to the right of Wellesley's flank, but it was too far away to be of any use in the assault, though he used it to pass over some of his scanty force of cavalry for the subsequent pursuit.

So far the resemblance between Assaye and Oporto went, and there it ended, but Wellesley had advantages which he had not enjoyed for the crossing of the Kaitna. He had the advantage of surprise and a favourable position for his covering batteries on the Serra Rock, and he had an opponent who was careless and overconfident. Scindia at Assaye had seized every available boat. Soult at Oporto had seized all but five.

The first of these came Wellesley's way by a stroke of luck. A party of the Buffs were searching for any sort of boat or raft, any baulk of timber which could be pressed into use for the crossing, when a barber from Oporto, quite unaware of the coming battle, got out a boat, which he had hidden for his own use, and began to row himself across to the south bank. As soon as it touched ground Colonel Waters, the commanding officer of the Buffs, snatched it, and with two of his men crossed the river and discovered four fair-sized boats firmly—inextricably it would seem—stuck in the mud under the north bank. Waters came back with the first of these, when his party had managed to heave it out, and reported to Wellington, who gave him the brief order: "Then let the men cross." With any other commander it might have seemed a mad venture doomed to failure, but Wellesley had the knack of making the most daring plans look commonplace and capable of fulfilment.

The boats, it was found, would take twenty-five men each, and so the Buffs began their hazardous crossing. Still no sentry from the Convent gave the alarm, no warning bugle or opening shot broke the silence. The French were taking their time from their marshal, who was at that moment sitting down to a late breakfast inside the Convent.

The first warning that he got of the impending attack was the crash as the opening shells of the bombardment from the batteries on the Serra Rock burst on the Convent roof and the panic-stricken rattle of the French drums beating the alarm.

The Buffs were already in the Convent, which they had entered by a small door at water level, and as more boats were found and released, Wellesley's infantry streamed across the Douro. The French guns at the Convent opened fire in reply, but the British from Serra Rock silenced them, while the British infantry swarmed across the river and into the city. The threat which finally broke Soult's nerve and ability to resist was the appearance to his left of the leading troops of Murray's little cavalry party which had crossed at the ford. He saw his line of retreat threatened and took flight while there was still time.

Murray might have caused untold damage had he risked an attack on the flank of the retreating French, but his force was small and the French were in great strength and not too demoralized to defend themselves. Sensibly perhaps, he let the chance slip and joined in the pursuit. Two squadrons of the 14th Light Dragoons attempted a charge, burst in among the enemy and captured General Laborde, but they were only a handful against a multitude and were beaten off, suffering some casualties. Soult's army fled in confusion down the road which led to the Spanish frontier, abandoning guns, baggage and wagons, with Wellesley on their heels and two other British detachments, one of them mixed British and Portuguese under Beresford, racing to cut them off from Amarante on the one side and from Galicia, where Ney might have relieved them, on the other.

On May 18 Soult halted and tried to re-form at Orense, from which he had marched only ten weeks earlier with a strength of over 20,000 to conquer his kingdom of Portugal. Now his army was beaten and disorganized, had suffered more than 6,000 casualties and lost all its baggage. In the action at Oporto, Wellesley had lost exactly 100 officers and men. In a campaign of little more than ten days with negligible loss he had achieved his first objective of driving the French out of Portugal.

On June 27, after a pause for refitting and rest and to allow newly landed troops to join him, he led his army into Spain. Any man might excusably have felt elated after so rapid a success in his opening campaign and might even thereby have been led into a rash move, but it had never been Sir Arthur's habit to let himself be carried away by an emotion, however justified. He had cleared Portugal of the enemy but he had to hold it, and for all his victory, the odds against him were heavy. Soult's army was regrouping on his left flank and had been joined by Ney and Mortier, while before him Victor stood, with yet another corps hurrying to his support. Wellesley knew how dangerous his position was, commanding as he did a total strength of 58,000 British and Spanish troops against some 100,000 French. He did not yet know his Spanish allies well enough to realize that his position was, in fact, not so much dangerous as desperate.

The Spanish commander was General Cuesta, who was senile, incompetent, arrogant and shifty. He was so fat and decrepit that he could not ride a horse so was conveyed, on the march and the field of battle, in a carriage drawn by six horses. Wellesley already had his suspicions about the value of his Spanish allies, but may have consoled himself with the thought that they could not be worse than the Portuguese.

If so, he was soon to be disillusioned. Cuesta promised and broke his promises, blustered and lost his head, made grandiose plans for fighting and suggested instant flight. When they conferred he went to sleep and remembered nothing of their discussions; when Wellesley was ready to make a concerted plan he went off to bed and could not be disturbed.

He ruined one favourable opportunity for action by refusing to fight on a Sunday. Worst of all, he seemed content to look on while the British came near to starving because they lacked both supplies and the money to buy them, while the Spanish storehouses were filled to bursting and their troops were in nearly the same state. The two armies joined hands on July 22, and during the following month the British had only ten days' issue of bread and even less meat, while over 2,000 horses died for want of fodder. Wellesley's correspondence during these days of July is a mounting crescendo of protest and irritation, freely expressed to his government at home; to Frere, the British minister with the Spanish junta; and to Cuesta himself. On July 24 he wrote to Frere: "I find General Cuesta more and more impracticable every day. It is impossible to do business with him, and very uncertain that any operation will succeed in which he has any concern. . . . He contrived to lose the whole of yesterday, in which, although his troops were under arms and mine in march, owing to the whimsical perverseness of his disposition . . ." So great, in fact, was Wellesley's anger and anxiety that he wrote a few days later both to London and to the Spanish saying that unless he were supplied at once and in plenty with food and fodder, he would march his army out of Spain and back into Portugal and leave Cuesta to cope with the French as best he might.

The threat stirred Cuesta to a show of action. His cavalry had had a brush with the French at Alcabon and had come off worse. It was a very small affair but it spread a general alarm through the Spanish army, who were ready to give up the war and go home without more ado. Cuesta, who could be relied on to do what no one in his senses would as much as contemplate, then announced his intention of attacking the French instead of following Wellesley's plan of letting the French attack and receiving them in a good defensive position. Cuesta was obstinate, and only Wellesley's personal visit to him and his insistence on the agreed plan, backed by his threat to leave Spain unless it were adopted, at last moved him. He gave the order to retreat, a move which the Spanish were accustomed to carrying out, though usually in a less orderly manner than suited Sir Arthur's taste. Victor was approaching with some 55,000 men and 80 guns, and Wellesley had chosen and reconnoitred a position which gave a good chance of stopping him, provided that the allies could take up their positions there before Victor came up to hustle them out of them. His chosen line ran at right angles to the river Tagus, which covered his right flank. It extended along a series of small hills to a mountain range and a deep ravine on which his left was to rest. Behind his right flank lay the village of Talavera. His 20,000 British were to hold the whole line from the left flank to the sector in front of Talavera.

This sector, the right of his line, was a position as nearly impregnable as favourable ground and protection both natural and artificial could make it. It was covered by broken and irregular ground, seamed with ditches, and strengthened by a tangle of breastworks and the stout stone buildings of a convent. Not even the Spanish, he thought, could fail to defend it, though he was soon to find that he had miscalculated, not having counted on their promptness in abandoning it without putting its possibilities to any thorough test.

The French moved to the attack in the afternoon of July 27, and all through the rest of that day and the whole of the twenty-eighth, the bloody and remorseless fighting went on. Half the Spanish fled during the first hours of the battle, and the rest of them were useless and would, no doubt, have been destroyed had not the strength of their position kept Victor from seriously assaulting it. The whole weight of the defence rested on the British infantry through the long hours of the two-day fight. Napier wrote, "30,000 French infantry vainly strove for hours to force 16,000 British soldiers, who were for the most part so recently drafted from the militia that many of them still bore the distinctions of that force on their accoutrements." The British lost in killed and wounded 6,200 men and officers, nearly one-third of their number. The French lost in their defeat 7,500, a loss much less serious in proportion to the numbers engaged. Even the Spanish brightened up as the guns fell silent and put in a claim to a loss of 1,200 killed and wounded, making no mention of the far greater number absent without leave. Cuesta proposed to add to his casualty list by shooting 60 officers and 400 men from his own force for the crime of running away and only at Wellesley's earnest and personal entreaty contented himself with 10 per cent of the intended sacrifice. Wellesley knew how futile was any such vengeful gesture, short of shooting the entire Spanish Army, which he personally might have welcomed rather than fight with it on his side once more. From that day forward he never again trusted a Spaniard or counted them as anything but a heavy entry on the debit side of his tactical accounts. "I have fished often in troubled waters," he said later, "but in Spanish troubled waters I will never fish again."

XXI

WELLESLEY had cleared Portugal, but no one knew better than he that he had only begun a task which would take several years and cost thousands of lives and immense fortunes in money. Even to hold Portugal itself would tax all his efforts and resources while such preponderant strength threatened him from beyond its frontier. How far ahead he looked and what a bitter struggle he foresaw was made clear in his instructions of October 20, 1809, to his chief engineer, Colonel Fletcher, to prepare a fortified position where his army could resist as long as resistance was possible and from which—he was not the man to refuse to look at any possibility—they could be taken off by sea when all else had failed. His unfailing eye for country had taken in the hilly region of Torres Vedras, where a natural fortress could be made practically impregnable by military art. "The great object in Portugal," he wrote, "is the possession of Lisbon and the Tagus and all our measures must be devoted to this object. There is also another connected with that first object to which we must likewise attend, viz., the embarkation of the British troops in case of reverse."

It was an immense task. There were chasms to be bridged, breastworks and strong points to be built, roads blocked and bridges destroyed. All was to be done by civilian labour, and as the work went on more than 10,000 Portuguese labourers were continually employed with such effect that the whole immense system was built in a little over twelve months.

He could spare no troops to help with it, beyond the engineers to direct the work, and of these he had pitifully few. His army, before the work was finished, might have to fight to cover Lisbon and the Tagus and to keep open their line of communication with Britain by sea.

He was, in fact, committed to the defensive for a period which turned out to be two years, for though he was to fight actions at Busaco in 1810 and at Barrosa, Fuentes de Oñoro and Albuera in 1811, it was not until the beginning of 1812 that he felt himself secure enough to begin his thrust into Spain by attacking Ciudad Rodrigo and Badajoz.

His first and most important task was to make his army fit for the work and to see that it was properly fed, equipped and paid. At the same time he had to make such use of his allies as might be possible. From the Spanish he hoped nothing, now that he had seen them in action. His main preoccupation with them was to prevent them from stealing the rations meant for his own men and steadily to keep out of any plans for concerted action with them. He saw slightly better possibilities in the Portuguese, and he handed this task to General Beresford, a man of gigantic stature and strength and a stern disciplinarian.

The view which Wellesley took of his own troops was nearly as gloomy. They had fought well for him at Vimeiro, at Oporto and at Talavera, yet from the moment that they had landed in Portugal, he had never ceased to rail at them in his reports to Castlereagh, nor did his tone become any more favourable after their victories. As he wrote to Castlereagh, it was his opinion that the British soldier could "stand neither defeat nor victory." He knew as yet nothing personally of defeat, but he had read the reports of the retreat at Corunna and had spoken with officers who had seen Moore's fine corps turned into a flying, disordered, unruly mob, blind to duty and discipline, thinking only of safety or plunder and of drink. He had seen the British soldier in victory and knew how superficial was the appearance of discipline which covered his innate rascality and how little fit he was for an extended campaign or for facing hardship and deprivation. The troops could fight when they were under his own hand and knew exactly what they had to do. No more than that could be expected of them, since both officers and men were ignorant, half-trained, wholly incapable of looking after themselves in bivouac, on the march or in a friendly town. Their lack of discipline was appalling, he wrote. They robbed and murdered the natives, strayed from their lines, lost their arms and equipment, insulted their officers and struck their N.C.O's. He turned his provost-marshals and their assistants loose among them, schooled them with the lash and the cells, hung them when they robbed and shot them when they deserted. His courts-martial were in continuous session, driven on by the knowledge that the Commander-in-Chief, whose duty it was to confirm or upset every verdict, had no hesitation in sending back to a court for reconsideration any verdict which displeased him—nor did he hesitate to increase a sentence which he thought inadequate. He held the opinion (one by no means uncommon in military circles) that the duty of a court was not to try, but to pass sentence, and in one letter home he deplored the tendency of courts to "proceed according to the evidence." "They seem to think," he said, "that they were courts of justice bound to enquire into every detail of an accusation brought before them," whereas, in his view, they were "courts of honour," before which a soldier had an opportunity of clearing himself. It was a legal theory unfamiliar to British jurisprudence and misapplied to his courts. It amounted to little more than treating any accused as guilty and asking him if he had anything to say for himself before being shot, hanged or flogged. It is fair to Wellesley to say that he was equally ready to refer back the proceedings of courts in cases where the conviction seemed to him unjust or the sentence excessive.

It was not only the rank and file who gave him trouble about discipline, or who were brought before his courts. The offences committed by officers were a little less crude but no less damaging to discipline. The most usual were absence without leave, employing an enlisted soldier as a private servant, drunkenness, duelling and "embargoing" mules and horses belonging to civilian Portuguese, "embargoing" being much the same as the process known to a later British expeditionary force as "liberating." Occasionally there was a trial for a more eccentric offence, such as that held in Lisbon in March 1808 on an officer for "most un-officer-like and ungentleman-like conduct, in being concerned in an affray which took place in the city of Lisbon on March 3." The uproar had happened in a brothel, and the officer's plea, which was not without ingenuity, was that, happening to be on the spot on private business, he had interfered to stop the fighting and became unavoidably involved.

The court, feeling perhaps more sympathy than they should with the accused, accepted his defence and gave him an "honourable acquittal," a verdict which brought down on them an immediate rebuke from the confirming officer, who did not mind the accused being found "not guilty," but reacted violently against the use of the word "honourable" in that setting. "No man," he wrote, "can exalt in the termination of any transaction, a part of which has been disgraceful to him; and, though such a transaction may be terminated by an *honourable* acquittal by a Court Martial, it cannot be mentioned to the party without offence or without exciting feelings of disgust in others. . . . The honourable acquittal of Lieut. —— as recorded in this sentence . . . will have the effect of connecting with the act of going to a brothel the honourable distinction which

it is in the power of a Court Martial to bestow. . . ." He ends by directing the court to omit the word "honourable" in their sentence.

The officers of his army presented Wellington with the greatest of his
many problems because, though he was in chief command, he had little
or no power over their appointment, promotion or posting. It has always
to be borne in mind that, in these matters, he was entirely dependent on
the wish of the home government. Even his divisional generals and his
staff-officers were sent to him without previous consultation, which
opened the way to all sorts of favouritism and nepotism in a society which
had long been masters of these arts in political and private life. When,
for instance, Generals Erskine and Lumley were sent to him, he reflected
bitterly on the "character and accomplishments of the generals of this
army," adding, of these two, "the first I have always considered a madman." (As a matter of fact he was perfectly right. Poor Erskine, after
making a muddle of every job which he had to do and being relieved of
his command, went mad and took his own life.)

On rare occasions even junior subalterns were sent to him as special
presents, as happened in July 1810, when he was informed that the
Duchess of Richmond had arranged for a young kinsman of hers, Lord
March, to be released from his regiment at home and posted to the 13th
Light Dragoons in Portugal. Wellesley apparently saw nothing odd in his
interest being bespoken for a cavalry subaltern and replied almost hum-
bly, "The 13th Dragoons are in the Alentejo and I think that it would
be better that you should send him up here in the first instance and I
will take care of him." One would have hoped that the man who bore so
immense a load of responsibility might have been spared these trivial
additions to it, but perhaps the care of the young Lord March seemed to
him no more unreasonable than the commission to secure and send
home some orange trees for Lady Castlereagh, an errand which he had
scrupulously fulfilled as soon as he landed. The truth was—astonishing
though it seems to us today—that the Commander-in-Chief in the Peninsula was looked upon as no more than an employee of the government
at home, whose duty it was to do their fighting for them when, where and
how they told him, but not to trouble them too much with suggestions
and certainly not to take on himself more responsibility than would be
expected of a senior civil servant. The age was that which saw the last
fine flowering of Privilege and Aristocracy before their imminent wither-
ing and decay. The great families still placidly governed the country and
regarded the forces of the Crown as they regarded the closed boroughs
or the customs and excise. The Wellesleys—though admittedly good
sort of people—were not of the dominant aristocracy, and Sir Arthur,
though a very great man in Portugal, carried much less weight in White-

hall. He was not even a well-known soldier, since all his achievements had been in the Indian wars, of which the great ones in London knew little. Had it not been for Castlereagh's authority and his steady advocacy, he might never have been selected for the command. The aristocracy had for long looked on army appointments as their right and the forces as their private preserve. Efficiency was less a consideration in appointing an officer, even a general, than family connection and influence.

Even more strange does it seem that Wellington should have not only tolerated the system but actually approved of it. He stood to be the chief loser by it, and any failure which it might cause would be his responsibility. Yet on August 4, 1810, he wrote to Colonel Torrens, Military Secretary: "I have never been able to understand the principle on which the claims of gentlemen of family fortune and influence in the country . . . should be rejected, while the claims of others, not better founded on military pretensions, were invariably attended to. It would be desirable certainly that the only claim to promotion should be military merit; but this is a degree of perfection to which the disposal of military patronage has never been and cannot, I believe, be brought in any military establishment. The Commander-in-Chief must have friends, officers on the staff attached to him, etc., who will press him to promote their friends and relations, all doubtless very meritorious, and no man can at all times resist these applications. But, if there is to be any influence in the disposal of military patronage, in aid of military merit, can there be any in our army so legitimate as that of family, connection, fortune and influence in the country?"

Sir Arthur was the most convinced supporter of the old order of life in Britain and the least likely to have patience with any attempt to change it. He probably did not realize that his preference for "family, connection and influence in the country" were known and resented in the very large part of his army which did not share in those blessings.

It was remarked that among the earliest sentences of a court-martial which he rejected was one of "guilty" on a marquis of a famous house and that some of the aristocracy were often more successful than their fellows in getting home leave. One of his departmental chiefs, Sir James McGrigor, wrote to a friend, "One morning I was in his lordship's small room, when two officers came to request leave to go home to England. An engineer captain first made his request; he had received letters telling him that his wife was dangerously ill, and that the whole of his family were sick. His lordship quickly replied, 'No, no, sir, I cannot spare you at this moment.' The captain, with a mournful face, drew back. Then a general officer of noble family, commanding a brigade, advanced saying, 'My lord, I have lately been suffering much from rheumatism—' without allowing him time to complete his sentence, Lord Wellington rapidly said, 'and you want to go to England to be cured. By all means. Go there immediately.' "

Perhaps there was more reason for Wellesley's apparent unfairness than appears. He was always desperately short of engineer officers, while he was lavishly supplied with members of noble families. His promptness in acceding to this general's request may indicate anything but reluctance to get rid of him. Also, Sir James McGrigor, like most senior officers, had had his own experience of Wellesley's blistering rebukes, as he did one day when he had taken some perfectly reasonable action without getting permission and was asked, "I shall be glad to know who commands this army—I or you?" It is recorded that officers sometimes left his presence in tears, as did Charles Stewart on one memorable occasion—and Stewart was of noble family if anyone in the Army was. Other men were less sensitive. Picton, whom Wellesley called "a rough foulmouthed devil, as ever lived," could be embarrassed by nothing less lethal than the explosion of a mine. Craufurd of the Light Division, after an acid rebuke, remarked cheerfully to a friend, "He's damned crusty this morning." No one from general to private was immune from the blast of that cold anger, that terse reprimand. It kept them alert and obedient, but it did not make them love their commander. But Wellesley was not there to be loved. His job was to make soldiers of them, and he did it, thoroughly and most successfully, in the only way that he knew.

XXII

THE BRITISH ARMY in Portugal had never stood in greater danger than during that year of 1810. Napoleon had won the battle of Wagram in 1808 and had made peace with Austria, so that he had troops in plenty to spare to finish off the Spanish venture, which he was now heartily regretting. Once more the long blue-clad columns crawled through the passes of the Pyrenees, and his cavalrymen cantered across the open plains of Spain. With them came Masséna, the ablest of his fighting marshals, to take command in a sector which had suffered till now from too many generals and too little co-operation. Masséna was aging and not as active as he had been a few years ago. He was not only the ablest but the most rascally of the marshals, and he had amassed enough loot during his service to enjoy soft living and to dislike exertion. But he had lost none of his cunning. He was as good a tactician as Soult, without Soult's fatal tendency to hesitation at a decisive moment, and as fierce a fighter as Ney, without Ney's bull-headed impetuosity. Wellington, who knew his reputation, called him "an old fox" and said that he was as careful and as thorough as was he himself. Wellesley was committed to the defensive for many months ahead, till, at any rate, his army was more fit to take the field in a long campaign and till the works at Torres Vedras were ready to receive him in case of failure. But, as he had written to a subordinate in India, "By defensive, I do not mean that you should wait in any particular place till you may be attacked, but that you should attack any party that may come within your reach." By July

1810, the French strength in Spain was 370,000 men with 80,000 horses. There was nothing to keep them from the Portuguese frontier except the wholly unreliable Spanish army and the three forts, Badajoz, Almeida and Ciudad Rodrigo, which guarded the approach to it and which, garrisoned as they were by Spaniards, might as well be given up for lost.

Wellesley had to look helplessly on and to refuse the appeals which came to him from Spain to save the forts. "Better lose a fort than a campaign," he said grimly and remained in his position near Beira, so close to the frontier that his outposts could hear the musketry and the roar of cannon as the French assaulted Ciudad Rodrigo. The Spanish garrison, under the Governor, Harrasti, made an unexpectedly gallant resistance, but they had no chance against such strength and the fort fell on June 11.

On August 18 Almeida, which had made only a token resistance, was surrendered to the French.

Masséna was not going to waste time and men in assaulting Badajoz. He had enough troops to be able to spare a force to contain it and to leave it to be picked up later. In fact it fell by Spanish treachery the following year.

Wellesley felt his position now to be almost desperate. His army still stood in their lines not many miles inside the Spanish frontier, with for their only protection Craufurd's Light Division, which was strung out over an immense frontage, watching the passes and the bridges for Masséna's coming. Their defensive line was the River Coa, and Craufurd used his ground and his troops with such skill that for some time he managed to deceive the French about his comparative weakness. He took frightful, though necessary, risks to carry out his duty of screening the main army, operating sometimes with his division on both sides of the Coa and his battalions so far from each other that concentrating to fight might be a matter of days at a time when hours would hardly be granted.

If Wellesley needed anything to make him feel his danger more acutely, it was supplied by the knowledge that the government and his fellow citizens at home had already written him off as doomed to defeat and destruction or to an ignominious scramble to the coast in the hope of evacuation by sea. "It is probable," Lord Liverpool said in public in England, in the early days of that year, "that the army will embark in September." In March, he wrote to Wellesley, "Your chances of successful defence are considered here by all persons, military as well as civil, so improbable that I could not recommend any attempt at what may be called desperate resistance." Parliament, forgetting their courage and their duty to the men who were fighting for them, freely criticized movements which they did not understand, and the opposition demanded an inquiry into the conduct of the war. One speaker in the Commons declared that it was "melancholy and alarming" that Wellesley should "have the impertinence to think of defending Portugal with 50,000 men of whom only 20,000 were English," and asserted that the only British soldiers left in the Peninsula before six months were over would be the prisoners of war. Even the Common Council of London joined in the chorus of yapping and sent an address to the King, accusing Wellesley of "an incapacity of profiting by the lessons of experience" and referring to "equal rashness and ostentation during the recent Talavera campaign."

Fortunately, Wellesley had a stouter heart than had his employers, or the men who should have supported him in the country, and also more knowledge of the situation and of what he could do to cope with it.

Day after day he hung on, trusting to Craufurd to give him warning of an attack and to delay it during its passage of the Coa. Behind that brave but tenuous screen, he hastened the training and provisioning of his troops and drove on the engineers and the Portuguese labourers who were toiling at the lines of Torres Vedras.

At the end of July, Masséna was ready to advance, and on the twenty-fourth, Ney struck at the crossings of the Coa. He caught Craufurd himself, with the centre of his division, on the east bank of the Coa, so that Craufurd had not only to defend the bridge but to extricate himself and get back to the west bank before he could fight. With enormous skill he achieved this and checked the French advance for a whole day, managing to draw off in the darkness, having lost nearly 300 killed and wounded.

He had won much-needed time for Wellesley, and it had not been wasted. Masséna, a little taken aback by so stubborn a resistance and overestimating the numbers which had shown it, hesitated before crossing and gave Wellesley time to concentrate and to move to a position from where he could march against Masséna by whichever road the French chose to come. Masséna did not know the country and rashly relied on the advice of Portuguese guides who, probably deliberately, misled him and steered him onto the worst possible road for his purpose. "There are certainly many bad roads in Portugal," Wellesley said when it was reported to him, "and the enemy has decidedly taken the worst in the whole kingdom." It was a narrow, winding road, boggy when wet, and rock-strewn always. It was impossible to move even cavalry along its surface, so that it became crowded with troops of all arms, with guns and baggage, men and horses. But worst of all for Masséna's purpose was its route, which led directly to the wild and rocky heights of Busaco, a ridge which extended for eight miles across the valley of the Mondego and barred Masséna's line of advance. By the time that the French advance guard reached the ridge, Wellesley's army were in position along the heights in such a good place for defence that their commander remarked, "If Masséna attacks me here I shall beat him."

Masséna was more sanguine or less prudent. He had no one at home to discourage him, and, indeed, he knew that the Emperor not only expected him to rout the English but was capable of making his life a burden should he fail. He was not even deterred by Ney, who, after reconnoitring the British position, advised against attack, though any position which gave Ney pause must be grim indeed. "I cannot persuade myself," Masséna said, "that Lord Wellington will risk the loss of a reputation by giving battle; but if he does, I have him."

Once more it was an infantry fight. The ground was too steep and broken to allow Masséna to make much use of his fine cavalry. It was the old story of column against line, impetuous attack against steady defence, French valour against British tenacity, and above all of the terrible power of the controlled British volley. At last the French broke off the fight and retired, leaving behind them 6,000 dead and wounded. The British loss was 1,200. It pleased Wellington also that there had been a few Portuguese battalions from Beresford's force among his troops and that they had shown unexpected courage and steadiness under fire.

Masséna was in no hurry to renew the fight, nor did Wellington wait for him. When, at last, Masséna felt ready to resume his advance and moved on Coimbra, he found that Wellington had anticipated him. Masséna had hoped to turn the flank of the British march but instead, when he reached Coimbra, found them well ahead of him and still retiring.

Wellington was satisfied with the blow which he had struck, and his lines at Torres Vedras were ready to shelter him. There he meant to spend the winter, leaving Masséna to the cold shelter of an unfriendly and denuded country. He would waste no more lives when cold and hunger would do his work for him. As he marched, he laid waste the country between Coimbra and Torres Vedras, bearing off such crops and animals as he could use or could carry, driving a vast number of Portuguese inhabitants before him to share his winter shelter, burning and destroying buildings and such crops as he had to leave.

Masséna, over-confident as he had been, had entered Portugal with only fifteen days' rations, and when he reached Coimbra, these were already exhausted. As soon as he had passed through Coimbra, leaving there his hospitals and depots, an independent force of Portuguese, under Trant, a British officer, sprang on it, capturing nearly 5,000 French prisoners and a mass of baggage and transport.

Masséna was left naked in a naked land to get through the winter as best he might. It was a maxim of his master's that war should support war. Wellington had seen to it that there should be little left in Portugal to support his enemy; nor could supplies easily reach Masséna from the rear when every mile of his line of communications was threatened and often ravaged by Spanish and Portuguese guerrillas. The Spanish were poor enough troops when pressed into formal battle, but banditry was their second nature, if not their first, and they were as cruel as they were elusive. So through the long winter months and into the spring of the year 1811, Masséna's men starved and shivered in the desolate lands of Portugal, while Wellington's army watched them from their impregnable heights. The British were well supplied by the sea routes and through the port of Lisbon, and were quite content to wait where they were till Masséna should risk a hopeless attack or starve to death.

Masséna held on till September and till he had proved the hopelessness of trying to keep his army supplied. On September 15 he sullenly withdrew to Santarem, having lost 6,000 men in front of Torres Vedras, principally by starvation. Wellington cautiously left his lines to pursue, but as soon as Masséna turned about to fight, he declined battle and retired behind his lines. Masséna was left in the district about Santarem, somewhat less exposed than he had been before Torres Vedras, but no better supplied and with no better prospect than holding out where he was and trusting to a change of fortune in the spring.

It was a bitter winter of storm and rain, but spring did not bring the relief for which Masséna hoped. It brought him instead some reinforcements and from his master one of those plans which look and are so much more feasible when they are drafted many hundreds of miles away than they become on the immediate scene of action. The reinforcements included 12,000 of the Imperial Guard and another marshal, Bessières, though the French were already suffering from too many commanders, none of whom was anxious to combine with any other. Soult was in Andalusia and in no hurry to leave it, having decided that since he could not be King of Portugal, he might as well set up a throne where he happened to be. Ney was with Masséna, but there was no love lost between them and more than once they quarrelled violently.

The French had the advantage of numbers and held all the key positions, except Badajoz. That, too, they gained when Soult was at last persuaded to move to undertake its reduction. An act of treachery gave him the fort on March 11. The three great fortresses barred Wellington's way into Spain, and until he could reduce them he could look for nothing more than another winter behind the Torres Vedras lines.

The whole campaign of 1811 hinged on his attempts to break the chain which confined him and on the French determination to repulse him. Once more he showed that his idea of defence included aggressive action whenever he saw an opportunity to use it. It was the strength of the French forces covering the fortresses which prevented him through the year from capturing them by formal siege. He did not have the heavy guns needed to batter them. Meanwhile he would take every chance of hitting the covering forces, and for the first time he felt strong enough to split his own strength and let his generals undertake separate movements.

Unlike Napoleon, Wellington was near enough to his divisional commanders to control them, and had enough confidence in them to detach them for special operations. During the long winter months in the lines, he had been able to watch his army and their commanders. Now he had collected round him the band of senior officers whose names were soon to be so famous and would always be linked with his own. There was Picton, the rough Welshman whom his men respected for his wild bravery in action, feared for his savagery in discipline and almost loved for the blasphemy and obscenity of his language when he addressed them. There was Hill, whom all the Army loved and called "Daddy Hill," a typical country squire, with his fresh complexion and trimmed whiskers, and his engaging habit of giving a coin and a meal to men who arrived at his headquarters with messages. Wellington, who liked and trusted him most of all of them, said that Hill "would do anything that he was told and nothing that he was not," which Hill afterward disproved by brilliant independent action at Arroyo and Almaraz. Craufurd, who still commanded the Light Division, was a man to be relied on in sole command of an operation, apart from a tendency to take a higher risk than was sometimes wise. Beresford was untried as a commander, but had scored a notable success by making the Portuguese into soldiers, so that battalions of them were now beginning to be incorporated in British brigades. Graham, the furthest away, at Cadiz, was the oldest of the general officers by many years and the least experienced, though he soon showed himself to be a shrewd leader and a determined fighter. Two years of war had begun to make the British army in Portugal a formidable and close-knit fighting force, and they were in good heart, having watched their enemies starve and fade away while they sat in comparative safety and comfort. The years had brought, too, a better understanding between the men and their exacting and unrewarding commander. They still did not like him—probably they never would—but they trusted him and felt happier when he was among them. Above all, they knew that he would not harry them with unnecessary detail. Anyone who is familiar with soldiers knows how important to them is so apparently trivial a matter. His attitude to their dress was typical. "Provided we brought our men into the field well appointed," wrote Grattan of the 88th Foot, "with their sixty rounds of ammunition each, he never looked to see whether trousers were black, blue or grey." He required them to be clean and neat and warmly clad for the winter, but he was never one of those officers who set store by military display. That could safely be left to the Prince Regent, the most adventurous of military milliners, who regularly staggered the cavalry in Portugal with samples of the new uniforms which he had designed for them.

Wellington himself set the example of neatness, combined with simplicity. His invariable dress in camp or in action was a blue or grey frockcoat, trousers of the same colour strapped beneath the instep, and a plain cocked hat with an adjustable waterproof cover, because, "I never get wet if I can help it." His sword and spurs were of plain steel and he carried, rolled before his saddle, a plain greatcoat with a wide cape.

It had been a foible of many great commanders to dress more plainly than their staffs or their men, whether the garment of simplicity be a blue frock, a grey redingote or corduroy trousers and a black beret. It serves perhaps to establish them in the minds of their troops as men who are not devoted to ceremonial or to what a modern army calls "bull."

During the winter months on Torres Vedras, the men got used to the sight of that trim figure, always so immaculately clean and well-shaved— he shaved always once and often twice a day, even on active service— mounted on the chestnut thoroughbred "Copenhagen." They began to call him by a nickname, "The Beau." A commander who has gained a nickname among his troops—always provided that it is not an opprobrious one—has gone some way to winning their confidence. When the campaign of 1811 began, Wellington and his army were beginning to know each other.

XXIII

THE YEAR 1811 was one of frustration. The campaign, which opened with some brilliantly successful actions, came to grief on the failure to take the fortresses, and December found the British once more in Torres Vedras. It was no comfort to them that the French were in worse plight, because they did not know it. Ciudad Rodrigo and Badajoz still stood grimly on guard where the line of advance into Spain beckoned to Wellington, and all his efforts to break the chain were unavailing. The French were always in such strength that they could combine against the British when they attempted a siege, and Wellington had to abandon his trenches and batteries to drive off the relieving forces.

It had been a spring of promise and hope for Wellington. Masséna hung on at Santarem until March 6, when he marched out in obedience to his master's orders to join Soult on the frontier. Napoleon, with the blithe confidence which comes from absence from the scene of action, had ordered Masséna to cross the Tagus and march south and west to join Soult coming up from Andalusia. But he had ignored the chief objection to that route, which was that the whole of Wellington's army could easily be thrown across it to prevent the junction. Masséna, resourceful as ever, decided to march to his flank to the Mondego, thus increasing the distance between him and Soult, then to turn westward again to Guarda and move by way of Ciudad Rodrigo. He covered his departure so well that four days had passed before the British were on his track, but as soon as they knew his plan, they were after him by forced marches, Picton with the Third Division racing ahead to turn his flank.

It was fortunate for Masséna that he had Ney to command his rearguard. Ney, as he was to show so gloriously in Russia two years later, was a master of delaying tactics. He made the British deploy to fight him and handled them roughly at Pombal on March 11 and at Cazal Novo on March 14. He tried again on the fifteenth at Foz d'Aronce, but with less success, since there he had made the same mistake as did Craufurd the year before on the Coa, being caught with his corps astride of the river and hustled back by Picton with support from the Horse Artillery.

Wellington halted on the sixteenth to rest his troops and to allow his supplies to catch up with him, but within twenty-four hours he was on the move again and came up with Masséna at Sabugal on the Coa, where Craufurd and Picton drove the French back and forced the crossing of the river. Masséna crossed the frontier into Spain and fell back through Ciudad Rodrigo to Salamanca.

He had entered Portugal on September 6, 1810. He left it on April 5, 1811, having lost during those six months nearly 40,000 men killed, wounded or taken prisoner. It was the end of his service in the Peninsula. Shortly afterward he was relieved of his command and ordered home to face his master, who never forgave failure. At the same time, Marshal Marmont was sent to Spain to see whether he could do what Masséna, Ney and Soult could not.

While this fighting had been in progress, Graham, whose division was in Cadiz, struck a clever tactical blow at Victor, whose role was to support Soult when Soult marched to join Masséna. Graham knew that a Spanish army under La Pena was somewhere near Algeciras.

His move was a good example of the strength which the British could always draw from their command of the sea. He embarked his division at Cadiz and landed them at Algeciras, from where he set out to join La Pena. La Pena had some 7,000 Spanish troops and about as much courage and ability as any other Spanish general. When Graham met him he was marching his force up and down the countryside in a vague manner, apparently looking for an enemy to run away from.

The combined British and Spanish force amounted to 12,000, which, as less than half of them were British, meant that when they fought they might be able to count on only some 4,000 effective first-line troops. Against them Victor had 20,000. He had moreover got wind of the whole plan and was ready to fall on La Pena before Graham could join him. He came upon him at Barrosa and, without delay, attacked. The head of the leading British column of route was within sight of the battlefield when most of the Spanish, including their general, fled into the distant countryside. Graham, without hesitation, deployed his division and attacked Victor. The fight lasted for little more than an hour and a half, but it was bloody and savagely fought. Once more the French columns withered away under the weight of the British volleys, and Victor broke off the fight and retreated in no good order. La Pena, who had watched the battle from a safe distance, arrived when it was over and claimed his share of credit for the victory, which so much annoyed Graham that he marched his troops right off the field and told La Pena that in future he could look after himself. Later he refused a Spanish dukedom which they offered in the hope of appeasing him and of keeping him in the district in case La Pena should want to run away again.

The chief benefit to the British of this brilliant little operation of Graham's was that it alarmed Soult, who stopped his march to join Masséna and moved back for some distance to support Victor.

Badajoz had fallen by treachery to the French on March 11, and Wellington sent Beresford with 20,000 infantry and 2,000 cavalry to take charge of the operations for its capture, while he blockaded Almeida. Beresford had a brush with the French at Campo Mayor, which was chiefly remarkable for a headlong cavalry charge by the 13th Light Dragoons, and on May 3 Wellington himself, to cover his operations against Badajoz and Almeida, fought a three-day battle at Fuentes de Oñoro.

Almeida fell to him on May 10. Six days later, Beresford, still trying to gain time for siege operations at Badajoz to be completed, met the French at Albuera and fought one of the most important and most fiercely contested battles of the campaign and, indeed, of the whole war. He was opposed by Soult, but it was a fight where tactical skill counted for little and the fighting powers of the men engaged for everything.

It was above all an infantryman's battle, though the French cavalry did much damage, all but destroying a British infantry brigade. The share taken by the British infantry in the victory had been immortalized by Napier in one of the most famous of his prose passages: "Suddenly and sternly recovering, they closed on their terrible enemies and then was seen with what a strength and majesty the British soldier fights. . . . Nothing could stop that astonishing infantry. No sudden burst of undisciplined valour, no nervous enthusiasm weakened the stability of their order; their flashing eyes were bent on the dark columns in front, their measured tread shook the ground, their dreadful volleys swept away the head of every formation, their deafening shouts overpowered the dissonant cries, as slowly, and with a horrid carnage, it was driven by the incessant vigour of the attack to the farthest edge of the hill."

It was the last big battle of the campaign of 1811, though Hill had a smaller fight with Girard at Arroyo on October 27. The campaign had lost its rhythm, and Wellington realized that he could do no more until the following spring. The British retired again to their Torres Vedras lines, leaving behind them the two great fortresses still unsubdued, while the French, badly mauled but still strong in numbers, lay beyond the frontier. Wellington still held Portugal, but Madrid and the Pyrenees were as inaccessible as ever, and he had to face the prospect in the New Year of renewing the attempt to reduce the forts which still defied him.

He had, if he had only known it, better prospects for 1812 than any-one in his army yet imagined. During the winter months some hint of it began to trickle into the British lines by means of spies and French deserters, of whom there was generally a regular stream outside the campaigning season. Often the men themselves did not know or guess the importance of the information which they offered to ensure a friendly reception. They spoke of the regiments and brigades which were in the French lines and of occasional movements of troops, naming certain fa-mous formations or units which the British were accustomed to meeting in the French line of battle. Gradually the British officers began to build up from these casual reports a coherent picture of the whole French position. As the weeks went by they heard of brigades being withdrawn from the French lines and put under orders for France, and these were often such troops as the Imperial Guard or cuirassiers and dragoons.

Spanish peasants came into the lines with tales of long columns of lancers and batteries of galloper guns moving westward along the road to Salamanca and Madrid. The French were not pulling out of Spain, but they were plainly reducing their strength there and taking from it most of the regiments which contained the veterans of the Emperor's earlier battles.

Napoleon had made up his mind to invade Russia, and all through the winter, his outlying garrisons were reduced to build up the huge army which he would need in 1812 for so great an enterprise. He was tired of Spain, where his armies had been dissipated without achieving any victory to speak of and where one after another of his once-trusted mar-shals had blundered and failed. Masséna had failed so badly, after so much had been hoped for from him, that he was unlikely ever again to find employment, and Bessières was withdrawn when the Guard left. Victor was under orders, and last of all Ney, the fighting man indis-pensable to any great task, turned his horse and rode homeward. In Ma-drid, Joseph, by the will of his brother King of Spain, was still in nominal command of all the French forces, but the next year's fighting would be the supreme responsibility of Marmont, who had not yet had the chance of grappling with the peculiar difficulties of war in the Peninsula.

What Wellington thought of the prospect no one knew because he kept his own counsel and, as was his manner, told no one of his plans, still less of his feelings. He cannot but have felt disappointment that another winter should find him still at Torres Vedras with the frontier fortresses still barring his road into Spain. Above all, he must have felt the weight of responsibility which lay on him commanding, as he was, what he always called "Britain's last army." When first he had landed in Portugal he had said, "If I lose 500 men they will bring me on my knees before the bar of the House of Commons." His force had grown to more than twice the size that it had then been, his infantry were battle-hardened and beginning to understand his ideas of discipline, his artillery and cavalry were slowly building up. But it was still Britain's last army, and a disaster to it would have incalculable consequences for Britain and the whole of Europe.

He had not even the assurance of a united and determined government behind him, as Lord Liverpool had fairly warned him, though Castlereagh was his strongest and most faithful supporter. His Spanish allies were as bad as he had known them to be, but his Portuguese gave promise of being worth their pay and rations and even useful in the line of battle. His divisional generals were proving themselves, though he was yet very far from satisfied with the standard which the regimental officers had reached—his comment on their worth as he looked back over the fighting of 1811 was the typically ungracious one, "There is nothing on earth so stupid as a gallant officer." It is little to be wondered at that during the latter part of the year many of them had found him even less approachable than ever or that, during the fighting, his rebukes had been more frequent and more obliterating. It was particularly noticeable that the most savage of them were reserved for his mounted troops, of whom he habitually spoke with contempt and something like hatred. During 1811 cavalry had, for the first time, come to represent an important branch of his army, as regiments were sent out from England, only too often after insufficient training and under woefully ignorant officers.

It is natural, when one thinks of the Army of the Peninsula, to think of them as infantry, so high was their reputation and so noble their record. Wellington himself was an infantryman, and it is doubtful whether he ever really understood cavalry or welcomed their presence on the battlefield. His complaint about them, frequently and forcefully expressed, was, "The only thing that they can be relied on to do is to gallop too far and too fast." They could not look after themselves or their horses, were indifferent to their own protection when at rest, could not rally after a charge. Their officers were as brave as men can be, but all the tactics that they had learned had been those of a thruster in the hunting field. If they charged successfully, they pursued too far, with the result that they eventually ran into a superior force and were destroyed or at best dispersed. Nothing, as Napier said, could stop that astonishing infantry. Wellington at times must have longed for someone who could stop his astonishing cavalry before they committed suicide.

His introduction to cavalry fighting had been unfortunate. In India he had seen and dealt only with native auxiliaries, ignorant of drill or discipline, unreliable in battle and useless for other duties, such as reconnaissance. His first encounter with the problem in the Peninsula had been at Oporto, when Murray, being in a position to attack the flank of the retreating French, had blundered, not in launching the whole of his few squadrons or in refusing to commit any of them, either of which might have been the right tactics, but in weakly allowing a small party of them to attempt a gallant but useless charge.

He had seen more of their ways at Talavera when he had ordered a charge of the 23rd Light Dragoons and some German Hussars, and the whole detachment had lost much of their strength by riding straight into a deep and hidden ravine which crossed their front. (It was probably not their fault—a cavalry commander cannot reconnoitre every possible route he may be ordered to take—but it did not increase Wellington's confidence in cavalry as an aid to winning battles.) On the same day, such of the 23rd as had survived the ravine had charged a square according to orders and, having been beaten off, had continued on their wild course and attacked three lines of French cavalry, losing nearly half their strength in men and horses. At Campo Mayor, the 13th Light Dragoons had followed a successful charge with a headlong thrust into the enemy's main body, earning for themselves his rebuke that they were "an armed rabble" and his promise that if they did it again he would take their horses from them and make them march in the infantry column. At the small engagement of Maguilla, Slade's Heavy Brigade did much the same thing, so that Wellington wrote angrily to Hill: "I have never been more annoyed than by Slade's affair. Our officers of cavalry have acquired a trick of galloping at everything. They never consider the situation, never think of manoeuvring before an enemy and never keep back or provide a reserve."

At Fuentes de Oñoro it was the Horse Artillery who came under the lash of his tongue. (They were, after all, the men whose guns went with the cavalry, and subject, in his opinion, to the same defects.) Captain Ramsay's battery, being in a forward position, had been overrun by the French cavalry and had quite disappeared from view as well as—in most people's opinion—from the army list. They cut themselves out, showing great courage and dash, and brought back all their guns and horses. The

THE BATTLE OF WATERLOO

From a contemporary engraving

WELLINGTON IN LATER LIFE

From a portrait in the House of Lords

feat was done in full sight of the army, who cheered the gunners as they broke away from the French and galloped to safety. Perhaps Ramsay and his men felt that they deserved the welcome, perhaps they even fondly hoped for a word of commendation from Wellington, but if so they were disappointed. He rode up to them, beckoned to Ramsay to come to him and said, "If this happens again, I will send you back to England." Not unnaturally the cavalry felt that Wellington treated them less than fairly and rated them below the infantry, to whom they felt themselves immeasurably superior.

In the next two years they were to be of more service to him and to contribute much to his victorious battles, as Le Marchant's Heavy Brigade would do at Salamanca. By the time that he reached Vitoria and the Pyrenees they were well up to the normal strength of the cavalry arm when serving with infantry. At Quatre Bras and Waterloo they fought well, though there was still the fatal tendency to press a successful charge too far. Even so, he still viewed them with suspicion, for as late as 1826 he was writing to Lord John Russell, "I considered our cavalry so inferior to the French from want of order that, although I considered one of our squadrons a match for two French, yet I did not care to see four British opposed to four French. . . . They could gallop, but could not preserve order."

It may have been all true. Much of it obviously was. But his freedom in expounding it did not make him popular with the cavalry nor—which was worse—did it give the cavalry the confidence that they were valuable and trusted.

G.

XXIV

FIVE YEARS EARLIER, Napoleon had said of one of his generals, "Ord-ner is worn out. One has only so long in one for war. I have six more years and then I shall have to stop." But at the end of 1811, when the sixth of those years was running out, he found, as most dictators find out sooner or later, that he could not stop. He had, as he said later, found the crown of France in the gutter and picked it up on the point of his sword. It was only by his sword that he could hold it aloft and defy his enemies and his own subjects, whom he had fed with victories and who would not welcome a change of diet.

He would, it may be, gladly have stopped, if it were possible to achieve his object, the complete domination of Europe, without further fighting, but he was in no position to dictate a peace treaty as absolute victor and he could not afford to offer anything else. His only recent successes had been against Austria, whom he had beaten at Aspern-Essling and Wag-ram. He had tried to make a friend of her by divorcing his wife, Jose-phine, and marrying the Princess Marie Louise, the daughter of the Austrian Emperor, but he was not sure that he could count on anything from Austria beyond neutrality. It was hardly likely that she could be got to march against her old allies Russia and Prussia.

The thought of Russia obsessed him. He could not turn his mind from those immense spaces, the endless plains with the pine woods and the dusty, muddy tracks which served for roads. Somewhere in that remote region, perhaps in fabulous Moscow, the city of gilded domes and frozen rivers, the Czar, that incalculable creature, might be planning good or ill for the French. Somewhere in that grim expanse enormous armies wheeled and marched, stiff and old-fashioned in their discipline, brave with a dour bravery of endurance, ruthless and half-savage. And somewhere across the infinite steppes there trotted sotnia after sotnia of the Cossack light cavalry, little men on little horses as tough and wiry as themselves—not to be compared on the battlefield with his own dragoons or lancers, but a menace and a pestilence to bodies of troops on the march or a detachment temporarily separated from the rest or an infantry battalion in bivouac. There was something about them of the cruelty and elusiveness of the Spanish guerrillas who never stopped harassing his troops in their own country.

Napoleon could not rest easy with that threat always at his back, and yet his resources were strained almost to the limit with his commitments in Europe. His armies were so widely scattered that they were for weeks at a time out of his control, and he could not trust his marshals to act sensibly—perhaps to act honourably—when they were acting independently. It was his own doing. Once more, like so many dictators, he would suffer no one to approach him in dignity or in the reality of power. He had trained his marshals to act promptly and efficiently on his orders with the result that, in his absence, they hesitated and shirked responsibility. Had he been able to stay longer in Spain, he would, he was confident, have crushed the resistance of the Spanish and have driven the British into the sea. He had, it was true, driven them out of Portugal at Corunna, but after their impudent fashion they had come back and, so far, in his absence no one had succeeded in dislodging them, though several of his best marshals had tried. Soult had started well with his storming of Lisbon, but then had tamely allowed Wellesley—the Sepoy General—to chase him out of Portugal with a trick which a child should have seen. Victor had failed at Talavera, Masséna at Busaco. Ney—as usual—had run his head bull-like into a barrier at Foz d'Aronce. Victor, trying again, had done even worse at Barrosa, and Masséna blundered at Fuentes de Oñoro. Then it was Soult's turn again, and he threw away his chance of victory by his hesitation in the bloody fight of Albuera. The Spanish campaign which Napoleon had designed as a demonstration of his strength had turned into a bitter struggle which promised to go on endlessly as long as the marshals were left to their own devices. So far from the Leopard having been driven into the sea, he was now across the border and into Spain, and his trenches and parallels were open against Ciudad Rodrigo and Badajoz, the two fortresses which controlled the way into and out of Portugal. Even if the British should be forced back again, they had behind them those impregnable lines on the Torres

Vedras heights, a natural fortress guarded by every device of the military engineer. Behind these the British could winter in comfort, drawing their supplies by sea and secure from attack, while his men must either freeze and starve in an enemy country or retreat into Spain with the work to do again next year.

He could not be everywhere himself. He tried to direct operations in Spain from his headquarters on the Danube, but by the time his courier arrived—if he ever arrived—the situation might have altered and rendered the orders useless. The only gain which he could count as coming from the Spanish venture was the closing of the Spanish ports to Britain's trade, but the Portuguese ports were open and there had been signs lately that the Russian Emperor was chafing against the loss of his own trade with Britain.

It all came back to Russia, to that immense and shadowy threat which was always at his back, the one power which could ruin all his plans and from which he dared not turn away to finish his work in Spain or to control what he already held. It was the same threat which, in 1941, drove Hitler to the venture which began his undoing. Napoleon knew that he must deal with it, whatever risk he had to take. He was like a man who fears that a ghost is behind him and forces himself to turn and face it rather than fly or hide from it. Slowly and as secretly as possible, he began to assemble his army of invasion and to move it onto its starting line behind the Niemen.

The army was ready by Midsummer's Day 1812 athwart the Vilna road and on the west bank of the Niemen. Late in the evening Napoleon put on the uniform of a Polish cavalry officer and, taking Berthier with him but no escort, rode forward to the river bank to an isolated house which stood there opposite to the village of Kovno on the Russian side. From the window he surveyed the crossing place and stared out in the failing light to get his first glimpse of Russian territory. There is a story, told but not vouched for by Hilaire Belloc, that as he rode back again into his lines his horse stumbled and nearly threw him and that an unknown voice said, "A Roman would have turned back." There could be no turning back now for him, and three days later, when his engineers had laid bridges across the river, he sat by the roadside and watched his army cross into Russia. It was the largest army that he had ever commanded—well nigh half a million men, French most of them but also allies, willing and unwilling, Prussian, Polish, Westphalian, even Italian. The columns went over all that day and all through the moonlit night and still on the next day were crossing. The Emperor spent many hours of both day and night watching the steady flow of the streams of men and horses, guns and wagons and—or so it is said—whistling to himself the old tune, "Malbrouck s'en va't en guerre," breaking off once to observe that all this multitude of armed men was worth less than a song sung by a girl in a Paris street. (The story may be true but sounds unlikely.)

The news grew worse that spring, with the fall of Ciudad and Badajoz to Wellington's storming parties, but there was a gleam of hope in a dispatch which reached him during—or it may be just after—the crossing of the Niemen and told him that the British were at war with America.

It was the inevitable result of the British Orders in Council which had forbidden trade between America and French-controlled countries and especially of the instructions to British ships to stop neutral vessels and search them for deserters. The British government had, it is true, ordered their sea captains to treat American ships with as little hostility as possible, but ships were long at sea and far away from the control of statesmen sitting in London. It was too much to expect captains to show very much restraint when they had an opportunity of recruiting their crews by impressing American sailors whom it suited them to believe were British deserters.

Negotiations went on for nearly three years, but the spirit of the States was rising while Britain's cooled, especially after a change of ministers which followed the murder of Spencer Percival, the Premier, and brought Castlereagh to the foreign office. Castlereagh, who was always conciliatory in his dealings with foreign powers and was a diplomat by nature and training, saw the futility of allowing the situation to drift into war and on June 16, 1812, announced the immediate suspension of the Orders in Council. Unhappily he was too late, for his announcement was made only two days before the United States' declaration of war. Yet, even if Castlereagh had been able to deal earlier with the naval position, it is unlikely that war would have been averted, though it might possibly have been postponed. America wanted war with Britain, not for the sake of her rights on the sea so much as because of her desire for Britain's colony of Canada.

It is seldom difficult for those who covet a territory to see themselves in the role of deliverers. When war broke out in 1812, the United States was ready to march into Canada and proclaim her liberation from British domination. The French and British were so much at odds with each other that they would surely not combine against a friendly invader. The French regarded the British—with some justice—as interlopers and robbers, while the British—with none at all—blamed the French for being French. So confident were the Americans of meeting with a cordial welcome that they prepared their invasion almost lightheartedly, forgetting that in Canada there were four regiments of British troops and some 4,000 Canadian Militia with the probable help of not less than 4,000 friendly Indians, while the strength of the United States Army was less than 7,000 men all told, and they would get no help from any Indians, since all their progress westward had been made at Indian expense and had cost dearly in Indian lives.

The United States troops were soon to find that they were unlikely to get help from the French Canadians. General Hull, with a force of 1,500 men based in Detroit, invaded Canada, proclaiming his mission to liberate the unhappy inhabitants from British tyranny, only to learn, as other liberators have learned, that to fulfil his mission he needed some sign of co-operation from the intended recipients of his generosity. The French Canadians disliked the British, but they were not discontented with their living conditions and they did not want to leave their profitable trade in furs and timber to waste time in being liberated. The Indians, indeed, were glad to see the invaders and showed it in no uncertain way by massacring any detached body of troops and cutting up communications. Finally, General Brock, the British commander, marched to bar Hull's further progress and summoned him to surrender, accompanying his demand with a wholly insincere expression of his regret at his inability to restrain his Indian allies unless the surrender were made without delay.

The first invasion of Canada ended ignominiously for the United States, but there was compensation in a series of small sea-fights, in four out of five of which the United States ships were victorious. One of the distinguishing features of the war is the number of engagements which were fought between single ships, usually frigates, of each side. One of the most famous was that between the United States *Chesapeake* and the British *Shannon,* one of the few which the British won, but quite as noteworthy and even more successful was the American frigate *Constitution* which destroyed the British *Guerrière,* a recent capture from the French, and the *Java,* while the United States sloop-of-war *Wasp* accounted for the British *Frolic, Hornet* and *Peacock,* all within the same month.

Whatever of interest and of credit there is about the whole war rests with the naval forces on both sides. The military movements were inconclusive and half-hearted, with both sides willing to abandon the fight if only someone would tell them to. It was nearly accomplished in 1812 after informal negotiations in London, which only broke down because the British refused to give up the right of impressing seamen from neutral ships, and the miserable squabble had to drag on for two more years.

Each side had some success and some disaster. The Americans penetrated as far as the mouth of the St. Lawrence River and destroyed part of Quebec. The British raided Washington and burned some of the government buildings. The only people who got any profit or enjoyment out of the war were the Indians, whom the British—naturally to their great and expressed regret—were unable to restrain from their tribal sports of massacre and destruction. There seemed to be no way of stopping a war which no one wanted to go on with, and Britain, at any rate, had lost all interest in that theatre and became even more sparing of reinforcements and supplies than earlier.

There was much in Europe to distract British attention during the winter of 1812, when it was hardly possible to doubt that France's wave of power had reached its crest and was beginning its downfall.

While this war in miniature was going on in Canada and round her shores, the destruction of France was slowly taking shape as a possibility in Spain and in Russia. In fact, two years later when Napoleon was, so it seemed, safely locked away on Elba, it was with something like mild surprise that the British remembered that they were still at war with the United States.

XXV

IT SEEMED that the Continental war would never stop. By the beginning of the winter of 1812 there was no feeling in any country in Europe other than great disillusion and weariness. It may have been that Russia alone saw a glimpse of light, but even she had not much more than faith to sustain her. Her armies had steadily fallen back, according to plan, in front of the advancing French, refusing battle and drawing the enemy on through a scorched and stripped countryside with communications which stretched now some two thousand miles back into France. Yet Russia could not feel certain of victory, since they had stood to fight at Borodino on September 7 and had the worst of a murderous battle which left the Emperor Napoleon free to enter Moscow on the fifteenth. The Russian retirement might have been according to plan, but there was no avoiding the fact that their Army had been defeated and their capital occupied. The French, however, were in a very dangerous situation and, if they failed to act promptly, might find themselves forestalled by the bitter cold of a Russian winter.

There was no reason to think that Napoleon, who always acted promptly, would fail at this crisis in his affairs. He still commanded an enormous army which, after deducting the casualties of the march and the battle of September 7 and the troops left to guard the line of communications, numbered almost a quarter of a million men, and their depleted stores were being replenished from the stocks of food left behind in Moscow. Even if Napoleon should decide to winter there he would be more formidable than ever in the spring with his troops rested and refreshed and probably reinforced, as long as his communications through Smolensk were maintained. On the other hand, if he should decide on an immediate retreat to somewhere like Smolensk, he could hold a fortified line for the winter; and if he were to move at once it was unlikely that the Russians, who had been badly shaken at Borodino, would be able to obstruct his retreat, and they would have to face him again in the early months of 1813. The one thing for which they had neither right nor reason to hope was the thing that happened: Napoleon, faced with the choice of retreat or staying in Moscow, did nothing at all and came to no decision for more than a month—a month which was vital, since it brought the winter by so much the nearer.

It was natural that he should halt for a time in Moscow to rest and feed his troops, but it was a rest such as those who had known the French Army in earlier campaigns had never seen before.

In earlier days the Army had used their rest time for re-forming battered units, replacing casualties among men and horses, and reinforcing such discipline as had lapsed owing to weariness or disappointment, and all the time the brain and heart of the Army at Imperial Headquarters had throbbed unceasingly with plans for the next move and with orders for the necessary drafts and transport.

In Moscow the Army's rest was like a stagnation or a coma. Discipline fell away before the opportunities offered by a rich and undefended city, and the men plundered on a grand scale, loading themselves with furs and jewelry, tearing down curtains and hangings, rolling up carpets and stripping the churches of ornaments and draperies. They gave no thought to the question of how they were to get all these treasures home again, though they must have known that there was no transport for anything but food and ammunition and not nearly enough for those. They had been outraged in the first days of the occupation by the fire which raged through Moscow and which was almost certainly caused by heroic Russian incendiaries, who had stayed behind in hiding when the main body of their Army marched through and out of Moscow. Most of the houses and buildings in the city were of wood, and a fierce east wind which rose on the evening of the battle at Borodino and blew without relief for at least a week sent the flames roaring through the empty streets and across the squares till even the Kremlin, where Napoleon had taken up his quarters, was threatened. The Army saw the shelter being destroyed and the riches of the city being snatched from their grasp, and they thought of nothing but enriching themselves while there was still anything left to loot. Only the Imperial Guard, the best-disciplined unit of the Army, stood firm at their duty, and there was still some semblance of order in the corps commanded by that ruthless martinet Marshal Davout. The rest were little else but a disorderly, drunken and rapacious mob. The only troops to escape the contamination, except the Guard, were Murat's cavalry reserve, who had been pushed through the city and formed a screen to the east and north of it to watch the Russian Army. Even they were ruined, not by indulgence but by senseless overuse. Their horses were all but foundered when they arrived in Moscow, and the chance of getting remounts was small, since the Russians had driven off with them every horse which could possibly have been used to pull a gun or a wagon or to mount a trooper. It would have been no more than plain common sense to give them as much rest as possible, leaving the duty of observing the enemy to patrols and vedettes as small and as few as would be consonant with safety. But common sense was never one of Murat's distinguishing qualities. He was fearless in battle and an unmatched commander of large bodies of cavalry in action, but he needed the spur of battle to rouse his interest in anything but his personal dignity and his wardrobe. He would quarrel or sulk for a month if he thought that another marshal was being favoured by the Emperor or getting more credit than he for a victory, and he would devote to the design of a new uniform for himself as much thought as most marshals gave to a campaign. He was a magnificent horseman but a wretched horsemaster, and till the trumpets sounded for action, he was quite happy to leave the command of his division for all practical purposes to anyone who would take it on. The cavalry reserve were posted some miles to the east of the city, and Murat, having no idea what to do with cavalry, except to move them as fast and as far as they could go, exhausted them with rapid marches and sweeping reconnaissances which could as well have been carried out by a few squadrons or even troops. In earlier and better days, the Emperor, who respected Murat as a fighter and in no other capacity, would have put a stop to such dangerous nonsense, but the orders which came from Moscow were very few and dealt with little but routine. The Emperor had sent Murat out to take up a position and to do a certain task and seemed content to leave it at that.

That indeed was the whole cause of the rapid deterioration of the French Army. There were no orders and no sense of central control. It was a feeling which no previous French Army had known when the Emperor was with them, and now that they met it for the first time, it frightened them more than anything, more than the fire, the thousands of miles which separated them from their homes, the weariness of the march and the agonies of the battle. The Army was rotting as the human body rots when the heart has ceased to pump lifeblood through the veins and arteries. So seemingly invincible had been that central control and

so absolute their reliance on it that its removal, even its temporary removal, paralyzed them. It was as though the Emperor himself had died.

And to those who were closest to him, to such men as Berthier, Caulaincourt and Bertrand, he seemed like a man in a trance or a sleepwalker.
He had always been able to face reality and to accept facts, often to
turn them to his advantage when they seemed to be against him. Now,
so changed was he that he seemed to live in his dreams and turn the facts
to suit the vision of his nights and days. After the fight of Borodino,
when Murat's advanced squadrons clattered into the suburbs of Moscow
to be met with no challenge, no shot, nothing but silence and emptiness,
the Emperor had shown a strange reluctance to follow them. He had set
up his headquarters in a small house outside the gates, where he waited
for the keys of the city to be delivered to him by Russian grandees and
civic officials, who would come—as others had come from almost every
European capital—to beg for his mercy and to learn his will. Day after
day he waited but no surrender came, while his troopers rode through
the empty streets and the main body of the Army chafed and fretted for
orders and for the imagined delights of the city.

It was the same when he entered the city and took up his quarters in
the vast emptiness of the Kremlin. There was so much to be done for the
good of the Army, so many orders to be given and plans to be made,
but he seemed unwilling or unable to turn his mind to them. It was not
worthwhile; they would only be here for a few days longer. An ambassador would come—would come any day, probably tomorrow—from the
Russian Emperor, announcing his submission and asking for orders. It
had always been that way, the Emperor of Austria had bowed before
him, the King of Prussia had fawned upon him, the Pope of Rome had
been glad to do his bidding. Something extraordinary must have delayed
the Russian messenger, but it could only be a delay of a day or two. He
would certainly be here tomorrow. So Berthier and the others—Murat,
Ney, Davout, Mortier—attended his levees and wondered to see him so
calm and so absent-minded. It seemed sometimes that he was waiting,
listening for something—perhaps for a sound of a trumpet and the hoof-
beats of the ambassador's horse. Occasionally he roused himself and inspected the Imperial Guard or one of the corps. Once, to show how he
kept his grip over every detail of life in France, though France was two
thousand miles away, he dictated a plan for the reorganization of the
French National Theatre. There was much silence in the bare halls and
rooms of the Kremlin, where spurred boots rang loudly on the floors of
empty chambers and the Emperor sat by the window watching the
swirling smoke and the flying sparks as Moscow burned. They had
warned him about the danger of fire reaching the Kremlin, and at first

he seemed to take no notice, but later he agreed to move to a safer lodging in another palace. It did not much matter to him, they would only be there for a few days more; the Russian ambassador must be very near the city by now; he would surely come soon, perhaps tomorrow.

One morning—it was still September but toward the end and the nights were getting a little chilly—he mounted and rode out to inspect Ney's corps. While he was riding round the ranks the sky became overcast and a few flakes of snow fell. It was nothing, they melted as soon as they reached the ground and gradually the sky cleared. Winter was still a long way off, and there was no one to warn him that the Russian winter was incalculable in its arrival but that it seldom delayed long after the warning given by the first light flakes of snow.

Long before the first heavy frosts began Alexander would have made his submission, especially since Caulaincourt had been sent to hasten him. Caulaincourt was of the old nobility of France and would be persona grata with Alexander, would make it easy for Alexander to accept the inevitable and fall into line behind all the other European kings who had bowed to the Imperial will. Had there not been at Dresden three kings and seven princes waiting in the Imperial antechamber till they were sent for to get their orders? Who was Alexander of Russia that he should escape the common fate of princes who opposed the will of France and her Emperor? Caulaincourt would explain that to him; Caulaincourt would be back any day with the submission—probably tomorrow.

When at last Caulaincourt returned, empty-handed and despondent, the old Napoleon came to life again and issued the orders for a retreat from Moscow by a route which would take the army many miles to the southward of the way by which they had come and bring them, by a shorter journey, to Poland and friendly lands. The retreat was to begin on the nineteenth of October. They would be out of enemy country before the onset of winter and ready to resume the attack in the early spring of 1813. Something like the Imperial anger flashed out again, too, when he saw the divisions falling in for the march and realized the state to which indolence and indiscipline had brought them. There were hardly enough horses to drag the guns, yet many of them were harnessed to carts which were filled with loot of officers and men, and men were standing in the ranks burdened and festooned with as much as they could carry, wearing costly furs and jewelry, carrying clocks and pieces of furniture, strips of copper from church roofs, icons and candlesticks from church altars. Imperial anger blazed hotly into orders for the destruction of most of the loot and for the return of all vehicles taken for private carriage. Imperial rebukes fell like hail on the heads of marshals and generals. But that anger, which had once been so terrible that even men like Ney did their best not to incur it, blazed now hotly and short-livedly like a fire of dried sticks with nothing else to keep the flame alight. There was the same fatalism about the Emperor now as there had been in the days in the Kremlin before the news from Alexander had struck the spark. He mounted and rode ahead of his escort and round him and behind him trailed the army, grotesque, burdened, soft with easy living, resentful of the breaking of their rest, a little overawed by Moscow with its silence and its emptiness followed by the raging of its fires, and by the emptiness of the vastness of the thousands of miles which lay between them and safety, between them and their homes. Most of the men and the officers—at any rate the junior officers—had been too much taken up with the securing of their own comforts and lodging to wonder what the Emperor was thinking, and in any case he was too remote from them for them to feel anxiety about his plans or his ability to carry them out. Only the most senior officers watched the slouching figure with chin buried in the collar of the grey coat, the hat pulled over the eyes, and wondered what had come over the Emperor, and, in wondering, felt a touch of chill at the heart more ominous than the first snowflakes of a Russian winter.

They marched out of Moscow on October 19—a fine sunny day of autumn which made the threatening snowflakes disappear from men's memory as swiftly and completely as they had vanished from the earth, and they took the southward road, the shortest way to safety. But there was to be no safety for them. Murat's exhausted cavalry had failed in their task of keeping the Russian Army under observation and Kutusoff, the Russian Commander-in-Chief, had slipped away from his lines and was, unknown to Napoleon, marching also southward on a parallel road. What was worse was that he had gained just enough start to enable him to throw his whole force across the French line of march and so to intercept them. At one moment, only a few miles separated the flanks of the opposing forces, neither of whom was as yet aware of the nearness of the other. The French were in good heart, once they had been torn away from Moscow and had been persuaded, or forced, to shed most of their burdens of loot. They were heading for home and they had been told that not far away, in the town of Kaluga, were enough stores to support them till they should reach friendly country. Even Napoleon's depression seemed to have lifted, and he rode, for part of the time, ahead of his advance guard, with only his staff and a small cavalry escort. Indeed, so narrow was the gap between the armies at one point that had the Russians not been as ill-informed as were the French, they might, with a swift diversion of only a mile or two with their cavalry, have captured the Emperor with all his staff.

It was not until they had been marching for four days, on October 23, that the French learned of their danger, and then there was nothing for it but to press on and cut their way through to Kaluga and so to Poland. Kutusoff had turned sharply north and flung his troops into the little town of Maloyaroslavetz, through which ran the only road leading to Kaluga. Napoleon had no choice. He must fight or turn back to take the old line of march by which he had come through Borodino from Smolensk—a shelterless track of a road beside which nearly every village and building had been destroyed by the Russians during their retreat, or wantonly looted and burned by the advancing French; a road on which there was no supply dump east of Smolensk, and which crossed several streams, any of which, with the coming of winter, might be in flood or covered with ice, which might be strong enough to afford them safe passage, or might be broken and more treacherous than open water; and beyond these lay the wide and unbridged river, the Berezina. Their engineers had brought them safely across by pontoon bridges, but how would they fare if they retreated under pressure, since the pontoons had been removed, or should the enemy succeed in reaching the river first and occupying its banks before the French could reach them.

With all this in mind, Napoleon threw all that he had into the attack on Maloyaroslavetz, and the French, seeing their only hope of safety vanishing, fought with reckless valour and tenacity. (It was remarked at the time that no troops were more impetuous in their onslaught or more grim in their hardihood than the Italians, those most unwilling allies on the eastward march. Their backs were turned at last on the dreary plains and their faces were set southward. Kutusoff's men stood between them and the olive trees and vineyards, the blue skies and the white villages of their own country.)

But the Russians too were in good heart, and Kutusoff knew the value of the position which he held. They fell by hundreds under the fierce onslaughts of the French and their allies, but they held the town and its suburbs. They plugged every gap in their line as soon as it had been made, and they exacted a heavy price in casualties for every yard of ground which they yielded and then retook. Maloyaroslavetz had never been ranked among the great fights of the Imperial legend. It does not stand with Jena, Austerlitz, Wagram, Friedland and the other victories, nor even with Waterloo, the supreme defeat, but that day of October 24, 1812, did as much as, or more than, any day in the Napoleonic calendar to destroy the legend and to bring nearer the inevitable end of the First Empire. At the close of it, Napoleon did what he had never yet been forced to do in any of his campaigns. He broke off the action and ordered a retreat in the face of a victorious enemy.

The Russians made little attempt at pursuit, though they had won the battle. They had been roughly handled and Kutusoff, that master of slow movement, had no mind to incur casualties when he foresaw that the enemy must almost inevitably perish without fighting before they could reach safety. His plan was to shadow them rather than to press them, and he entrusted this work to his Cossack cavalry, hard-bitten little men on harder-bitten little horses, who were to hang round the rear of the retreating French like a cloud of stinging insects, cutting off stragglers, threatening every halt and every period of rest, appearing suddenly in the rear or on the flank, a perpetual threat and reminder of the power that followed up behind them.

When, later, survivors of the retreat talked of its horrors, one of their chief memories was of these terrible Cossacks. The cold, the snow, hunger, weariness—all would take their toll, but the abiding horror of memory was of the everlasting threat of these shadowing, half-savage horsemen. They spoke of the snow-covered plains, the occasional birch woods, the eternal vista of white nothingness; but above all they remembered the sudden appearance of the dreaded Cossacks, springing, as it seemed, out of the ground, giving no warning of their approach, disappearing as suddenly and reappearing from a different direction. The men who returned to France could never afterward quite rid their memories of the thought of these ghostlike pursuers, who were to be with them until the Berezina had at last been reached and crossed.

The French turned northward, a sullen and defeated army, to take again the road by which they had advanced, now stripped bare of food or shelter or safety, littered with the debris of their passing a few weeks earlier. Before they had marched for more than a few days, they had a grim reminder of what had been and grimmer foreshadowing of what might still be to come. The first warning came as they turned from a northerly to a westerly direction and it came in the form of a revolting smell, faint at first, but quickly becoming overpowering, a smell of death and putrescence. Their road led them across the battlefield of Borodino, where thousands of men on each side had fallen whose bodies still lay on the field. In some places, especially round the great redoubt which had been the key of the Russian position, the corpses lay in heaps and piled up like walls. Nearly all of them were naked, having been stripped by Russian pillagers after the battle. All of them were rotten, bloated and stinking in the treacherous warmth of that lovely autumn.

The Grande Armée trailed across the battlefield as best they might, sickening at the smell and shattered by the sight. With diminishing hope they plodded on westward toward Smolensk and the Berezina and beyond those to France and a safety in which they no longer believed and for which they hardly dared to hope. A few days later, snowflakes began to drift lazily down from the sky, like those first flakes which had fallen so lightly in Moscow in September. But unlike those flakes, these did not vanish with the warmth of the sun but lay on the ground and were quickly covered by more and more flakes as the Russian winter took up the task of annihilating a beaten enemy.

XXVI

THE BRITISH were heartily tired of the seemingly endless war. They were as resolute as ever to see it through, but after all, they had been at it for twenty years with hardly a break. Almost every other European nation had at one time or another submitted to Napoleon or had, at least, made a dishonourable bargain with him. The British had been in at the start and they meant to be there at the finish.

That finish, so long desired and so often deferred, had seemed suddenly to be very near during the first months of 1812. Wellington's army had wintered in safety and in comparative comfort behind the lines of Torres Vedras, while their commander matured his plans for the next campaign. It was time now for Britain to take the offensive, and he meant to leave Portugal, never to return to it, to drive through the heart of Spain to Madrid, and perhaps further still.

The roads into Spain were commanded by the two fortresses of Ciudad Rodrigo and Badajoz, and Wellington knew that he must secure these before he could risk an advance. They were formidable obstacles, solidly constructed, well-manned and provided with every sort of defensive arm, and it would be no light work to storm them. He lacked a proper siege train and enough heavy guns, and since he must take the fort, he had no choice other than to send his storming columns against walls which had not been sufficiently battered and were manned by soldiers who had not felt the effects of heavy bombardment. The siege of Ciudad began on January 8, 1812, and the fort was stormed on the nineteenth.

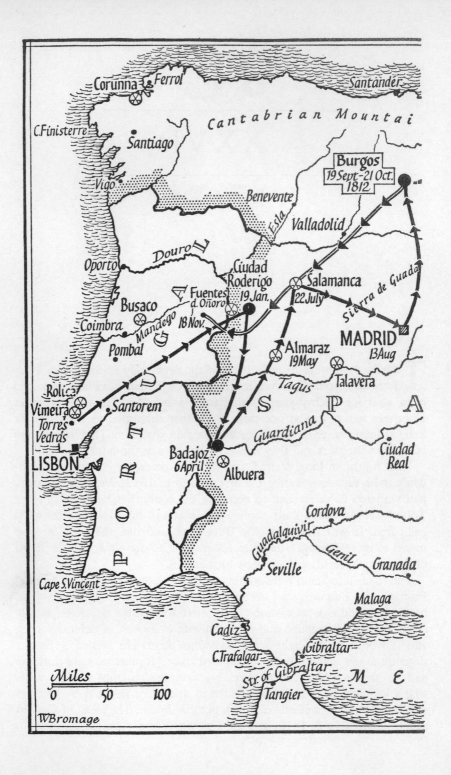

Corunna
Ferrol
Santander
C.Finisterre
Santiago
Cantabrian Mountai
Vigo
Benevente
Valladolid
Burgos
19 Sept–21 Oct.
1812
Esla
Oporto
Douro
Ciudad
Roderigo
19 Jan.
Salamanca
22 July
Busaco
Coimbra
Fuentes
d. Oñoro
18 Nov.
Mandego
Pombal
Almaraz
19 May
Sierra de Guada
MADRID
13 Aug
Rolica
Santorem
Tagus
Talavera
Vimeira
Torres
Vedras
Guardiana
LISBON
Badajoz
6 April
Albuera
Ciudad
Real
Cordova
Cape S.Vincent
Guadalquivir
Genil
Seville
Granada
Malaga
Cadiz
C.Trafalgar
Gibraltar
Str. of Gibraltar
Tangier
PORTUGAL
SPAIN
M E
Miles
0   50   100
W.Bromage

San Sebastian
13 July–10 Sept. 1813

Bayonne
Feb. 1814

Orthez
27 Feb. 1814

Toulouse
10 Apr. 1814

F

R

A

N

C

E

R. Nivelle
10 Nov. 1813

14 Dec. 1813

9 Dec. 1813

Savroren
27–28 July 1813

ns

Pyrenees

Mts

Vitoria
21 June 1813

Segre

Saragossa

Lerida

Barcelona

Ebro

Tarragona

Tortosa

rrama

S P A I N

Jucar

Valencia

Alicante

M E D I T E R R A N E A N

SPAIN & PORTUGAL
1808–1814
Shewing Wellington's Campaigns
of 1812 & 1813–14
Advance ➡ Retreat ⇐
Battles ⊗ Sieges ●
1813 Advance ----➤

Badajoz was an even tougher task, and its siege lasted from March 16 to the storming on April 6. "Nothing," Napier was to write of the Fusiliers at Albuera, "could stop that astonishing infantry." It was the same astonishing infantry which captured the two fortresses, but the price in casualties was heavy, for the two sieges between them accounted for some 5,000 officers and men killed or wounded—and it must be remembered that few who were badly wounded escaped death in those days of primitive surgery and complete ignorance of antisepsis and hygiene. It is said that when Wellington saw the casualty list after Badajoz he broke down and wept.

At the beginning of the year, his strength, including Portuguese, was not quite 55,000, while the French, even after the Imperial Guard and other regiments of veterans had been withdrawn for the Russian venture, amounted to 300,000 men with some 50,000 horses. He could ill afford the 5,000 men whom the two fortresses had cost him, but, whatever the cost, he was in Spain again and on the offensive. The French were in retreat and in May, General Hill captured Almaraz. Wellington, driving forward, met the French at Salamanca on July 22 and entered Madrid on August 13. On the twenty-fourth the French, who had been investing Cadiz, abandoned the siege.

It almost seemed in the high summer that victory was within the grasp of the British, but the year was to end in disappointment, which was the more bitter for the early successes. Wellington felt bound to exploit his advantage and to press forward while the French were shaken and in retreat, but he knew well how dangerous was his true situation and how faint were the chances of reaching the Pyrenees before winter. There were three French armies in the field against him, each of them stronger than his own. Joseph with the force which had withdrawn from Madrid was at Toledo, Soult was marching up from Andalusia and Suchet held southern Spain. If the three armies could combine against the British, Wellington would have much difficulty in extricating himself.

Yet the odds were not so much against him as they appeared. The French were numerous and well-armed, but they were not well-commanded, now that their Emperor was marching eastward into Russia. Joseph, who was supposed to hold the chief command, knew nothing of soldiering and had no desire to learn. Soult was leisurely in movement and had found a comfortable home in Andalusia, of which he had a dream of becoming king. There was no urgency among the French and no one to instil it, nor was there anyone to co-ordinate their plans and to give orders. The directives which arrived intermittently from the Emperor were, by the time that they reached Spain, so out-of-date and impracticable that they were best left unregarded. And, all the time, the

Spanish guerrillas hung on the flanks and the rear of every French army, killing and plundering, capturing messengers, whom they first tortured and then killed, disturbing the night's sleep of the armies and keeping their nerves stretched taut.

Wellington took his opportunity and drove onward toward the Pyrenees. His lines of communication, which stretched back to Lisbon and Corunna, grew longer and needed more men to guard them, but if he could reach Burgos and, after Burgos, San Sebastian, he would have cleared the northern coast of Spain and would be able to transfer his base to Santander, or some other port on the Bay of Biscay, where ships could reach him from England in a short time and without danger of being intercepted.

His fortunes had reached their high tide at Salamanca and the ebb was beginning. Four days after the French had ridden into a silent and empty Moscow, Wellington flung his storming columns against the fortress of Burgos as he had flung them at Ciudad Rodrigo and Badajoz. The attempt was a complete failure. He still lacked the heavy guns and the siege train, and in once more using his infantry to storm an almost unbreached wall, he incurred heavy casualties without effecting an entrance. The siege began on September 19 and went on for a month before the final and calamitous attempt to storm it compelled Wellington to abandon the task until the next year. The winter was coming on and he could not keep his army where it was when such strong enemy forces were threatening him. On October 21—it was two days after the French had marched out of Moscow—Wellington began his retreat to the Portuguese border. With the two great fortresses in his hands he would have no more need of his lines at Torres Vedras, and even though he had retreated, he would winter for the first time on Spanish soil.

The horror of the French retreat from Moscow has so captured the imagination of historians that Wellington's retreat from Burgos has almost passed unnoticed. It would be well that it should, since it showed the British army and their commander at their worst. In many ways it was reminiscent of the more famous retreat of Moore's army to Corunna, in which discipline went to pieces under the pressure of fatigue and foul weather. Wellington's men, on the retreat from Burgos, suffered terribly from the incessant rain and the mud which it caused, but in other ways they were luckier than Moore's had been. Their road led over no such mountains as Moore had had to cross, nor were they pressed, as Moore had been pressed, by the enemy cavalry. Yet, for a time, the army which had won Salamanca and captured Ciudad Rodrigo and Badajoz and had marched so proudly into Madrid was reduced to a straggling mob, sullen and resentful, slouching along the Spanish roads without more than a semblance of discipline. The men had tasted the delights of disorder in the sacking of the two fortresses and had been, as they thought, robbed of a third sack by their failure to take Burgos by storm. They were resentful and their temper was finally ruined by the usual failure of the supply service. "At one time," says the regimental record of the 44th Foot, "the men were without biscuit for eleven days and received only one small ration of beef."

At Torquemada they were further disrupted by finding a huge store of wine and brandy in the great wine vaults, so that it was estimated that 12,000 of them at one time were incapably drunk. Altogether, the siege and the retreat from Burgos cost Wellington 9,000 men, though his junction with Hill, when they met at Salamanca, raised his strength to 50,000 British and Portuguese, with some 12,000 raw and mostly useless Spanish troops. Wellington, as is well known, had never professed to like his men or to regard them as anything more than pieces to be manoeuvred on a board.

On the way back from Burgos to Salamanca they so much disgusted him that he gave free reign to his contempt for them and for their officers. His savage rebukes were familiar to his staff and to many officers who had in any way displeased him, and now as his sodden and miserable army trailed back toward the south, he issued a circular letter to all commanding officers in which he spoke most bitterly of the army which had done so much and endured so much under his command. "The officers," he wrote, "have lost all command of their men," a loss which he ascribed "to their habitual inattention to their duty. Discipline," he went on, "has suffered in a greater degree than I have ever witnessed or even read of. No army has ever made shorter marches in retreat, had longer rests, or been so little pressed by a pursuing enemy."

The retreat ended at Ciudad Rodrigo on November 18. Little more than a week later, the remnants of the French army reached the Berezina River, with the Cossacks at their heels and with Russian forces in rear and on both flanks—indeed, for all they knew, in front of them as well, since there was a strong rumor that Wittgenstein had already crossed the Berezina higher up and was hurrying down its western bank to cut their last communications. Behind the main body of the French and out of touch with it was all that remained of Ney's corps, whose heroic rearguard action had saved the main army and the Emperor. It took two days for the army to cross the Berezina, and the weary march went on. The Emperor refused all suggestions that he should save himself by hastening ahead with a small escort, and it was not until they were safely back in friendly country that he drove off to travel by night and day in the hope that he might reach Paris before the whole truth of the disaster became known.

In London, the news that Wellington, after his brilliant exploits, had turned tail and run before the French was received at first with incredulity and then with anger, and finally with the realization that there might yet be several more years of war to be endured. Even now there was no thought of a negotiated peace or of compromise of any sort with the Corsican bandit. For twenty years Britain had poured out her gold and her goods, sacrificed her liberty and her young men, stood firm when all else was shadowy and shifting. She was not going to forego the benefits for which she had worked and suffered if it took her ten or twenty more years to achieve victory. Britain's mood was one of grim determination, but there was no enthusiasm.

Her task was made even harder by the unrest and misery among her own people, especially in the north and the Midlands. Trade, especially the textile trade, was bad and getting worse, and there were unemployment and starvation. The Berlin Decrees and Britain's Orders in Council had put a stop to traffic with the continent of Europe, and the American War of 1812 ruined the trans-Atlantic trade. At the same time, the new machines were coming into use in the mills and throwing more and more men and women out of work. Since the Combination Act and the other repressive laws still stood on the statute book, there was no way in which workmen could resist the continued drop in wages which came with bad trade.

In the Midlands the workers, driven beyond endurance, began to attack the mills at night and to break up and burn the frames, if, indeed, they did not fire the whole building. During the winter of that year there began the first rumours of a certain "King Ludd" or "Ned Ludd," from whom eventually the rioters took the name of "Luddites." No one knew whether King Ludd was a real man or not, though the frequency and regularity of the attacks and something in the efficient way in which they were carried out suggested a controlling mind behind them. It was said that King Ludd had his headquarters in some forest in the Midlands— the more romantic, perhaps with a backward look to Robin Hood, Will Scarlett and Alan-a-Dale, swore that he held his court in Sherwood. The movement spread from Nottingham to Yorkshire and Lancashire, and now it was the new machinery which suffered under the blows of "Great Enoch," the heavy hammer which Enoch James had made to destroy the frames of his own invention as well as the new machines which were replacing them.

The millowners were hard and grasping but they were not, for the most part, cowards. It must have needed a stout heart to sit through the night in the empty and echoing mills with a few friends, waiting for the red glare of the torches and the angry muttering of a mob working themselves into a frenzy of vengeance and, as they drew near, yelling their terrifying song of battle:

> Great Enoch still shall lead the van,
> Stop him who dare! Stop him who can!

Yet many of the millowners stood to fight it out with firearms. Mr. Burton's mill at Middleton, in Lancashire, was one of the first to be attacked. In April 1812, the owner of Rawfields Mill in Yorkshire fired on the Luddites, who ran off, leaving two of their number wounded on the ground. The owner—or so the story went—refused to give them water or to allow a doctor to see them unless they would reveal the names of their ringleaders. They refused and died where they lay. The Luddites, not unnaturally if their story were true, made several attempts later to murder the millowner, but they were less successful than the men who actually killed another owner, William Horsfall, less than a month after the affair at Rawfields.

Obviously it was the government's duty to suppress the riots; no less obviously it should have been an equal duty to inquire into the reasons for them and to do what they could to remove the cause. They neglected the second duty but effectively carried out the first with the help of magistrates and judges who were sent out on special commission to the affected areas. They could not find "King Ludd," though one of their spies, a blackguard called Lawson, swore that he was actually the Scottish chieftain, Lord Lovat. The last time that a Lovat had taken part in public activity had been in 1745, when he was hanged for his pains, but Lord Sidmouth, who was as senseless as he was cruel and cowardly, actually issued a warrant for his arrest, though no more was heard of it.

The men who were arrested found short shift and little mercy at the hands of the special commissions. The commission in Cheshire sentenced fourteen men to death, two of whom were executed, the rest being transported for life, an almost more terrible fate. In Yorkshire, seventeen men were hanged, one transported for life and six for seven years.

In Lancashire, four people, including a woman, were sentenced to death for forcing dealers to sell butter and cheese at a price below the ordinary one; fifteen men or boys were sentenced to transportation for seven years for accepting or administering oaths. For the burning of Westhoughton Mill, three men and a boy of sixteen were hanged. "The boy," G. D. H. Cole and Raymond Postgate write, in their The Common People, 1746–1938, "Abraham Charlston, had three soldier brothers, and had acted as a sort of sentinel at the burning, pacing up and down with a scythe. He was young for his age, and when he was brought to the scaffold he called on his mother for help, thinking she had the power to save him."

No such terror had been abroad in England since the days of the abominable Judge Jeffreys.

The official leaders of the Whigs—Grey, Grenville and the rest—made no protest against this inhumanity, and only a few of the back-benchers like Whitfield and Burdett raised objection to the free use of the death penalty.

Yet, perhaps because it was in England, where justice comes as often from the ordinary man as from the politician and where the poet and the artist have often the truest view of human rights and needs, a few brave efforts were made to resist this tyranny. In Lancashire, one honest juror, whose name deserved a better fate than the obscurity into which it has passed, by his obstinacy prevented any convictions for the riot at Burton's Middleton Mill. In Manchester, where the case against the men had been worked up by the ruffianly Nadin, the corporation's chief constable, later to be prominent in the affair at Peterloo, the defence was undertaken by Brougham, Scarlett and Williams. All were later to be successful and famous, but at that time they risked their professional advancement by undertaking such defences. Between them they tore Nadin's evidence to pieces, and the judge, after the manner of English judges putting justice against party or expedience, directed the jury to acquit the accused, which the jury promptly did.

The greatest act of defiance of the government's policy came not from a judge or a juryman but from a poet, Lord Byron. Much evil has been thought and written of him—much of it, it may be, justly—but against it should be set his words in the House of Lords when they were debating the bill to impose the death penalty for rioting and conspiracy in the working districts. "Suppose it passed, suppose one of these men, as I have seen them—meagre with famine, sullen with despair, careless of a life which your Lordships are perhaps about to value at something less than the price of a stocking frame—suppose this man (and there are thousands such from whom you may select your victims) dragged into court to be tried for this new offence by this new law, still there are two things wanting to convict and condemn him; and these are, in my opinion, twelve butchers for a jury and a Jeffreys for a Judge."

Yet it would not be fair to condemn Grey and Grenville and the other Whig leaders for indifference. They cared as deeply for liberty as any men in England. But they were politicians and therefore judges not only of what was right but also of what was expedient. They believed— and were soon to show that they could act on their beliefs—that parliamentary reform was the best, if not the only, hope of redressing the wrongs of the working men and women and of establishing equity for all free men of whatever class they might be members. But, as politicians, they also knew that almost everything depends on the timing of an action or a movement. In the false atmosphere of wartime, with its artificial hatreds and restrictions and with its repressions masquerading as safeguards, they could get no hearing for any scheme of reform. In all times of stress, in all countries, the oppressor has always been able to prevail with the simple statement, "This is not the time to consider reforms." The Whigs knew that it was not the time. They must be content to wait until the war was over. And it seemed in that dark year of 1812 that the war would never stop.

XXVII

S UDDENLY—it was in the midsummer of 1813—it seemed that the war might stop very soon. The old Grande Armée lay buried on the Russian plains but, by the beginning of the campaigning season of 1813, Napoleon was in the field again with a new army wrung from France by a ruthless use of conscription and a reduction of the age for service to seventeen.

All over France the forges and ironworks were toiling as they had through the previous winter, day and night, to replace the weapons which had been lost on the retreat from Moscow, from which only nine cannon had been painfully dragged back across the Niemen. In every village, however small, the smithies rang with the blows of the hammers that were forging shoes for the new cavalry; in every little workshop there was the incessant whirr of grindstones, sharpening swords and bayonets. In the fields and on the farms parties of dismounted cavalrymen were seizing and training horses, since of all the thousands which had gone into Russia barely enough to mount a squadron had returned.

There was little other activity in the fields that spring and summer, for every farmboy who could ride or could carry a musket had been taken and the crops were left to the old and the unfit. There would be time to think of the harvest later, when France had driven back the threatening tide of invasion.

It was a fantastic task, this rearming of France in a matter of a few months, and no one knew better than France's master how fragile were the defences which he was building. Many of the boys who were called to the colours were undersized and weak after many years of wartime life and food; still more of them were unwilling; all of them were untrained in the use of arms.

Any of them who could ride were drafted into the cavalry and given some perfunctory drill on horses, many of which were as green and unfit for battle as were their riders. The older soldiers laughed at the raw recruits and called them "Marie Louises," after the Empress, because of their girlish complexions; and their master complained ungratefully of their habit of falling sick on the march and in camp. It was not the least of his achievements that he managed to put an army into the field at all that summer and to equip, arm and mount them. Yet, raw as they were, they were an army and they served him well against the overwhelming strength which was facing them as the Allies tightened the ring round France and prepared to move in for the kill.

Napoleon had two invaluable assets, which saved him during that summer—his own supreme military ability and the complete lack of co-operation of the Allies.

The Emperor did not underrate his own skill and the terror of his name. "I have myself and 50,000 men," he said during the campaign, "that makes 150,000," and it was no idle boast. Wherever he was in command in person he triumphed, as he did in May at Lützen and Bautzen. Whenever he had to leave the task to one of his marshals, the battle was lost. So great was his name as a soldier that even so fierce a fighter as Blücher preferred to decline battle against him, and manoeuvred to face one of his detached forces.

The Allies were without unity of command or even an agreed plan and, by failing to combine, gave Napoleon the chance of beating them in detail, which he was in all Europe the man most capable of using.

In none of his campaigns did he show anything to surpass the sheer tactical brilliance with which he held half Europe at bay in 1813 and the following year. After his victory at Bautzen, he seemed so much in the ascendant that the Allies offered an armistice to last until August 16, to allow for the discussion of possible terms of peace. Napoleon, who had no intention of making peace except on his own terms, gratefully accepted the chance to regroup and refit his troops. He was hopefully negotiating a renewal of the armistice when news came from Spain which put new heart into the Allied commanders then assembled in Dresden and stiffened their attitude toward any gift of a further breathing space to France. At the beginning of July, messengers from Spain brought the story of Wellington's overwhelming victory at Vitoria and of King

Joseph's headlong flight with all his army across the Pyrenees into France.

Twice before, Wellington had left Portugal and entered Spain, and twice he had been compelled to go back and winter in his old quarters at Torres Vedras because the fortresses on the frontier remained unassailable as long as French armies, in overwhelming strength, covered them and prevented siege operations. In 1812 the forts had fallen to him, and he wintered behind their protection just within the Portuguese border. He could set out again in 1813, knowing that his rear and his communications would be safe.

He knew now, as well, how much the French strength in Spain had fallen during the winter, and how fast it was still falling, as Napoleon called brigade after brigade of his veterans back to join France's last army, which was to defend her borders. Suchet, whom Napoleon said was the best of his marshals after Masséna, was still at Saragossa, and Wellington sent Sir John Murray with a corps to contain him there and to prevent him from marching to Madrid to join Joseph's main army. Murray mishandled the operation and involved himself in a court-martial, but the diversion occupied Suchet's attention and kept him separated from the rest of the French.

Joseph was in nominal command of all the French troops in Spain, with Marshal Jourdan as chief of staff. Soult, the best tactician of the senior marshals, had gone back to France after a quarrel with Joseph and was commanding the Imperial Guard in Germany.

Napoleon had his hands too full with his own problems to send any more of his grand schemes to Joseph, whom he ordered to forget that he was a King, to remember that he was a general (which he most emphatically was not) and to leave Madrid and to concentrate his army at Valladolid. Wellington moved too quickly for him and, indeed, has never been given enough credit for the rapidity and daring of his advance that spring. His plan was simple and had the additional advantage of being opposed to all the best strategical principles and thus incomprehensible to the enemy, who looked for him to advance with his whole force under his hand ready to be promptly deployed for action. Wellington, who knew when to take a risk and had formed a shrewd estimate of the ability which might be expected from a combination of Joseph and Jourdan, left Portugal by three separate roads, with his left, under Graham, leading by three days' march. He was offering Joseph the chance of attacking Graham while he was unsupported, or of swinging his army round to crush Hill, who formed the right wing of the advance. Looking at the ground at Fuentes de Oñoro after the battle, Wellington had observed, "If Boney had been there we should have been beat." Had

Napoleon been at Madrid, Wellington would not have attempted a dispersion of his force, but he counted, as he had every right to do, on Joseph's incompetence and feebleness and drove his three columns forward into the heart of Spain.

One of his staff noticed that when he rode across the border of Portugal, he waved a hand and called out "Farewell Portugal," and indeed he was never to see it again, though it seems doubtful whether he yet hoped to advance up to and across the Pyrenees into France. An order of his, dated in the winter of 1812, suggests that he was still uncertain, since it gives instructions for unloading certain war material in Portuguese harbours for "the winters of 1812 and 1813," and he told Croker some years later that he had not made up his mind to try to force the Pyrenees crossing until his arrival at Burgos on June 12, a month after his departure from Portugal.

There is something a little unlike him in Croker's story, which was that when the French abandoned Burgos after blowing up the fortress, he had a sudden inspiration that he would go straight forward and not halt until he was on French soil. It may have been that he had expected to have to storm Burgos, which had defied him in the previous year, and he must by this time have known of the hurried retreat and partial demoralization of the French. But he was not given to sudden inspirations, which he was willing to leave to more mercurial temperaments like that of Napoleon. At any rate he cannot have failed to realize in June, when he stood at Burgos, that his strategy had completely succeeded. He had advanced so far without firing a shot and had so manoeuvred that the French were in full retreat before him and apparently thinking of nothing but getting home to France in safety. He drove forward in the same echelon formation and came up with the enemy at Vitoria on June 20.

Wellington always afterward classed the battle of Vitoria with Salamanca and Waterloo as his three greatest victories. The end of the day's fighting was the complete defeat of the French and the destruction of their last power in Spain. The tactics which had brought Wellington's army to the battlefield were to serve for the battle itself, with Graham racing ahead on the left to cut the French line of retreat by the main road to Bayonne, Hill assaulting on the British right, and Wellington with the main attack in the centre.

The two armies were evenly matched as to numbers, being about 70,000 strong each, but the French, bravely though they fought, were at a hopeless disadvantage. They had no one to command them. Joseph had long ago given up any pretense at giving orders; Jourdan did not feel that it was his place to give them when Joseph was in command. Their position was cramped for manoeuvre and hemmed in by hills, and there was only one good road leading to the rear. When Graham cut this, all that remained was a narrow and flooded track, not wide enough to take a retreating division without congestion. Above all, their army was in no shape for a desperate defensive battle. A captured French officer said to Wellington, after the battle, "The difference, my Lord, is that you are an army and we are a walking brothel." Among the French column were hundreds of carriages crammed with officers' private baggage, much of it being the result of looting in Madrid. There were carts and wagons piled with the spoil of an army which, as long as it was in Spain, had systematically carried off anything which could be carried. Among the press of vehicles, too, was the transport of Joseph's royal household, his private loot, his travelling kitchens, the wagons with his plate and wardrobe, and one consignment which held the whole of the remaining funds of his deserted kingdom. Riding, driving and walking among these were officers' and men's wives and mistresses, civilian servants, Spanish civilians who had befriended the French and dared not lag behind them when they went—an immense mass of vehicles, mules, horses, foot-travellers, every variety of useless lumber which could impede a defeated and retiring army. Joseph himself only escaped from his carriage by one door as British soldiers wrenched open the other, and he left in it all the valuable paintings which he had stolen and packed away there to accompany him back to France. There, too, the British found Jourdan's marshal's baton, which Wellington sent as a present to the Prince Regent, who wrote very prettily to thank him and announced that in return he was sending to Wellington the baton of a British field-marshal—a graceful gesture which caused confusion at the Horse Guards, since no such baton had ever been carried in the British Army and they had to invent and manufacture one in haste.

The unwieldy mass choked the one remaining road, and Wellington ordered up his horse artillery, who mercilessly shelled this ideal target from the high ground on each side, while the British dragoons charged them repeatedly from the rear. Tomlinson of the 11th Hussars, who took part in several of these charges, reported afterward that the French rearguard resisted gallantly and that the whole mass was so tightly packed on the road that cavalry could hardly penetrate beyond the first or second rank.

The French casualties were not excessive, considering that the fighting had been fierce and prolonged before the final collapse.

The British and their allies lost nearly as many men, but the French left behind them all their artillery, except for two guns, nearly all their ammunition, 2,000 carriages and most of the rest of their transport. Greatest of all was their moral loss. The last army of the Spanish kingdom, as set up by Napoleon, was nothing but a mob of fugitives, running for their lives, not to be checked or re-formed, had there been anyone to attempt it.

It was that news which was brought to Dresden where the Allies were in consultation and to Napoleon's headquarters in the field, where he was hopefully demanding an extended armistice. There could no longer be any question of that. The Allies would have been mad to give it a thought, and finally, Austria, which had hung back out of a lingering tenderness for Napoleon's Austrian Empress, threw her weight into the already overladen scale. The French were beaten at last, it seemed, even though it might take one more campaign to bring Napoleon to realize and admit it. The ring round France tightened and was welded solid. The next move would be a combined march on Paris and the end of the war.

For Wellington there would be no return to Portugal and, without waiting, he made his plans for forcing the passes of the Pyrenees. There was to be more delay than he had foreseen because, for more than a week, his troops were too happily engaged in plundering and pursuing various parties of fugitives to think of their duties. He had lost some 3,574 British troops in the battle, but after it more than 6,000 were absent from the roll calls, until slowly they trickled back when they could carry no more loot or had drunk all the wine and brandy which they had captured. Some of them had delightedly fallen on the royal treasure chest and had helped themselves generously before they were stopped. A British army on service lived hard, were poorly paid and that not regularly, and knew no such luxuries as leave. It was expected that they should indulge in a reasonable amount of looting and not all Wellington's provost marshals, not all their gallows and lashes, could stop the practice. For once, not even he could find it in his heart to say of them anything other than, "I never saw troops behave better."

In August he had them in hand again. There was hard and difficult work for them before they could reach the French frontier. There were the forts of San Sebastian and Pamplona to be reduced, rivers to be crossed, mountain passes to be scaled. Before them lay the great barrier of the Pyrenees, ideal ground for defence, not unlike his own old position at Torres Vedras. There could be no return this year to winter quarters, no let-up in the advance, no loss of impetus in a campaign which so far had moved smoothly. It had always been his way, as he said, to like to know what was going on on the other side of the hill. Now the hill, which was the range of the Pyrenees, lay in front of him. He knew what was on the other side. There lay France, victory and peace for Europe.

PART V

1814-1819

XXVIII

I N APRIL of the year 1814 the war was over. On the fifth Napoleon was
compelled to ask the Allies for an armistice, and this time there
would be no bargaining, no discussion of terms and no proposals for ex-
tending the armistice. The Allies would hold no discussions with France
until the Emperor had been removed from his throne and put where he
could do no more harm.

Even his own marshals would fight no more for him, when the only
end of it could be the destruction of France. Marmont, with his whole
corps, deserted to the enemy, and even Ney, whom Napoleon had called
"the bravest of the brave," had had enough and told his master that the
fighting must stop and that the Army would obey not the Emperor but
its generals.

The war was over, except in the south, where Wellington and his old
adversary Soult faced each other at Toulouse. No one, it seemed, had
thought of telling them about the armistice until some days after it had
been signed, and the news did not reach them until April 12.

The news came to Wellington while he was dining in his headquarters
mess. There were some forty officers with him, including Picton, Alava,
the Spanish general attached to his staff, and Alten who commanded the
King's German Legion. It was not, one may believe, a festive meal up to
that point. They were tired, had been in the saddle all day and looked
forward to nothing other than another day of fighting. Nor was Wellington's headquarters mess ever a scene of much comfort or of any luxury.

Even his men in their lines and bivouacs knew that the Field-Marshal lived as sparely as did they and lay on no softer bed. Alava said, long after the war had ended, that the two English remarks which he had come to dread were "At six o'clock" and "Cold meat," those being Wellington's usual answers to the questions at what hour the troops would move and what he would have for dinner that night. He had always lived simply, even in luxurious India, and lately his ways had been almost ascetic. He never seemed to care what food was put before him, drank only a single glass of wine after his dinner, lay in bed for what few hours he could spare when the evening's work was over—for even when he had been with the front-line troops all day, there was still a mountain of correspondence and paper work of all sorts to be disposed of in his own quarters. He did not smoke, having, it is said, made only one attempt at it in his life, when the Prince Regent gave him a cigar which he did not finish. Since he had landed in Portugal in 1809 he had not had a single leave, and his only relaxation had been an occasional day's hunting with the hounds which had been brought out from England to give his officers something to do during the long winter months behind Torres Vedras. (They had followed the advancing army at a safe distance, and while the army had rested and re-formed at St. Jean de Luz, after Vitoria, there had been more hunting, at which Wellington had appeared, after his custom, in the sky-blue coat of the Salisbury Hunt and a top hat.)

The uniforms of the men who sat round the mess table that night were worn and bleached with sun and rain, and their hair was greyer and their faces more lined than they had been at Torres Vedras. They were sitting over their meagre supply of wine when the message was brought in and handed to Wellington. It came from Lord Burghersh, who wrote ecstatically, "Glory to God and yourself, the great man has fallen," and went on to give details of the Emperor's abdication. Wellington read the message and called for champagne. When it had been brought, he rose and said that he would give them the health of His Majesty King Louis XVIII of France. (It was typical of him that at one of the greatest moments of his life he should instinctively have turned to an old-established order, something which had existed when he was young and the world was sane.)

They drank the toast decorously, even with enthusiasm, though few of them felt any regard for Louis XVIII or had given much thought to France's new government. It was enough for them that her old ruler had come to the end of his career of crime—or so they thought in that year of 1814, in common with the rest of Europe. And, the news being what it was, anything was good enough as an excuse for celebration. But there was real enthusiasm for the next toast, when General Alava rose and proposed the health of Field-Marshal the Marquis of Wellington. (He had been raised to that rank in the winter of 1813, and when they told him, being preoccupied with the preparations for Vitoria, he had asked a little testily, "What the devil is the use of making me a Marquis?") Perhaps now it seemed strange that his health should have been proposed by a Spanish general and not by one of his own officers, Picton or his military secretary, Somerset, or some other who had known him and served with him in his own army. It may have been that they doubted whether he would appreciate such a display of enthusiasm, pardonable as it might be from an excitable foreigner.

There was no lack of enthusiasm when Alava gave the toast. They sprang to their feet and drank, cheering him with "three times three" and with musical honours. The foreign officers, of whom there were several, hailed him in their own separate tongues, calling him "Liberador da Portugal," "Liberador de Espagña," "Libérateur de France," and calling on him for a speech.

He sat at his place at the table, wearing his plain grey frock-coat, looking, one of his staff remembered, "a little confused," and shook his head when they called for a speech. But they would not be denied and at last and very unwillingly, he rose and bowed to them. They cheered him again, and then, as he still stood silent, the table was hushed and they waited for his words. He looked down at the rows of faces turned up toward his own, bowed again and told the servant to bring in coffee. Shortly afterward he went to his quarters and sat down to his evening's work.

Next day he entered Toulouse in triumph. Since July of the year before, his army had been almost continuously on the move, fighting their way out of Spain through the appalling conditions represented by the Pyrenees in winter. They had reduced San Sebastian and Pamplona, crossed the Bidassoa, the Nive, the Nivelle, the Adour, fought the two battles of Sorauren, the nine days' running fight in the Pyrenees, the battles of Orthez and Bayonne and smaller engagements almost innumerable. They had taken the shock when Soult had launched his counter-attack at Roncesvalles and thrown him back whenever he tried to pierce their front in another spot.

In Spain, during the days before Vitoria, their advance had been all but a triumphal progress, with the people in the liberated towns throwing flowers to them and singing hymns of praise—of which Wellington had observed somewhat ungratefully, "This psalm-singing wastes a lot of time." There had been no flowers and no singing when they came to the Pyrenees—nothing but bivouac in the cold and wet, fighting almost daily, endless marching and climbing, hunger and cold, danger and death. Now they were on the threshold of what they believed to them to be the promised land, with orchards full of fruit, inns full of food, cellars crammed with wine, lovely girls who would be grateful to the liberators. The Pyrenees had long been a place of starvation and misery, but their reward was within sight. Their commander did not share their enthusiasm or their illusions and, in his unreasonable way, seemed to think that there was no less reason to behave properly in France than in Spain. He had issued orders and warnings in his familiar style, promising the lash and the rope for anyone who in any way offended or robbed the inhabitants of France. To make his point perfectly clear he had sent back to their own country 10,000 Spanish troops whose discipline was not, in his opinion, equal to the strain which would be put upon it. "Wor Arthur," it appeared, did not distinguish between a friendly country like Spain and Portugal and a conquered enemy country like France. But they knew him well enough now to know that however unreasonable his views might be, his methods of enforcing them would be drastic and uncompromising.

There was much celebrating in Toulouse, which showed no regret for the loss of an Emperor, though little enthusiasm for the return of a King. There was *Te Deum* at the Cathedral and a grand ball in the City Hall, at which Wellington put in a brief appearance, and when the hounds arrived, there was more hunting, though it was nearly summer and it seemed almost improper to be following the hounds when the trees were in leaf and the countryside bright with flowers. It was all gay and exciting and yet somehow unreal, for the war was over and no one quite knew what was to happen next. So many of them had known nothing but war for what seemed a lifetime and wondered what niche there would be for them in a world at peace.

As it happened, the same question was agitating the minds of the government in England. Their first instinct being, as usual, to rid themselves of a large and expensive Army, they did not stop to reflect that no peace had yet been signed with France and that it might be as well not to dissipate the Army till the war was officially over. Fortunately they recollected that they were still at war with the United States of America and at once began to send orders to the best of the infantry battalions to proceed directly to join it. It was a decision which they were bitterly to regret within twelve months, but it offered a present solution. Besides, though the country rang with praise of Wellington's heroes, it had not to be forgotten that large and extremely well-trained armies if not kept busy and preferably at a distance are apt to begin to think for themselves, to demand arrears of pay and, in extreme cases, to indulge in politics. The British had never forgotten—would never forget—the New Model Army outside London after the Civil War, the regime of Cromwell's major-generals or James II's menacing camp on Hounslow Heath.

There remained the question of what to do with their commander. It was easy to heap honours and titles on him, to vote him vast sums of money and to thank him in Parliament. But successful generals when not actively employed can be nearly as embarrassing as their armies, and it was essential to find something to keep Wellington from developing his own ideas, whatever they might be. It might be as well for him not to come back to England for a little while, till things had settled down, but they could hardly send him off to America, even if he would go.

Castlereagh, who had always been Wellington's most constant supporter and who knew him well enough to know that personal or political ambitions were very far from his thoughts, found the solution.

In the Europe of that year no one had more prestige or commanded more respect than Wellington. Any government would listen to him, and since every country would soon be suffering from the after-effects of war, it was essential to keep him where he would be immediately available when his advice or his authority was needed. France was the obvious place, though perhaps there was a more urgent if temporary need in Spain, whose restored King and government were displaying alarming tendencies in revising the recent methods of government and liquidating their private enemies. The Allied cause, which had triumphed as the opponents of tyranny, was not to be invoked for the wholesale destruction of those who in Spain were known as the "Liberales" nor for the restoration of the Inquisition which the tyrant Napoleon had abolished.

Castlereagh wrote to Wellington, proposing to visit the Continent, and there to confer with him about diplomatic missions. Wellington answered at once and characteristically, "I must serve the public in some manner or other and as, under existing circumstances, I could not well do so at home, I must do so abroad." As he had told Mr. Croker in 1809, he was still "nimmukwallah". He had eaten the King's salt and he still considered it his duty to serve him cheerfully wherever he might be asked to go. In the first week of May he was in Paris, a Paris wild with enthusiasm for the restored monarchy, or at any rate for the return of peace, filled with uniforms and state equipages, loud with military music and the clatter of hoofs and wheels. All the Allied sovereigns who had met and debated at Dresden were in Paris to see the completion of their work and vied with each other in reviewing their troops and showing themselves on balconies.

Wellington arrived in time to witness the greatest of these displays, the combined review of the Allied armies and their march past their assembled sovereigns. The long columns marched behind their brazen bands past the window in the Louvre where Louis XVIII of France sat with the Emperors of Russia and Austria and the King of Prussia. Lord Castlereagh watched the parade from the street where he sat on horse-back with Field-Marshal the Duke of Wellington, who wore a blue civil-ian frock-coat, white trousers and a top hat. They had made him a Duke a week or two earlier and he had added a postscript to a letter which he was writing to his brother, "I believe I forgot to tell you I was made a Duke."

XXIX

H IS GRACE was unduly diffident about his entry into the world of diplomacy. It was, he wrote, "a situation for which I should never have thought myself qualified," but he did himself less than justice. His military life, nearly all of which had been spent abroad, had been very different from the ordinary routine followed by so many officers, and he had continually been obliged to deal with governments and ministers no less than with armies and generals. Any man who had experienced the tortuous diplomacy of Tippoo Sahib and of the Spanish and Portuguese governments had served no mean apprenticeship to the slightly less blatant but no more scrupulous ways of Talleyrand and Metternich. If he lacked something of their skill and experience, he was their equal in determination and more than their equal in honesty. Years later, he said to Lord Stanhope that "with nations, depend on it, the only way is to move straight forward, without strategems or subterfuges," and he followed that line unswervingly in his short diplomatic life. His first task in Spain was one from which he could hardly have expected success, since it lay in trying to persuade the most reactionary power in Europe to show something more than lip service to the ideals of liberty and decency which the other Allied nations were beginning to profess, if not to pursue. He found Ferdinand, it is true, "not quite such an idiot as has been supposed," but Ferdinand's advisers were intolerable and the whole aim of the administration seemed to be to reintroduce the principles of the time of the Spanish Armada.

One of his duties was to press for the abolition of the slave trade, and his way was not made easier for him by the intemperate way in which the British advocates of abolition clamoured for its instant adoption. Britain had profited handsomely from the trade but, having suffered a genuine change of heart, was displaying perhaps a little too blatantly the white sheet of repentance for the admiration of her neighbours. The British abolitionists, as Wellington wrote to Lord Holland, were pressing him "with all the earnestness, not to say violence, with which we are accustomed to urge such subjects without consideration for the feelings of others." They were, in his view, fanatics, though perfectly honest fanatics. The chief of them was Wilberforce, who combined a real and burning compassion for the unfortunate Negroes with a bland indifference to the sufferings of his own countrymen, for whose benefit he was strongly in favour of the restoration of the death penalty where it had been removed by recent legislation. The Spanish King and government were unsympathetic, and Wellington came away from his first diplomatic post with an unjustified feeling of failure.

He can hardly have looked forward with much more eagerness to his next duty, which was to represent his country at the Court of Louis XVIII in Paris, where he was also to press for abolition in a society hardly more liberal and humane than that of Madrid. Also he was uneasily aware that France might not altogether welcome as ambassador to her court the man who had done more than anyone to defeat her armies. The Emperor Napoleon, now at Elba and watching the European stage with rather more interest than was necessary for one who had made his last bow there, saw the same objection and commented on it, "No one, least of all a Frenchman, likes to be reminded that he has been defeated."

Wellington realized that he must be at the heart of Europe until peace had been restored because, as he said, "in case of the occurrence of anything in Europe, there is nobody but myself in whom either yourselves or the Country or the Allies would have any confidence." In that he spoke no more than the simple truth. He had always been modest about his own abilities, but this was no question of ability. Europe needed his courage, his honesty and his moderation, even though they might not be prepared to admit it.

He was strengthened in his determination to go to Paris by a new suggestion from the British Cabinet that he might take over the command of the army in America, where a war, though pursued by both sides with a marked lack of enthusiasm, lingered on. He did not refuse the invitation outright but suggested that no more should be heard of it until, at any rate, March 1815. He still distrusted the French, believing that, after such a history of triumph, they would not easily settle down to a life of

peace relieved only by the mild activities of raising barricades and throwing paving-stones. Bonaparte, as he said on more than one occasion, was
"a sad fellow," "a damned intractable fellow" and "no gentleman," but
round that diminished figure in his tiny kingdom of Elba there still hung
an afterglow more alluring and more dangerous than the restored daylight of the Bourbons. His marshals and generals had been turned off,
and his old soldiers discharged, so that they spread among their fellow
countrymen a feeling of grievance and of fierce longing for the old days
when France dominated Europe. It is not to be supposed that Wellington
had any definite foreboding of an attempt to bring back Napoleon and
to renew the glories of the Empire. But he knew that France was seething
with discontent and would seethe for many years ahead. It was no time
for the absence of the one man whom all Europe trusted.

In July of 1814 his time at Madrid was over. Before he took up his
new duties in Paris, he was to pay a short visit to the England which he
had not seen for five years. (There could be no danger, surely, in a
purely private visit to his family, as long as he left for Paris within a few
weeks of his arrival in England.) He was to sail from Calais, and on the
way he stopped at Bordeaux, from where he addressed his final order to
his army. It said little more than the formalities usual in such a document, except that in the last paragraph he assured them that "he shall
never cease to feel the warmest interest in their welfare and honour; and
that he will be at all times happy to be of any service to those to whose
conduct, discipline, and gallantry their country is so much indebted."

It would have been well had he not written those words; better still if
he had written them and tried to live up to them. The sad truth remains
that never, by speech or action, in public or private, did he make any
attempt to give reality to these generous sentiments. Other soldiers in
his position—the late Earl Haig is an honourable example—exerted themselves and devoted their days of retirement to an attempt to get justice
and gratitude for their men from a country which was never forward in
showing either. Wellington did nothing. The country heaped honours and
wealth on him, and he took them, as indeed he had every right to take
them. His old soldiers were turned off to live or starve as best they might,
without even their arrears of pay in many cases, and he did nothing for
them, nor did he ever show the smallest sign that he was interested in
what became of them. It was a pity that he left them at Bordeaux with
the sound of that empty promise in their ears.

He called in Paris for a few days and then left for England by way
of Calais. It was not an official homecoming and no arrangements had
been made for his reception at Dover. (After all, the war was over and
soldiers were not quite what they had been a few months ago.) The bulk

of his army were embarking for America. There seemed to be no need for any more formality for their commander when he came home. But the people of Britain were more grateful and less apprehensive than their rulers. As soon as the ship came in sight of Dover, he could see the immense crowd waiting for him, and as soon as he was within ear-shot, he heard the great waves of cheering come rolling across the water to welcome him home. There was a carriage waiting at the harbour, but the horses had been taken out of the shafts and men fought and shoved for the honour of dragging it through the streets. They brought him to the Ship Inn, and long after he had gone inside, the cheers went on in the packed street, as they called for him to come out and let them see him. But he was tired and, it may be, a little impatient of all this fuss. Also, he was hungry and he had not eaten a meal in England since that last hurried breakfast before his ship sailed for Portugal five years earlier. He ordered tea and buttered toast.

There was the same enthusiasm next day all the way to London. Crowds packed the sides of the streets and the country roads, and mounted men appeared at every village to ride beside and behind his carriage as it ran through the Kentish lanes into Surrey and as the first houses of London stretched out down the road to meet him. He wore his usual plain clothes and top hat, and those who caught a glimpse of him as he passed told less fortunate friends that he sat very stiff and up-right and did not seem to be looking out of the carriage windows. Did he, one wonders, think that it was all a lot of "damned nonsense"? At any rate, when they were crossing the Thames and he saw a great crowd on the far bank awaiting him, he told his coachman to take the nearest turning which led to a suitable side street and to drive like the devil to Piccadilly, before another crowd had time to collect there, and from Piccadilly into Hamilton Place. There Kitty would be waiting for him. She was a Duchess now, a little puzzled by her new dignity. He had not seen her for five years, and, as for the boys, he had never seen them since they were babies. The Duchess was still the same simple Kitty who loved him and was afraid of him and wondered, perhaps, how much these five years might have changed him. The carriage pulled up before his door in Hamilton Place, and he was at home again.

He was not to have much time to spare for his family. The five weeks, which were all that he could have at home, were filled with various en-gagements which he could not well refuse. Kitty went with him to the balls and receptions and to the Opera, but they had small opportunity of being together in their home. There was hardly any time at all for the two boys—Arthur, Marquis of Douro, who was seven, and Charles, who was six. No doubt they found this new figure in the household rather alarming, especially as Kitty had told them of what a great man their father was and of how important it was not to get in his way or to speak to him until they were spoken to. The advice so impressed young Arthur that for years afterward, whenever he found himself in his father's company, he was quite unable to keep awake. He would drop off to sleep at the table, or when out driving in the carriage, till his father wondered whether the poor child was quite right in his head. Child psychology was almost unknown in those days and no one recognized that the boy's persistent sleepiness was a defence against being left alone with his alarming father. The Duke had no wish to be a frightening father, but he came to the children as a stranger and never had time afterward to make up for the loss of those early years when they might have got to know each other.

In August he was in Paris again and busy with his new trade of diplomat. Once more he was obliged to try to press the abolition of slavery on a government which was, if possible, less enthusiastic than the Spanish had been. The French, always with a keen suspicion of anyone who professed disinterested motives, suspected that Britain's new-found detestation of slavery—for after all Britain had done remarkably well out of it—sprang from a desire to curtail France's colonial power and to steal her overseas trade. Only Louis himself was sympathetic, but he had not the will power to stand out against the rest of his family. The Duke viewed the entire company of them with a contempt, which he later expressed to Lord Stanhope, after dinner at Walmer Castle: "Louis was a walking sore—a perfect sore—not a part of his body was sound—even his head let out a sort of humour. . . . I had a very bad opinion of Louis XVIII—he was selfish and false in the highest degree. I always thought better of Charles X, but you see what he came to at last." He thought even less of Louis Philippe, whose "conduct during the Revolution was bad—very disgraceful indeed. . . . His own policy has completely changed since June last year. I always said it would." Strangely he thought that Philippe Égalité was "not so very bad a man as we commonly believe."

XXX

CASTLEREAGH was at Vienna where all the statesmen of Europe were in congress, settling the terms of peace with France and the outline of a new Europe, but at the end of 1814 he found that he could not longer be spared from his place in Parliament. The Opposition was strong, and the feeling in the country, as so often happens in Britain after a war, was inclined to favour a change—almost any change as long as there were some new faces on the Treasury Bench and some different recipients of government patronage. The affairs of Europe could wait while Castlereagh came home to defend his policy and confute the Opposition, but someone must be found to replace him and there could be no one with higher prestige or more influence in Europe than the Duke of Wellington; he left Paris early in 1815 and arrived at Vienna in February.

He did not like Vienna. He complained bitterly of the overheated rooms, which gave him a heavy cold as soon as he arrived. Nor was he unduly impressed by the sovereigns of Europe, or even by the veteran Talleyrand, of whom he said, "He is not lively or pleasant in conversation, but now and then he comes out with a thing that you remember all the rest of your life." Apart from that, Talleyrand was "not a good man of business—no, not at all, nor, to say the truth, does he pretend to be so. It is quite astonishing how much he depends upon others; for instance, others write for him." It may well be that His Grace, always the most fastidious of men, was disgusted by Talleyrand's personal habits, his deplorable table manners, his dirty fingers within diamond rings and the unpleasant smell which was the result of his indifference to the elementary principles of personal hygiene.

There was much discussion and bargaining among Russia, Austria and Prussia, all of whom were determined to reconstitute the kingdom of Poland in such a way as to conduce to the enlargement of their own possessions. Britain and her representatives incurred all the unpopularity of those who counsel moderation when they want nothing themselves and view revenge with the dispassionate eye of a secure and unravaged country and people. Castlereagh had insisted on what he called "the just equilibrium" of Europe, meaning what later statesmen would call the "balance of power," and Wellington dutifully followed his predecessor's policy.

There were lighter moments at Vienna between conferences and private talks, and Wellington, when he felt well enough, took his full share in them. There was much waltzing in the great ballrooms, *Fidelio* at the opera and, one night, the première of Beethoven's new descriptive piece, *The Battle of Vittoria,* with full musket and cannon effects. (There is an agreeable, though almost certainly apocryphal, story that a Russian diplomat asked Wellington whether it was anything like the battle and got the hearty reply, "By God no, if it had been, I should have run away myself.")

The congress lasted through the spring of 1815, and the final act was signed on June 9. But Wellington was not there to see it signed, for before then he had left for the Low Countries to command the Allied armies against the Emperor Napoleon, Emperor no longer of Elba but once more of France.

The news of Napoleon's escape had reached Vienna in the very early hours of March 7. The message came to Metternich from the Austrian Consul-General at Genoa, and at ten o'clock that morning the plenipotentiaries met in full conclave to decide on their joint course of action. Talleyrand, whose agile brain was now faced with the purely personal problem of which side of the fence to favour, asserted that Napoleon would make for either Italy or Switzerland, but Metternich, with a more acute sense of reality, said that his objective must be Paris. For a few more days they waited for news from France, and Wellington was understood to hope that the French Army would settle the business. But the hope was vain, and Wellington had not been mistaken when he suspected France's unwillingness to be satisfied with her present status and the negation of her past glories. French troops indeed had barred the way to Paris but the sight of the short figure in the old grey redingote was too familiar, the appeal to old days too strong for their loyalty. Ney deserted

to the Emperor at Lons-le-Saunier, taking his troops with him; other
units joined in as the advance on Paris became a triumphal procession.
The whole royal family, without hesitation, ran away while there was
still time, and less than three weeks later, Napoleon's advance troops
were at the gates of Paris.

Inside, the streets were crowded and noisy as the mob surged toward
the centre of the city. In the Tuileries servants were hastily hiding away
the trappings of the departed Bourbons and bringing out the old decorations of the Empire, and above the roofs of palace, church and house,
the tricolor floated again. The Emperor arrived late on the night of the
twentieth of March and was borne into his palace on the shoulders of
his Imperial Guard. He looked white and exhausted, and it was said
afterward that, as he passed through the doorway, he muttered to himself, "They let me come just as they let the others go."

A week before that night, the powers of Europe had issued a manifesto
putting the Emperor Napoleon outside the law of nations and declaring
him an enemy to humanity, and a fit subject for the vengeance of Europe.
Wellington had no doubt as to what his own part in the coming struggle
would be. Castlereagh had written to him, "Your Grace can judge where
your personal presence is likely to be of most use to the public service.
The Prince Regent, relying entirely upon your Grace's zeal and judgment,
leaves it to you, without further orders, either to remain at Vienna or
to put yourself at the head of the army in Flanders." On March 22 Wellington had already made up his mind and had written to Lord Burghersh,
"I am going into the Low Countries to take command of the army." On
April 4 he reached Brussels, which in that summer of the year 1815 was
like London during the Season or the Prince Regent's Brighton. All the
fashionable world had come in the Army's wake. Noblemen and members of Parliament rode in the parks or walked in the gardens, the carriages of great ladies took them up and set them down at rout or concert
or card party. Her Grace of Richmond was planning a ball which was
to be the event of the summer and had fixed it for June 15—provided,
of course, that that tiresome Bonaparte did not interfere with Her Grace's
arrangements.

Somehow it seemed easy to forget Bonaparte in those brilliant days of
pleasure. Certainly there was no need to worry about him when there
was the familiar figure of the Duke of Wellington, always in plain clothes,
riding with a party of ladies or looking benignly on at a race meeting or
a cricket match. True the city was full of red coats and there were grim-
looking gun parks in some of the squares, but the officers seemed always
to be available for escort or as dancing partners. Had there been immediate danger, surely His Grace would not have looked so genial or, ap-

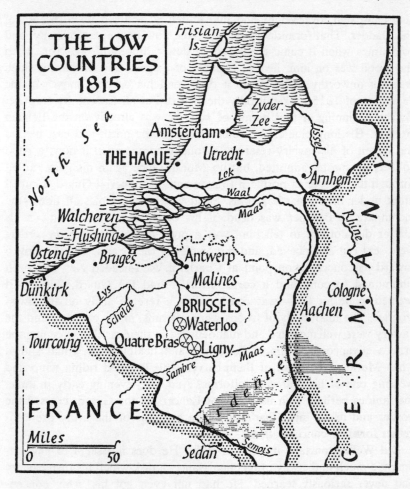

parently, have done so little apart from the social round. Bonaparte must still be far away, and he would be dealt with in due course.

But he was not far away, and for once in his life Wellington had badly miscalculated. As he himself admitted, "Bonaparte has been humbugging me. He has stolen forty-eight hours on me." Did the Duke, one wonders, rate Napoleon too lowly, prepare too carelessly, to meet him? That was not—had never been—his habit. He had fought against the best of the French generals except their master, and well as he knew the French tactics and their strength and weakness, he had not yet had personal experience of the Emperor's lightning speed and silent movements. Napoleon was not the man of Austerlitz, still less of Arcola. He was a man prematurely aged by war, suffering still from the effects of his Russian campaign, overweight and intermittently troubled by a disease of the bladder. That formidable energy came now only spasmodically, and sometimes when it came it seemed to desert him suddenly. Yet, when the mood was on him, he was capable of a speed and brilliance which was not unworthy of his greatest days, and his opening moves in the campaign of 1815 took not only the British but all Europe by surprise. By the beginning of that month of June he was already on the Belgian frontier. His long blue-clad columns were rolling north and east behind the screen of his cavalry reserve—Grouchy commanded it now, a good soldier, his master admitted, but no Murat. Once again his guns rattled through the villages of northern France and the Imperial Guard tramped afoot under their great bearskins. Soult was his chief of staff now—the incomparable Berthier was dead of his own hand—and Soult, as his master did not fail to tell him, was a poor makeshift. Yet the orders were sent out and obeyed, and remorselessly the Grande Armée moved toward its concentration point at Charleroi. Red-headed Ney had been summoned to command a corps, Mortier had the Guard, Suchet—it seemed to be his fate—was commanding a reserve army on the Swiss frontier. The main body of troops were veterans, many of them, and the cavalry were well mounted and manoeuvred in their task of screening the army's advance with almost the speed and flexibility they had shown when Murat rode ahead of them carrying his jewelled riding whip and wearing one of his fantastic uniforms. And, one evening early in June, the famous berline, with its escort of Lancers of the Guard, crossed the border and drove into Charleroi as the columns of the army drew together for their concentration.

Did Wellington take it all too lightly? He does not seem to have attempted much in the way of reconnaissance, a task which his own cavalry had never seriously learned. He had not even got his army concentrated, but held some 18,000 of them at Hal, having, for some reason, a presentiment that Napoleon would attempt an attack from that flank. There were no orders for that isolated detachment to join the main body for action, and indeed Wellington fought at Waterloo without them. Those who saw him at Brussels remarked on his apparent lack of care, but he was never given to showing his feelings and no one knows with what anxiety he may have waited for the first news of the enemy.

Yet he had plenty of cares on his shoulders before he had news of the Emperor. He was back at his old task of trying to get what he wanted out of a supine and apparently indifferent government—the troops, the staff officers, the supplies and armament which he needed. He said later that the army of Waterloo was "the most infamous army I ever commanded"—a graceless remark, since they had served him well, but one for which he has been overmuch blamed.

It was not a good army, judged by the standards of his Peninsular days. Too many of his seasoned troops had been shipped off to the Americas, and the ranks of his battalions were filled with recruits who had had too little training and, in many cases, no experience of battle. The old names and numbers were there—the 60th, the 95th, the 51st and 52nd Light Infantry—but they were second battalions, filled with the recruits and with reservists. The Guards were still the men of the Peninsular War and so were most of his cavalry—but he had never thought much of his cavalry. He had allies, Dutch and Belgian, but he thought even less of allies, having had bitter knowledge of them during most of his soldiering life. There were the Prussians under old Marshal Blücher, but they were not part of his command. He had said of his old army of Spain that with them he would march anywhere in Europe, but, surveying the motley force which was all that he had, it is little wonder that, as was his way, he should have spoken of them with contempt, though later he admitted, "I never knew infantry behave so well." So, when the ubiquitous Mr. Creevey buttonholed him one day and asked him whether he could "do the business," His Grace was guarded in his reply. He pointed to an infantryman, who was walking near to where they stood, and remarked, "It all depends on that article there." Mr. Creevey, anxious to be well-informed, then asked whether he counted on any desertions from the enemy, which was a question which he could answer without hesitation. "Not a man, from private to general inclusive. We may pick up a marshal or two perhaps—but not worth a damn." He was at the Duchess of Richmond's ball on the fifteenth when he knew at last that Napoleon was approaching—it was then that he admitted to being humbugged—and that night, having stayed at the ball as long as he thought advisable to reassure the minds of the British civilian guests, he left unobtrusively, ordered his carriage and drove out of Brussels. Next morning he was at Quatre Bras, after a visit to Blücher, whose position at Ligny he had inspected and dismissed with the comment, "I should expect to be damnably mauled if I fought there." He had driven out in plain clothes and now he changed into his usual battle dress, the blue frock, the famous cocked hat with its waterproof cover, in which, without enthusiasm, he had fixed the rosettes with the various colours of the allies. He sent away his carriage, and his groom led up Copenhagen, the chestnut gelding he always rode in battle. Not far away the Emperor's white horse, Marengo, was being saddled. The weather was fine, but as "I never get wet if I can help it," he had his cloak rolled and strapped across his saddle bow. A servant brought his sword in its plain steel scabbard and the telescope that all the army knew. Heaven knows what were his thoughts, but no doubt one of them was the same as that which he had carried to the Peninsula: "I at least will not be afraid of them."

XXXI

NAPOLEON'S rapid approach march had given him the initiative, and his mood of urgency was still on him. Since his army was stronger than either the British or the Prussian but weaker than the two combined, his plan was to attack each separately and to drive them apart, leaving him a clear road to Brussels. On the sixteenth of June, he sent Ney with a corps to contain the British near Quatre Bras, and in the evening he flung his main body on the Prussians at Ligny. Blücher was a fine fighter but he was no match for Napoleon as a tactician and his dispositions were so faulty that, before night, he had been, as Wellington had foreseen, "damnably mauled." The beaten Prussians withdrew from the field, and as they stumbled through the night, every mile that they marched took them further away from Wellington. It was a defeat and might have been a disaster, but Napoleon's feverish energy deserted him and he made no effort to press the retreat. Ten or even five years before he would have sent Murat's cavalry thundering on the heels of the Prussians and, by so doing, would have isolated the British until he could turn and deal with them. But now he fell into a strange lethargy and gave no orders for the pursuit till the next day. Even then the orders were carelessly given—Soult may have been to blame for that, for, though he was an excellent general, he had no liking for staff work. Grouchy, starting twenty-four hours late, made matters worse by losing his way and all trace of the Prussians.

Wellington remarked that "Old Blücher has had a damned good hiding and has gone eighteen miles to the rear. We must do the same." The fighting at Quatre Bras had been bloody but indecisive. Ney, who was never at his best in independent command, had shown a strange irresolution. There had been more bungled staff work and one corps, d'Erlon's, had marched and countermarched all day from one battle to the other without taking part in either. Wellington himself had as narrow an escape from death as he had ever known, when he was caught almost unattended in a sudden rush of French lancers and had to turn and ride for it. His retreat took him across the front which was held by a Highland regiment who were lining a ditch. He shouted to them to lie still and put his horse at the ditch and cleared it. (The brunt of the infantry fighting fell on the Highlanders of Picton's brigade, which consoled a great lady in Brussels, who observed, "The Scotch were chiefly engaged so there are no officers wounded that one knows.") Brussels heard the guns that day, and there was a general feeling that the holiday was over, while the more prudent made arrangements for horses to be ready in case they should need their carriages in a hurry. Wellington had sent a message to Blücher telling him that he proposed to stand and fight at Mont St. Jean, before the village of Waterloo, and urging Blücher to hurry to his support. Then he began to withdraw his army, which involved a sharp cavalry action at the village of Genappe. On the evening of the seventeenth they were in position on the slopes of Mont St. Jean with detachments holding the outlying farms at Hougoumont and La Haye Sainte.

It was a cheerless night, for it had rained unceasingly all that day and the fields were sodden so that the gun teams were hard put to it to bring their guns into position. All the night of the seventeenth it rained, and the eighteenth came in on a grey and cheerless dawn. From their positions the British could watch the French taking up their battle order on the slope in front of a little farm called La Belle Alliance. The Grande Armée moved into line with its usual pomp, with bands playing and colours flying, and took up its positions on the forward slope, so that the British could see every move and pick out the better-known units such as the Guard and the Polish Lancers. Wellington had his own men, as was his way, on the reverse slope, where they would be shielded from the opening cannonades of the battle. About eight o'clock in the morning they heard a storm of cheering from the far hillside, and some of them caught a glimpse of the small figure on the white pony as he rode along his line of battle. An enterprising gunner subaltern—or so the story goes—asked permission of Wellington to lay his guns on the French Emperor but was sternly told that it was no business of opposing commanders to assassinate each other. The story may well be true. If so, it provides an agreeable contrast with the later conduct of the Emperor in leaving in his will a small sum of money to a man who tried to assassinate Wellington in London. But, as His Grace always maintained, Bonaparte was no gentleman.

For almost five uneasy hours the two armies lay facing each other, waiting for the ground to become dry enough for the guns to be run into position. There was no cheering and no display on the slopes of Mont St. Jean—they were content to leave that sort of thing to the Mounseers.

Wellington must often during those hours have calculated how long it would take Blücher to come to his help. That Blücher would come with all possible speed he did not doubt. That tough and fiery little fighter had been ridden over by his own cavalry at Ligny and had treated himself with a medicine of his own devising, a compound of gin and rhubarb. Wellington believed him to be no more than ten miles away, but ten miles in those conditions was as bad as fifty on a good marching day. Blücher had to drag his guns along the vile roads which the recent rain had made almost impassable. He would come with all the speed that he could muster, but until he came Wellington had a little over 50,000 men and 156 guns against Napoleon's 72,000 and 246 guns. He could ill spare those 18,000 at Hal, waiting uselessly for the attack which never came.

Perhaps the uncertainty made him a little testy. When Lord Uxbridge, his cavalry commander, rode up to ask him what his plans were, he answered, a trifle shortly, "Bonaparte has not given me any idea of his projects; and as my plans depend on his, how can you expect me to tell you what mine are?" Perhaps he realized that he had shown his anxiety, for at once he laid his hand on Uxbridge's arm and added, "There is one thing certain, Uxbridge; that is that, whatever happens, you and I will do our duty." (A few hours later he had his more famous conversation with Uxbridge, when, as they were riding together, a cannon ball struck Uxbridge on the ankle. To Uxbridge's agonized, "By God, there goes my leg," the Duke, having inspected the damage, replied, "By God, so it does.")

The battle began between noon and one o'clock; and from then onward, for seven hours it was, as Wellington said, "Hard pounding gentlemen, we will see who can pound the longest."

As he said later, "Napoleon did not manoeuvre at all. He just moved forward in the old style in columns and was driven off in the old style." All day Napoleon was in one of his moods of lethargy. He had ordered a chair to be brought for him, and for hour after hour he sat watching the battle, making little effort to control it, leaving its direction to Ney, whose sole idea of tactics was a frontal attack with himself leading it. That was all in Wellington's favour, since all that his men had to do was to stand and fight with musket and bayonet, and it was work which they understood and did not fear.

So, for hour after hour, Ney's assaulting troops, horse and foot, surged up the slope, and again and again they were beaten back by the stubborn British infantry. Hougoumont was a blazing ruin but the Guards held on there, and Ney futilely threw in division after division, which would have been of more use against the main line of battle. At about two o'clock in the afternoon he launched the first of a series of cavalry charges against the British centre, a series which did not cease until he had thrown away the greater part of the splendid French cavalry on the British squares. Even Wellington could not refrain from paying a compliment to his infantry. "I had the infantry," he said later, "for some time in squares and we had the French cavalry walking about us as if they had been our own. I never saw the British infantry behave so well."

All through the day he was up with the front line. He was, it would seem, quite indifferent to personal danger, and at the end of the day, though he was untouched, every one of his staff who had ridden with him had been hit. It was a battle made after his own choice, where he could be in the middle of his men ready to take advantage of a piece of good fortune, to correct a mistake or check a momentary hesitation. The men who had served under him in the Peninsula felt at home with him, hearing his familiar and brief oral commands, seeing his absolute calm and self-possession. He spoke in few words and those such as any soldier could understand, as when he sent the Guards in to counterattack with "There my lads, in with you—let me see no more of you," or the Household Cavalry into a charge with "Now, gentlemen, for the honour of the Household troops," or, riding up to the 60th as the French cavalry retreated, asked them to "drive those fellows away." And Mercer's famous battery of horse artillery no doubt went more eagerly into action for hearing, as they swept past him, his approving comment, "Ah, that's the way I like to see horse artillery move."

Yet he must have had many anxious moments as the hours passed and still there was no sign of Blücher, no sound of Prussian guns. He heard the first of them about four o'clock in the afternoon, away on his left, but it would still be some time before they could come up in force, and now he was hard pressed. Hougoumont still held out, but Ney had stormed La Haye Sainte and once had all but pierced the British line. Now it was evening, and, in a lull in the fighting, Wellington saw through his glass a large body of French troops moving from the battle line and away to their right and knew that they had gone to meet Blücher's advance guard. Five o'clock came and six, and the gunfire on his left grew in intensity as more Prussians struggled on to the field. Again the French had to detach troops to try to hold them.

The light was failing when the French made their last attempt. Wellington sat on his horse among his infantry and watched the long columns of the Imperial Guard toiling up the hill, supported by every regiment of foot, every squadron and battery that Ney could summon for the last desperate effort to break the British line before the Prussians came in force. But the Guard failed where all others had failed before them, and when the Guard failed, the French army knew that there was no more hope for them.

As the columns wavered and stopped and began to turn back, the British could hear the horror-stricken cry which rose among the remnant of the French infantry—"La Garde se recule." Then Wellington was galloping along the line, bareheaded and with only one officer with him —the rest of his staff were disabled. They saw him standing in his stir-rups and pointing with his cocked hat toward the enemy, and they surged forward in the counter-attack with all the eagerness of men who had stood to be shot at for six hours. One officer, a little less intelligent than his fellows or, it may be, dazed by the long fighting, asked which way they were to go and was reassured by the common-sense answer, "Why, right ahead to be sure." The Prussians had broken through at last and soon Wellington was, a little reluctantly, submitting to the embrace of their little white-haired marshal, who smelled strongly of gin and rhu-barb and was ejaculating, "Mein lieber Kamerad" and "Quelle affaire," which, as Wellington remarked afterward, "was pretty well all the French that he knew."

Then Wellington rode slowly back to Waterloo and to the casualty lists which he dreaded. When he read them he wept, as he had wept at Badajoz. Of himself he said, "The finger of God has been over me." (The less devout-minded Copenhagen tried to kick him when he dis-mounted.) His servants, who knew his ways, brought him tea and toast and his civilian clothes, and he changed and went back to Brussels. There, inevitably, he met Mr. Creevey and told him that it had been "a damned nice thing—as near a run thing as ever I saw," adding, when Creevey asked whether the French had fought better than usual, "No, they have always fought the same since I first saw them at Vimeiro. By God, I don't know that it would have done if I had not been there." No one in his own time and few in ours will question the truth of that opin-ion or grudge him its expression.

He was back again in Paris in July, with his last and perhaps greatest victory behind him and with the fate of France and, to some degree, Europe resting in his hands. He was there now, not as Ambassador but as commanding the Allied forces of occupation and, no doubt he found the position less equivocal: he had negotiated an armistice with Marshal Davout, now Minister of War, which provided for the temporary settlement of the French problem (her greatest problem was well on his way to final solution at St. Helena), and his first care was to see it fairly and sensibly enforced. It was no easy task, and for anyone without the Duke's supreme authority and prestige it might have proved impossible. The royal family of Bourbon were intent on confirming Napoleon's opinion that they had "learned nothing and forgotten nothing," as well as Fox's maxim, "The worst of all revolutions is a restoration." Louis XVIII was a mild enough man, indisposed for revenge on his beaten enemies, but without the strength to withstand the ferocious instincts of the younger members of his family and especially of the younger women, such as the Duchesse d'Angoulême, who were all for proscription and persecution of the fallen figures of the Empire.

Most of these were, in fact, protected by the terms of the armistice, but there were certain, such as Marshal Ney, whose recent treachery was too gross to be overlooked. Ney was put on trial, first before a court-martial composed of his old colleagues who, to their credit, refused to condemn him. The House of Peers, many of whom were members of families of the old regime, were less merciful, and Ney was condemned to death and shot in the Luxembourg Gardens.

Wellington might have intervened to save him, and so great was his influence that he would probably have succeeded, but he refused, even in the face of a personal appeal from Ney's wife. He answered her passionate entreaty with a reasoned statement of the case against Ney—which can have been of small consolation to her—and a very proper disclaimer of responsibility in the matter. No doubt he was right—he always was right—but it is possible to wish that for once he had found himself able to show less regard for protocol and more for mercy.

It was his unfailing pursuit of his two ideals of fairness and moderation which enabled him now to dominate a scene in which few of the principal actors showed much regard for either. The Bourbons were for revenge and for restoring everything that had prevailed before the days of an Empire which they tacitly agreed to believe never to have existed. Talleyrand, having proved his indispensability to both Kingdom and Empire, was intent on continuing the demonstration. Fouché, the supreme spy, ancestor of all Gestapos and Ogpus, clung grimly to office in the assurance of his unmatched ability in directing the secret police and spy service of anyone who would employ him. Even Wellington, who must have loathed him, recommended his retention for the present, knowing his own ability to control him as long as necessary and to get rid of him as soon as possible.

Fouché seems not at first to have understood either how far his authority extended or what liberties he could take with the strange and silent man, who said so little and seemed to lack subtlety. But, if His Grace lacked subtlety he had, in profusion, two qualities which Fouché signally lacked, honesty and the ability to state plainly what was in his mind.

Fouché was sharply made aware of this when the question of the dismantling of the French fortresses came up for discussion and Wellington was informed that certain of them were still fully armed and garrisoned, the fortresses of Vincennes being one of the most notable examples. When Wellington brought this deficiency to his notice, in the presence of Mr. Croker, Fouché almost tearfully confessed that there had been an oversight but protested his inability to control the commander of the garrison and begged to be told what he could do to ensure the evacuation and dismantlement of the fortress. Wellington, so Croker recorded, replied without hesitation, "It is not my business to tell you what you are to do, but I will tell you what I am going to do. Unless the fortress is handed over to me by tomorrow morning I shall take it by assault. Do you understand?" And, when Fouché attempted to argue, there was a brusque conclusion—"The fort must be handed over by ten tomorrow. If not, I shall assault it at noon." Wellington thereupon turned cheerfully to Croker, asking, "Croker, you have never seen a battle, have you?" and offered to lend him a horse and take him out to see the storming. Fouché, who may well have been shocked at so casual an invitation, may even have thought that the threat was unreal. But Paris awoke next day to the sound of bugles playing an early reveille, to the tramp of feet and the rumbling of gun-wheels as the troops detailed for the assault marched out of the city. Wellington—as anyone who knew him could have warned Fouché—did not deal in idle threats. When the fortress was hastily evacuated before ten in the morning, the storming parties had been told off and stood ready, the guns were in position and the port fires lighted. The business of dismantling the remaining fortresses went forward without delay.

Wellington stayed in Paris, with hardly a break, for more than three years, and it was not until the year 1818 that he felt himself able to send away the last troops of the occupying armies and himself to return to England.

It may well be that he was in no great hurry to be at home. That we shall never know, since it was not the sort of thing which he would tell anybody. But perhaps England held fewer attractions for him than she does for most returning soldiers. He knew already that his married life was not to be a source of much happiness for him, though he would always be a good husband and, as far as he knew how, a devoted father to his children.

He must have wondered what employment there would be for him, now that Europe seemed to be set for a long period of peace. He did not want any more fighting. He had seen enough of it and he hated its waste and its destruction—as he said, there was nothing as bad as a defeat except a victory. But war was the only trade that he knew, though he had dabbled in politics and more than dabbled in diplomacy. He was to be made Master-General of the Ordnance, but that was little more than a sinecure though, in his case, it carried with it Cabinet rank. He was foreign to the ways of Cabinets, having mostly experienced them as assemblies of men out of whom he found it impossible to get what he needed. He cannot have felt much elation at the prospect of joining a body which had starved him of men and money and munitions, and had overloaded him with decorative and useless staff-officers. The worst of his handicaps was that he did not know England, having spent less than five years of his manhood there. Least of all did he know the new postwar England, with its restlessness and discontent, its violent but as yet unformulated desires, its hot resentments of what it had always taken for granted. Had he returned immediately after Waterloo he would have grown up with the postwar era, and though he would probably never have liked it, he might have understood it. England in 1818 was different from England in 1815. The triumph was over and the disillusionment had begun. The Industrial Revolution was in full growth, and the country was already at heart a part of the nineteenth century. It was to be his misfortune— it might almost be called without exaggeration his tragedy—that he came home as much a man of the eighteenth century as he had been when he left for India twenty years earlier.

XXXII

B RITAIN HAD, in Pitt's phrase, saved Europe by her example, but she had yet to save herself by her own efforts, a task whose difficulty Pitt did not, perhaps, fully visualize when he spoke in the midst of a war.

In European and world affairs, Britain was pre-eminent, and among her leaders Wellington was supreme. How great was the influence which he wielded in Paris is plain from his dealing with the Prussian, Marshal Blücher. Prussia had suffered much at the hand of Napoleon, and Blücher, after the manner of his race, was out for full revenge. He had no sympathy with the views of Wellington and Castlereagh, who counselled moderation in the terms of the treaty. His first attempt was to try to persuade Wellington to pursue and catch Napoleon before he could reach the French coast, and to hang him without benefit of trial, but all the response which he elicited was a chilly note saying, "Should the Allied Sovereigns decide to execute Bonaparte, they will doubtless appoint an executioner, who will not be I."

Blücher would willingly have taken on the duty single-handed and, in fact, nearly had the chance, when his dragoons rode into the courtyard at Malmaison not many hours after Napoleon had driven out. Now, as Wellington did not seem cooperative, he decided to make a demonstration on his own account, by blowing up the Pont d'Jena, a bridge which Napoleon had built across the Seine to commemorate the battle. Fortunately Wellington heard of the plan in good time and ordered one platoon of the Coldstreams to picket the bridge and to hold themselves responsible for its safety. When Blücher's sappers, in considerable force, arrived to do their job of demolition, they were stopped by the sight of a solitary red-coated figure, standing as sentry on the bridge. They did not pursue their task any further. Even Blücher knew and respected the power which lay behind the lonely sentry.

That was Britain in the first flush of her dominance of Europe. It would have been well for her had her domestic affairs prospered as strongly as her fighting men and her foreign policy. But, just at this time, Britain was like a red and shining apple which, when bitten into, is found to be rotten and maggoty. As usual, during a big war there had been plenty of people in England who looked forward to nothing so much as a return to what Sir Winston Churchill once called, "our old, decent ways." Equally there were people, though not nearly so many, who were determined to snatch the opportunity of doing away with old abuses and putting Britain's policy on to a just and free basis.

There will always be the many who fancy that, once the fighting stops, everything will become automatically the same as it had been and that trade will enjoy prosperity to make up for the uncertainties of war, and the few who foresee and try to warn their fellows that, after so huge a dislocation of the country's economy and of world trade, the more likely prospect is that of trade slump and industrial unrest, of hectic finance and of general insecurity.

All these Britain was soon to experience, and she was in no shape for battling her way through them. Her King was an old madman, fumbling his way through the passages in his Palace of Kew and strumming phrases of Handel's music on harpsichord or organ. The Prince of Wales was having wife trouble and the Princess of Wales was having husband trouble. The other royal dukes were conducting themselves as usual and had by this time, as Wellington remarked, "insulted—personally insulted— every gentleman in England."

In 1818, the succession to the throne was by no means assured, and had the King died then, there would have been twelve brothers and sisters who might succeed if they died one after another. Of the brothers, it is safe to say that not one of them but would have proved a disaster, with the possible exception of William, Duke of Clarence, who was promiscuous and not much more than half-witted but was not vicious and, having served in the Navy, had some conception of the meaning of the word "duty."

George III and his Queen Charlotte had produced fifteen children who reached maturity, yet of that generation not a single man had fathered a legitimate child. There was no lack of bastards. William himself had ten little Fitzclarences, the fruits of his alliance with Mrs. Jordan.

There seemed to be some hope of better things in this year when it was known that Princess Charlotte, the daughter of the Prince Regent, was pregnant. The Stock Exchange predicted that the funds would go up by 2½ per cent if the child should be a girl, and 6 per cent for a boy. The calculation was the measure of the British people's fervent desire to be spared the succession of any of the royal dukes. They were doomed to disappointment, for the child was stillborn and the Princess died in childbirth.

It was inevitable that the Prince Regent should succeed as soon as the King died, unless his régime of brandy and grandmothers should carry him off first. The people of Britain accepted this prospect without enthusiasm as an unavoidable fact. The Prince had few admirers in the country, outside his own small and raffish circle. He now weighed about twenty stone (nearly three hundred pounds), and his valet reported that he had at last given up the complicated system of corsets, which had for years restrained and done something to conceal that vast and growing bulk. "His Royal Highness," he reported, "has let his belly go and it now hangs down to his knees."

The Prince, to the alarm of his supporters and his doctors, was displaying signs of mental as well as of bodily weakness, though it would be unfair to suggest that his brain was dangerously affected. He talked sometimes a little oddly, as though he had let his mind go blank when his belly went. He spoke of things which could only be delusions, asserting that he had ridden the winner of the Ascot Gold Cup and that he had fought with the Brigade of Guards at Waterloo. "I charged with the Guards, did I not, Duke?" was a favourite question, to which Wellington could find no better reply than a gruff, "If your Highness says so." Wellington's loyalty was as impeccable as his manners, but, as he reminded the King of France, he was also an English gentleman and, in that capacity, he found the Prince Regent repulsive. "By God," he said once, "you never saw such a figure in your life as he is. Then he speaks and swears so like old Falstaff, that damn me if I am not ashamed to walk into a room with him." (He was equally outspoken about his old enemy, now imprisoned in St. Helena, where he had a most unsympathetic guardian in the Governor, Sir Hudson Lowe. There were endless complaints from sympathizers of Napoleon's about the harshness of his captivity, but as the Duke said, "By God, I don't know. Bonaparte is so damned intractable a fellow there is no knowing how to deal with him"; and, with memories of a few weeks spent there in 1805, he considered that Napoleon had no reason to complain of the climate, though he conceded that Lowe was "a damned fool.")

The death of Princess Charlotte and her baby stirred the royal dukes to hope and a sudden flurry of activity. Above all, they were, most of them, men in a half middle-age, fully competent to beget an heir to the throne. The first mention of this competition between them is found in an entry in Creevey's diary, on the day when Edward Duke of Kent sent for him and regaled him with a summary of the matrimonial and extra-matrimonial affairs of his brothers, mentioning his own prospects of finding a wife and founding a family. One after another the rest of them got the idea and began to try to qualify for the position as father of the heir with all the keenness of rival firms tendering for a contract. For himself, the Duke of Kent, who was living on an annuity of £12,000 and was in debt for £50,000, stated his terms succinctly and without undue modesty. He was prepared to give up his French mistress, Mme. St. Laurent, but "Justice must be done to her by the Nation and the Ministers." Her wants would not be unreasonable—a small house, a few servants, a carriage and a few horses, "so that her friends will treat her with respect. For himself, his annuity must be raised to £25,000 a year and all his debts paid." On these conditions and after having given his elder brother, William of Clarence, three months' start in which to produce an heir, he was ready, he said, "To obey any call my country might make on me (though God knows the sacrifice it will be to make it) whenever I shall think it my duty to become a married man." In order to show that he meant business, he announced the names of two German Princesses, either of whom he would be willing to marry if the government accepted his terms. They were the Princess of Baden and the Princess of Saxe-Coburg, the second of whom became his wife and the mother of the future Queen Victoria.

Frederick, Duke of York, and his wife were both over fifty—she, past the age of childbearing—so that he was not considered eligible to compete, but William of Clarence also made the mistake of pricing his tender too high for the dubious advantages of his person. He would send Mrs. Jordan packing, the country giving her a generous allowance for the rest of her life, and making ample provision for the ten little Fitz-clarences. For himself, all that he asked was the payment in full of his debts and such a settlement as he deserved for being willing to marry for the sake of ensuring the succession. There was a surprise entry by Adolphus of Cambridge, then living in Hanover as the representative of his father. He got away to a good start by marrying the Princess Augusta of Hesse-Cassel, the first of the brothers to make the great sacrifice, but as the elder dukes were just about to marry, Adolphus was not consid-ered a good bet and found few backers. Three weeks later, the Duke of Kent, resigned to his fate though sorely disappointed at the parsimony of Parliament, which increased his annuity to £18,000 instead of

£25,000 and indicated that he must provide for Mme. St. Laurent out of that, married his Victoria at Coburg.

William of Clarence was the last to get away from the start, but he early showed signs of making the running when in 1819 his wife, who had been the Princess Adelaide, daughter of the Duke of Saxe-Meiningen, bore him a child who lived only a few hours. William made another effort to come through in 1820, when his wife bore a girl, thereby changing the prospects for everybody, but the child lived only a few months.

In the year of 1820, the question of the succession was settled. It was a year which proved fatal to royalty, including, as it did, the deaths of Adelaide's baby girl, the Duke of Kent and George III. This brought the Prince Regent to the throne at the age of fifty-eight, and made of his brother Clarence heir-apparent, with an unusually good chance of succeeding, since the King's matrimonial difficulties prohibited the idea of any further issue by that marriage. The same events vastly increased the young Princess Victoria's chances of following her uncle, whose undoubted fertility seemed doomed to fail before the task of raising a legitimate heir.

His Majesty, King George IV, lost no time in further displaying the family talent for washing dirty linen in public. No sooner was he seated on the throne than he set about trying to get rid of his wife. He was a perennial optimist, and may even have thought of remarrying and getting an heir, preferably a male heir. Queen Caroline was abroad as she had been for many months, conducting herself with her usual levity and publicity in somewhat less than dubious company. On the advice of Brougham, whom she had appointed as her Attorney-General, she opened negotiations with her husband to secure her future position and comfort. After some bargaining she refused his final offer of £50,000 a year on condition that she reside outside Britain and announced her intention of coming home in time to be crowned with her husband. The King responded to this threat by ordering her name to be omitted from the Prayer Book whenever prayers were offered for the royal family, but even such a portentous and public punishment passed harmlessly over the head of the Queen's incurable frivolity. She greeted it with the comment, "Praying always makes me hungry; if they put me in the Liturgy, I shall be absolutely famished."

But, beneath that frivolous and sometimes scandalous façade, there was in the Queen great determination, and she meant to fight for her rights. The King was determined to get rid of her and consulted the law officers of the Crown about the correct procedure. They were not encouraging and said so. If His Majesty proposed to rely on the Queen's adultery as cause for divorce, he would run the almost certain risk of having his own affairs disclosed in court, and there would be no difficulty in getting evidence of his own promiscuity. (It was even possible—though of this the law officers knew nothing—that the whole story of his marriage to Mrs. Fitzherbert might leak out and endanger his occupancy of the throne because of her religion.) On the whole the law officers did not like it, and their distaste was perhaps deepened by the certainty that, if the case came to court, the Queen's leading counsel would be Henry Brougham, who could be expected not only to make the very best of her case, but also to involve the King in any amount of unpleasantness. George consulted the Prime Minister, Lord Liverpool, and the Cabinet, none of whom was any more anxious to make public so undignified and squalid a story, though Wellington countered the comment that a divorce case would degrade the King by remarking, "His Majesty is degraded as low as he can be already."

Nothing would turn the King from his purpose, and eventually the Cabinet promised to draft a bill which became known as the Act of Pains and Penalties, which Lord Liverpool reluctantly undertook to introduce to the House of Lords before the end of the year. Opinion in political circles, taking no notice of so abstract a thing as morality, fell into two groups, which corresponded accurately with the division between Whig and Tory. The Tories, following their government's lead, were for the King, the Whigs for the Queen. Had it been possible to take a census of their private opinions, the result would probably have been surprisingly unanimous. Both parties, in their inmost councils, thought that the Queen had probably committed adultery but that, as far as His Majesty was concerned, there could be no doubt at all; that a lot of mud would be stirred up and reputations would be torn to shreds all round; and that, in short, the whole business was a piece of irresponsible lunacy.

Yet if the King would have it, the Tories were not going to stand in his way. He had always been a sympathizer with the Whigs, and it was generally thought that he was only waiting for a chance to turn out the Tories in order to put in his friends. The Whigs had been happily counting on this for years and felt some reluctance to endanger their chances by opposing the King on a personal matter so early in his reign. Still, there was something to be said for it; it might serve to turn out the Tories, and in any case if it were to be a government bill they would automatically oppose it. Also there were many among the Whigs who shared the Tory view of the King's proposal, and there were even a few, such as Lord Grey, who believed the Queen innocent.

The bill, after having been introduced by Lord Liverpool, would have to be debated in the Lords in the same way as any other bill and would then be sent down to the Commons for similar treatment. If both Houses passed it, it would become law on receiving the Royal Assent, which was the only part of the procedure on which anyone could count with any confidence.

The bill never reached the Commons. The Queen was represented by counsel, chief among whom were Brougham and Denman, and they dealt drastically with the seedy array of witnesses which the King's advisers had collected at great expense (to the country) from the shadier ports on the Mediterranean seaboard. Brougham delivered one of the finest of all his fighting speeches, and Denman unwittingly added to British folklore with an inept quotation from the Bible. The Lords were unimpressed by the injunction to tell Her Majesty to "Go and sin no more," but it was eagerly welcomed by the makers of street ballads who sang to delighted audiences,

> *Most gracious Queen, we thee implore,*
> *To go away and sin no more;*
> *But if that effort be too great,*
> *To go away at any rate.*

There was a small majority in favour of the bill on its first reading in the Lords, a still smaller one on the second and a majority of only eleven on the third. Lord Liverpool dared not send it down to the Commons where an even smaller majority for it was probable, and withdrew the bill.

The King's fury was unbounded, and much of it fell upon the Whigs for opposing his royal will, though by this, they were not unduly alarmed, perceiving that they had not in any way improved their chances of coming into power, but that the Tories had done nothing to secure their tenure. It was perhaps with some idea of giving a cash compensation to the disappointed King that they voted the unusually large sum of £240,-000 for his coronation expenses. This was a project into which he could throw his heart and in which he could occupy his mind, and he planned the ceremony in such a magnificent style that it seemed unlikely that Parliament's generosity would suffice for its splendour. It won from the Duke of Clarence, who stood near the throne during the crowning, the heart-felt comment, "By God, I'll have everything just the same at mine!"

London's streets were packed with crowds, most of whom were prepared to cheer the Queen more heartily than her husband, whom they hated. Queen Caroline had not been invited to the coronation and, with her invariable and fatal lack of taste and good sense, drove to Westminster in a carriage and demanded admission, which was refused. It was to be almost the final action of her unhappy life, for within twelve months she spoke her last pathetic words, "I am going to die, Mr.

Brougham, but it does not signify." Only a few months earlier the King had been much encouraged by a report of her death, though his satisfaction had been premature. When the news of the death of the Emperor Napoleon at St. Helena had reached England, a member of the court rushed into the Royal Presence, announcing joyously, "Sire, your greatest enemy is dead," to which His Majesty, with equal delight, replied, "Is she, by God?"

This time there was no mistake. But, as she had said, it did not signify.

XXXIII

THE GREAT ONES of the Kingdom—the King, the royal dukes and their more or less disreputable friends—were acting out their shabby harlequinade on the stage before a bored and preoccupied audience. The political world and polite society had seen too many such performances to take much further interest, and, outside the privileged circle, most people took very little interest of any kind in the characters of their royal family. The general opinion seemed to be that they were ridiculous and sometimes indecent but that they were better than the Stuarts.

The working-class population took no interest at all. The masked figures might mouth and posture on the lighted stage, but they made no difference to work in the mine, the factory or the mill. The only realities there were the long hours of work, the intolerable working and living conditions, the prostitution of wives and children in the cause of another man's wealth. Few of them could read or write, or had knowledge of anything beyond the few square miles within which they lived, worked and died. In the little spare time which was left to them, few had the strength to do anything but sleep. It is doubtful that they had even heard of most of the royal antics. News travelled slowly and newspapers were far too expensive for workingmen's pockets. For all that they knew—or that most of them cared—the King and his brothers might have been disporting themselves in New York or Timbuktu. Such folk were like the strange characters in a fairy tale, though not many of the workers would have had much truck with fairy tales since the days when they ran free and happy in the countryside which they had abandoned for the town.

It was from the classes just above their own that the friends of the workingmen were drawn. They were the small traders, country lawyers, farmers, sons of fathers who had prospered and lifted their families out of the ruck by their boot-straps. They were near enough to the workmen to know their sufferings and their patience and far enough removed from them to take a wider view of the state of the country, and they were politically minded enough to plan and articulate enough to plead for better things.

They hoped for nothing from the King. The day when the peasant looked to the King for protection against his oppressors had died with the end of feudalism. These men were brought up in the tradition of parliamentary government and it was to Parliament that they looked for relief.

They had little to hope for in the years which followed Waterloo. The Tories were still in office, and there did not appear to be any immediate prospect of turning them out. The Whigs were suffering from too many years in opposition, and were quarrelling among themselves so continually as to obliterate any chance of concerted and vigorous opposition to the government. Meanwhile, the hand of Pitt's wartime restrictions lay as heavily on the country as it had done at the height of the struggle with Napoleon. Habeas corpus was regularly suspended every year, the Combination Acts were in force and imprisonment awaited any man who dared to speak openly against the government. The system of governmental espionage flourished, and half the magistrates in England were on the watch for the slightest sign of insubordination so that they might punish it in an exemplary way. Trades unions were still illegal and had to meet in secret and under pretence of being non-political.

The situation was made worse by the return and discharge of many of the soldiers who had fought in the late wars. In proportion to the general population of the country they were few in numbers but they were a powerful leaven to work in the dough of the farm laborers and the operatives in mills and factories. Not even the achievements of the armies in Spain and Belgium could break through the barrier of the British people's fear of military power and their contempt for the common soldier. The men of Badajoz and Vitoria, of Quatre Bras and Waterloo, came home with no prospect of employment, no money and no one to help them. Even those who had been wounded were discharged from the crude military hospitals as soon as they were on the way to being healed, and no thought had been given to their after-care, in either health or occupation.

It was not long before their influence began to make itself felt in the troubled districts of the North and Midlands. They had come back with a certain glamour about them, so that they could count on a hearing when they voiced their opinions in alehouse or at street corner. They were trained and disciplined men who spoke with authority, and they had a real and burning grievance in the country's cynical neglect and ingratitude toward her undoubted saviours. They were not violent men but they were tough and resourceful, accustomed to fighting for what they wanted, impatient of fine words and fine promises. It was, at any rate in part, with them that there began the feeling that things were so bad and the men in power so callous that violence would be not only inevitable but wholly justifiable.

They were not revolutionaries in the sense that a revolution means an overturning of an existing system, nor were they, on the whole, republicans by conviction. They did not admire the royal family, but they did not want to turn them out or cut off their heads or to behave in any way like the Mounseers. They believed most strongly in parliamentary government, and all that they asked for was that the system should be overhauled and brought into line with the changed condition of the country. For many years past Parliament had played happily at the game of reforming itself, secure in the knowledge that neither party dared risk the possible calamity of attempting it. It was no game to the workingmen and their leaders, and if Parliament would not reform itself the people of Britain would take on the task and, if necessary, would use violence.

During the years which followed Waterloo, there began throughout the country a steady movement of men pledged to work and if necessary to fight for reform. The leaders were, for the most part, level-headed men who would go to almost any lengths to achieve their ends constitutionally and peaceably, but they were also determined not to be turned from them by chicanery or force. The method which they first tried was that of holding public meetings in the larger towns and passing resolutions or drawing up petitions in favour of reform. These would be sent to Parliament and there presented by any sympathetic member who would undertake the task. (It was not always easy to find one but there were a few of the younger Whigs who were always ready to help.)

It was all peaceful and constitutional enough, but behind these decorous proceedings lay the growing anger of a frustrated people and the threat of a resort to force by desperate men who had little but their lives to lose and found even those hardly worth saving. Spies were kept busy, and their reports began to show a pattern of something more menacing than the burning of a few isolated mills. They told of the great open-air meetings which were being held in such towns as Birmingham, Leeds and Manchester, and all their reports agreed on the orderly and disciplined way in which the men marched to the place of meeting and formed up when they got there. The leaven of the old soldiers was beginning to bring results, and many of the columns of workers who assembled in the fields and open spaces near the towns had been drilled by the men who had stormed the breaches at Badajoz and Ciudad or had served the guns at Waterloo. The spies took fright at what they believed to be the beginning of organized armed insurrection, though the men's leaders gave out reassuringly that all this marching and halting and dressing was only a better way of getting the men to assemble and to form an audience and, in fact, that a little discipline prevented straggling and rioting and general misbehaviour by individuals.

It may have been true. In some parts of Britain it undoubtedly was true, but not in the angry and stubborn North, where living conditions were the worst in England. The spies saw, at the peril of their lives, assemblies of men who were indeed drilling, though not within miles of any place where a meeting was to be held. It was on the lonely moors of the Pennines and along the Scottish border that these nightly drills went on, often in almost total darkness, since the men in the ranks had only had time to leave their work and to go, unfed, to the drill ground. The men who watched them told, too, of more dangerous tendencies than would seem to be justified by the pacific purpose of drilling in order to form up as an orderly mass at a meeting. It was not, for instance, necessary for that purpose to practice the movements for preparing to receive cavalry, nor for advancing in skirmishing order. Still less was it necessary to practice arms drill, though the men were armed with nothing but cudgels cut from the hedges or stakes torn from fences. All these things were observed and reported with more or less accuracy to Lord Sidmouth, the Home Secretary, and by him to the Cabinet.

The government was thoroughly alarmed. Just as Pitt had expected to be murdered in the time of the Jacobins, so now the Tories had visions of huge columns of angry men, all armed to the teeth, coming from every county and marching together on London for an intensified repetition of the Gordon Riots. They knew how feeble were their own resources if they should be compelled to put London into a state of defence or to fight for their own lives in Westminster. There were no civilian police anywhere in the country. What order was kept in the towns was still in the hands of the watchmen, the Dogberry and Verges of Shakespeare, who were nearly always aging men and often useless even for the apprehending of a single malefactor. The Bow Street Runners, who were the first detectives, were brave and fairly efficient, but they were few in number and could not be spared from London itself. There remained only the Army, which could always be called out in case of serious trouble, but even the Tories hesitated to employ this weapon unless it were absolutely necessary.

Any brush between the troops and rioters must involve casualties, and however justified the soldiers' actions might have been, the death and the sufferings of the wounded would be laid at the door of the government who would be called tyrants and murderers. There was additional anxiety in the absence from the country of so many of the best-trained battalions, some of whom were still in France and Belgium, while others were dispersed in garrisons overseas. The business of demobilization had begun soon after Waterloo, and the units who were at home were not up to strength or very reliable as to discipline.

The government's anxiety caused an unhappy incident in 1819 at St. Peter's Fields, Manchester, the scene of what was ever afterward known as "The Peterloo Massacre." An open-air meeting had been arranged which was to be addressed by the famous Orator Hunt, one of the leading agitators for reform.

Samuel Bamford, who presided at the meeting, left a detailed account of it in his *Autobiography of a Working Man*. The crowd began to assemble in St. Peter's Fields an hour or two before the meeting was due to start, and the first comers were surprised, though not alarmed, to see mounted troops drawn up in line on two sides of the ground. The crowd were in holiday mood, the men wearing their best suits, the women and children gay with ribbons and favours. There were not many days of festival in their lives, and any outing was a treat to them. So happy were they at first that they even cheered the soldiers, not, apparently, anticipating any danger from them and imagining that they were there to keep order and make sure that the meeting was peaceably conducted.

As the day went on, the Fields became filled with a dense crowd, as one by one the deputations from various towns marched in in something like military order and wheeled to form up in their allotted place. Hunt was late and Bamford opened the meeting and spoke himself, till distant cheering and a movement in the outer ranks of the audience told him that the speakers' procession was approaching. Hunt and his red-capped escort drove on to the ground and were led through the crowd to the platform.

It was then that the magistrates, who were watching the scene from a window, sent orders to the troops to disperse the crowd and to arrest Hunt and the other speakers. To crown their folly they first gave the order to the Lancashire Yeomanry. The blunder lay in using these instead of the Hussars, who were trained men on disciplined horses and who, moreover, were disinterested, having no local connections. The Yeomanry were all local men, and many of their officers were the sons of millowners, so that there was from the start ill-feeling between them and the crowd. In addition they were less than half-trained, and the horses which they rode, being their own and for the most part hunters or farmhorses, were quite unused to manoeuvring with troops or to dealing with crowds. The Yeomanry rode into the crowd, laying about them with the flat of their sabres, but their line broke and they disappeared into the mass in little isolated groups or even as single troopers. They could not control their horses, and being frightened and angry, began to turn their wrists and use the edge of the sabre on the crowd. They made little progress. As they spurred into the crowd, the ranks at the back who were nearest to them pressed forward, and soon the whole assembly was locked in a struggling mass in which the Yeomen were embedded like currants in a cake. Men and women were pressed almost to death and some of them fell and were trampled by the horses, but the Yeomanry got no nearer to the platform and had all that they could do to defend and extricate themselves.

The second charge, made by the Hussars, was a different matter. They advanced at no more than a trot, in close formation, and cut through the crowd like a wedge till they reached the centre where Hunt stood. Even Bamford remembered that only a very few of them used their sabres at all, and those few only the flat of them. As soon as they could disentangle themselves, the crowd broke and fled in every direction while the furious Yeomen rode after them and tried to cut or ride them down. The Hussars, having done their duty, rode off escorting their prisoners. The infantry came as the crowd was dispersing and wounded a few with their bayonets. Mercifully, the guns arrived too late to be brought into action. Nine men and two women were killed and several hundreds wounded or injured, many of them by suffocation and the pressure of the crowd, some under the hooves of the horses.

The importance of the Peterloo massacre was its division of the country into two sharply contrasted factions, which, for once, did not coincide with the usual division of Whig and Tory. Though, for the most part, the Tories expressed approval of the action which the Manchester magistrates had taken, there were many who looked with horror on the use of troops to disperse crowds and on the excessive violence which had been employed. The Whigs, on the other hand, while mostly condemning the magistrates, included a number of men who wished for reforms and especially for parliamentary reform but shrank from the idea of violence as strongly as from the threat of revolution. The Prince Regent, with that lack of tact which so often distinguished him, sent a message of congratulation to the Manchester authorities, which roused the Common

Council of London, a body by no means radical, to send a protest to the Prince Regent. It was especially noticeable that many newspapers expressed their indignation at the action of the magistrates and that among them were papers which were generally far from supporting radical or liberal views and politics.

The most outspoken protest came from the Whig aristocracy, who, in many counties, organized or attended meetings and spoke against the excessive use of force at Peterloo. One of the biggest meetings was that held in the West Riding of Yorkshire and presided over by the Lord Lieutenant of the West Riding, Earl Fitzwilliam, whom the government deprived of his office for his contumacy. All over England there were riots and threats of violence. In Lancashire, as Bamford notes, there was a steady production of weapons made from the everyday implements of the farm and the workshop—scythes, hatchets, old sword blades, anything that could be converted to the use of killing. At Manchester the mob stoned a special constable to death, while Newcastle keelmen assaulted their magistrates with showers of brickbats and cries of "Blood for blood!"

These outbreaks, and the threat of yet more, alarmed the government into a panic of fresh lawmaking, and before the end of the year they passed six new acts prohibiting private drilling and arms-bearing and most kinds of out-of-door meetings, so restricting the freedom of the press as practically to silence the cheaper papers such as were likely to be bought and read by the working men's leaders, and by the few working men and women who could read.

The Army of Occupation was coming back from Belgium and France, and with it came the Duke of Wellington, now Master of the Ordnance and a member of the Cabinet. The hand of the government was much strengthened by having more troops to deploy in case of serious trouble. It was equally strengthened by the presence in the nation's councils of the Duke, who could be relied on to support discipline and to co-operate in quelling disorder. As he was grimly to remark on a later occasion, "The people of England will be quiet; if not, there is a way to make them."

PART VI

1820-1832

XXXIV

D UKE OF WELLINGTON, Marquis of Wellington, Earl of Wellington in Somerset, Viscount Wellington of Talavera, Baron Douro of Wellesley, Prince of Waterloo in The Netherlands, Duke of Ciudad Rodrigo in Spain, Duke of Brunoy in France, Duke of Victoria, Marquis of Torres Vedras, Count of Vimeiro in Portugal, Field-Marshal of Great Britain, a Marshal of Prussia, a Marshal of Spain, a Marshal of France, a Marshal of Russia, a Marshal of Austria, a Marshal of Portugal—they are only a few of his titles and honours when he came home in 1819 to a Britain which was already beginning to forget him and would, before many years had passed, execrate him. General Alava had shown his foresight in his regret that the Duke should be about to embark on the stormy seas of politics.

It is seldom—so history shows—that a successful general becomes an equally successful politician or statesman. It would, perhaps, be something of a miracle if it should happen. The two roles are too far apart, too fundamentally and mutually exclusive for any ordinary man to shine in both. The soldier is accustomed to definite orders and prompt obedience; the politician proceeds by negotiation and persuasion.

It was, perhaps, more difficult for His Grace the Duke of Wellington to succeed as a civilian than for any other soldier known to history. Every chance and circumstance was against him—his peculiar position as a soldier and a European figure, the country to which he returned, the times in which he lived and, above all, his own nature. His country was Britain, always suspicious of a soldier, whether he be field-marshal or private, and always a little too ready to discard in times of regained peace the man who has done most to regain it. Moreover, it was a Britain of which he knew little, from which he had been too long absent and with which he was out of touch, as he was out of sympathy; a Britain of new ideas and new movements, impatient of old restraints and intolerant of old privileges and distinctions; a Britain wherein every man noisily asserted the right to shout as loud as he pleased, whether he had anything to say or not.

Wellington was essentially a man of the eighteenth century, of the old aristocratic tradition, and it was his fate to be called to high political office at the time when Britain was breaking with the eighteenth century and all that it meant and that he represented. It would yet take years to accomplish the destruction of the power of the old landed aristocracy, but the process was beginning, and nothing could stop or delay it.

Now, at the beginning of the nineteenth century, Britain was passing into a new phase, an altered system of values, when ability, self-reliance and, above all, wealth were to replace the old values of aristocracy and the land. Pitt had given the first impetus to the movement when, in doubling the numbers of the House of Lords, he had admitted the first legislators to come from the world of finance and commerce. Before his time the Lords had, in fact, controlled the whole country by their own powers and through the influence of the Commons, which they virtually owned by skilful political management and unashamed bribery. Pitt, in increasing the number and diluting the quality of the Lords, had almost imperceptibly knocked from under them the first prop of their power and created a new type of peer whose values were totally unlike the traditional values of his predecessors.

This was the first sign to Wellington that the world which he had known and the values which he had unquestioningly accepted were no longer supreme. He was typical of the old aristocracy, so it is little wonder that he found the changes unwelcome. Still less did he, whose life had been based on discipline and absolute obedience, find anything pleasing in the new spirit of liberty and free speech which was spreading through Britain, and the growth of what, for want of a better word, was beginning to call itself democracy. He was sharply made aware of it soon after his return, by the outspoken championship of the Queen's cause by the London mob. It is often misleading to speak of "The People" or "The Workers," terms which can cover almost any section of the community that suits the writer or speaker, but the London mob was, in the early nineteenth century, a distinct entity and a frightening sign of the growing license of the times—so at least it must have seemed to him.

The London mob had felt their power during the Gordon Riots of 1780, when for days on end they terrorized the city and respected no authority but that of mounted troops or loaded muskets. The French mob, ten years later, showed what power lay in a spontaneous rising of men and women with a wrong to avenge or a grievance to remove. There was something in the violence of Londoners which was far more terrifying, because they were more compact and unanimous than the mobs in the provinces, who burned the mills and wrecked the machines, something which justified the prevalent fear of Jacobinism, of which they were often accused. Even when they did not proceed to actual violence and destruction they had a way of making their feelings and convictions felt as a reality and a threat. The government, which had no civilian force of police on which to rely, was somewhat at a loss as to how to deal with them. The only recourse, in time of real trouble, was to call out the military, and the aftermath of Peterloo served as a warning of how sternly Britain resented the use of armed force whenever it went beyond the absolute necessary minimum.

Nor was the new legislation of much help to the government, because the mob never seemed to assemble in any form, or in any way under which it could be touched, even by the spate of new Acts which Parliament in its panic passed. The mob, except when it was in action, was intangible. It assembled like a cloud of insects and, having worked off its violence, dispersed as insects do. It had no rules, no leaders other than those of the moment, no form which could be forbidden as trade unions were. It could not be charged with holding illegal meetings or passing seditious resolutions, because it was amorphous and irresponsible. It was extremely difficult even to arrest ringleaders or workers of damage to property, since the soldiers were generally too much occupied in restraining the mob in the streets and defending themselves to have time to arrest individuals, and were often set to guard streets or buildings without moving from them, so that the mob joyously marched off to destroy some other district. The Londoners were unruly, outspoken, excitable but not, on the whole and except for rare outbursts like that of 1780, wantonly destructive or murderous. They would gaily break all the windows of a house but seldom proceed to burn it down, as they would shout abuse at individuals whom they hated, yet stop short of actually assaulting them. The worst of them were always, as they had been in 1780, the ruffians from slums who joined a crowd without caring what its object was or what slogans it was shouting, as long as they had an opportunity for looting and drunkenness, so that they spent much of their violence on inns and wineshops. Even during the Gordon Riots, which were unquestionably anti-Catholic in origin and object, many chapels and houses of Papists were wrecked and burned by men who would have been hard put to it to say what the Reformation meant or when it had happened.

It was men such as these who were the real danger and supplied the real viciousness of the London mob, and there was no shortage of them. It was the time when rumour of great wealth in the cities, especially in London, was attracting crowds of men and women who had found life intolerable in the countryside because of starvation or lack of work. They came, during those years, in floods into the big towns, not knowing how or where they would live, where they could get work, where they could find a rotten roof to shelter them and some thrown-out scraps to feed them. They herded together in alleys and sheds, crowded, insanitary, lousy and rat-ridden, lacking anything that distinguishes a man's life from that of a beast.

One thing they never lacked and that was cheap and ruinous liquor. Drunkenness racked and destroyed them as much as did disease and filth. It was the era of cheap liquor, especially of cheap gin, when the lowest taverns displayed boards offering to make men drunk for a penny and dead drunk for twopence, with the luxury of free straw on which to fall and lie until they had slept off the fumes. They had nothing to hope for, nothing to live for, and the gin offered to them at least a few moments of false exhilaration and a few hours of forgetfulness. Also it made them as careless of their lives as madmen and as savage as wolves whenever they had a chance of destroying or killing in the streets. Apart from these, the drink-inflamed and the almost professionally ruffians, and except on the rarest of occasions, the excitement of the London mob was more apt to find expression in breaking windows and hurling abuse than in actual destruction and killing. They had one safety valve, which was always denied to the French peasant, in the outspokenness of their public outcries and a certain tradition of free speech.

Even His Royal Highness, the Prince Regent, was fond of telling a wholly apocryphal story of his epic fight with a bullying butcher on the Steyne at Brighton.

Both the Prince and Wellington experienced the mob's taste for free comment and for the threat, if not the actuality, of physical violence during the public excitement which followed the Bill of Pains and Penalties and the exclusion of the Queen from the coronation. When the Prince appeared at the theatre, shortly after the withdrawal of the bill, he was greeted by the occupants of the cheaper seats with shouts of, "Where's your wife, George?" and had the wit to advance to the front of his box and bow in acknowledgment, whereon the shouts changed to cheers at a sporting gesture of defiance. He had an experience which might have been serious when driving through London to open a session of Parliament. There was the usual jeering and abuse from the crowd which he could afford to ignore, but as the coach passed down the Mall, one of its windows was shattered by either a stone or a shot from an airgun. His Life Guards of the escort closed round the coach and a few cavalry rode into the crowd to search for the would-be assassin. They never found him, and little further fuss was made about the incident. It was generally accepted that there had been no serious attempt on the Royal Person and that the incident had been rather an excess of exuberant criticism than the work of a would-be murderer.

Wellington was known to be a strong opponent of the Queen's cause and during these troubled weeks had his first taste of the unpopularity which was so soon to be his constant lot. More than once as he rode, after his custom, unattended between his residence, Apsley House, and Westminster, parties of hooligans shouted at him and even, confident in their superior numbers, surrounded him and threatened to pull him off his horse. But His Grace, who had watched unmoved the slow approach of the French Imperial Guard up the slope of Mont St. Jean, was not the man to be frightened by a few ruffians, and it was only necessary for him to turn his horse and change his grip on his whip to send them flying to a safer distance. He told the story to Creevey: "The mob are too contemptible to be thought about for a moment! About thirty of them ran away from me in the Park this morning because I pulled up my horse when they were hooting. They thought I was going to fall upon them and give them what they deserved!" And, once, when he was surrounded by the mob who clamoured to him, demanding that he shout, "God save the Queen!" he obliged them by retorting, "Since you wish it, gentlemen, God save the Queen! And may all your wives be like her."

The mob admired courage above everything, and they were not yet in the ugly mood which was to make them really dangerous. A few years later during the riots in favour of the Reform Bill, they were so dangerous that, though the Duke rode about London unattended, he consented to have locks fitted to the doors of his carriage, in case the mob should try to pull him out of it. His courage was so absolute and indestructible a part of him, whether it was at Talavera or Vitoria, in Hyde Park or Piccadilly, and his contempt for the mob so complete that with nothing but his horse and his whip, he was ready to face any number of hooligans; but a man seated in his carriage is in a poor position for defence, and he yielded to the request of his wife and his servants to take such elementary measures of defence and protection. Brave as he was he had never been foolhardy, and no man knew better the use of parapet and

breastwork in defence. His unpopularity was intense, but short-lived.
There were yet to be years of comparative peace for him before he would
hear the mob screaming round his house on June 18—the anniversary
of Waterloo.

XXXV

I N 1822 the Tories suffered a grievous loss in the death of the Marquis of Londonderry. He had succeeded to the title in the previous year, but was and will always be better known by his courtesy title of Castle-reagh. He had been one of Britain's most distinguished and successful Foreign Secretaries, but overwork and nervous exhaustion had sapped his strength, and his friends had begun to notice signs of derangement in his mind. He was often melancholy, and though he worked as hard as ever he had done, he seemed to be without confidence in himself or hope for his policies. The next signs of his disease were his oddity of speech and, more than anything else, his fits of panic in which he believed that there were endless conspiracies against him and that he might be murdered at any moment.

One day in August, the Duke of Wellington had an interview with Castlereagh in London and was thoroughly alarmed by his symptoms at first. They discussed foreign affairs for some time, and, afterward, Wellington reported that "he never heard him converse upon affairs with more clearness and strength of mind than that day." He was therefore the more startled when Castlereagh broke off the conversation and began to talk about the danger which threatened him. "In the middle of the conversation," wrote Charles Greville, to whom Wellington recounted the incident, "he said, 'To prove to you what danger I am in, my own servants think so, and that I ought to go off directly, and they keep my horses saddled that I may get away quickly; they think that I should not have time to go away in a carriage.' Then, ringing the bell violently, he said to the servant, 'Tell me, sir, instantly who ordered my horses here; who sent them up to Town?' " The man answered that the horses were at Cray, and had never been in Town. Wellington was so much startled and distressed by Castlereagh's manner and appearance that he instantly took charge of the case and wrote to Castlereagh's physician, Dr. Bankhead, asking him to attend Castlereagh at once and telling him of his fear that his patient was going mad. A few days later Bankhead confirmed his suspicion and treated the patient, after the manner of the time, by bleeding him copiously. This drastic measure appeared to have done him good, or at the least to have quieted him, so that his people were able to move him from London to his country house at Foot's Cray, but it was only a temporary improvement. Almost as soon as he arrived he fell once more into the torment of his delusions and fears. His household took the sensible precaution of removing all—as they thought—his razors and knives, fearing that he might commit suicide. Wellington drove down to visit him and decided that his must be the ungrateful task of telling Castlereagh that his illness was too bad to allow him to continue in foreign affairs, or in politics at all.

It had never been Wellington's way to shirk a task, however unpleasant, but equally never to consider the feelings of an individual when the task had to be done. It cannot have been anything but an aggravation of Castlereagh's disease when the Duke said to him, without preamble or equivocation, "It is my duty to tell you that your mind is deranged." Having thus comforted and cheered the patient, His Grace drove back to London. A few hours later, Castlereagh cut his own throat with a small knife which his servants had overlooked when he, with a madman's cunning, had hidden it away.

The Tories had been in office for some twenty years and had every intention of staying there, but it was not to be an easy task. The loss of Castlereagh deprived them of one of their ablest men, a great Foreign Secretary and a man whom all the party respected. The obvious person to replace him was George Canning, but somehow nobody seemed to want him. He had been too free with his tongue and his pen, his jeers and sarcasms, so that by now he had more enemies than any other member of Parliament. A short time before Castlereagh's death, the Cabinet had had the really brilliant idea of sending Canning out to India as Governor-General and, to that end, had appointed him to the Board of Control so that he might learn a little of the business of ruling India. The vacancy caused by the loss of Castlereagh impelled a hurried change of plan. The Whigs were gathering strength, and the growing demand for reform was adding to it. Much as the Tories disliked Canning, they could not afford to let their best debater in the Commons go abroad for a period of years. They needed him in their councils but here was another difficulty. The King hated Canning, who had opposed him over the matter of the Bill of Pains and Penalties. Not only did Canning take the Queen's side but he openly objected to the country's paying the enormous Bill of Costs which the King incurred. Many thousands of pounds had been spent on searching in various Continental ports and towns for witnesses to the Queen's alleged misdemeanours and then on bringing them to England and there maintaining them during the hearing. Canning thought, and told the King, that as His Majesty was suing as a private person, he ought to bear the cost out of his own pocket. To this His Majesty, having by now seen the utter worthlessness of most of the witnesses, strongly objected, and Canning offered his resignation, though his colleagues persuaded him to withdraw it. Lord Liverpool, the Prime Minister, being a man of sound good sense, at once offered to Canning the Foreign Office and the leadership of the House, and Canning, with some hesitation, accepted.

Castlereagh's death broke a link with the traditions of the eighteenth century and its aristocratic predominance in home politics and foreign affairs. The strange thing is that this was still as strong as ever in the Whig party and so continued long after the Tories had begun to admit representatives of commerce and finance to high places in their councils. Pitt had started the movement with his lavish creations of new peers, and the new men in the Commons—men such as Canning and Peel— came from bourgeois families rather than from the aristocracy. It might have been expected that a party which was showing signs of moving with the times, and with the growing feeling for democracy, would have been the men to press for parliamentary reform, but it was not so. The reformers came mostly from the Whigs, who yet remained serenely patrician and looked with suspicion on even such a brilliant man as Brougham, because he was not of their class and was suspected of being what later came to be known as a "career politician." The rising men in the Whig party were still members of the landowning class, such as Lambton and Lord John Russell, who with their leader Earl Grey were soon to take the most prominent part in passing the first Reform Bill. It may be that men who themselves have risen from comparative security to high place are less generous than they might be to others who try to follow them and less considerate of the class which sired them—undoubtedly the harshest employers in the mines and the mills were men who themselves had risen, by their own efforts, from the loom or the coal face. They had fought their way upward and were inclined to look on their former equals as either enemies or weaklings. When Pitt's Com-

bination Laws were at last repealed and unions were legal again, there
was a concerted effort by most big employers to prevent their formation
by mutual agreement not to employ union men. The feeling was strongest in the Durham and Northumberland coal fields, and opponents of
the aristocratic tradition must have observed with some displeasure that
the only pits which freely allowed men to belong to unions were those
which belonged to the Marquis of Londonderry and the Earl of Durham.

The Whigs, secure in their own untroubled and patrician ways, felt
no fear of competition from men who were less fortunate, so that such
men as John Lambton were comfortably able to hold and express far
more radical views than such reformers as Cobbett or Hunt or old
Major Cartwright. So the difference between the two great parties grew
wider and their relations more strained as the Tories became less exclusive to persons and more resistant to ideas, while the Whigs became
wilder in their ideas and remained as confident as ever in the serene right
of their class to put the ideas into practice without help from outside.

The King was capricious, and neither party could count on enjoying
his favour for many weeks ahead. He had always favoured the Whigs who
had hoped to be called to office soon after his accession. But the years
went by and they were no nearer to their goal. He had not yet forgiven
them for the way in which they had opposed his effort to get rid of his
wife. On the other hand, he held it against the Tories that they had
failed to set him free by passing the bill. He had forgiven Canning's
opposition to his wishes in the matter, but he did not trust him and he
did not like Peel. In fact the only member of the Cabinet for whom he
felt any affection was Wellington, whom he would gladly have had for
Premier. The affection was not returned. Wellington despised his master.
He was further and continually provoked by the military airs which the
King gave himself and his tendency to dogmatize, over the dinner table,
on tactics and drill. Charles Greville quotes a typical conversation in his
diary:

"When the Duke was at Brighton in the winter, he and the King had
a dispute about the army. It began (it was at dinner) by the King's saying that the Russians or the Prussians (I forget which) were the best
infantry in the world. The Duke said, 'Except your Majesty's.' The King
then said that the English cavalry were the best, which the Duke denied;
then that an inferior number of French regiments would always beat a
superior number of English and, in short, that they were not half so effective. The King was very angry; the debate waxed warm, and ended
by His Majesty rising from the table and saying, 'Well, it is not for me
to dispute on such a subject with your Grace.' "

Wellington might dislike the King as a man but to the throne he was utterly loyal, and though he did not want to be Prime Minister, he would never refuse should the King insist on it. "The King's government must be carried on" was one of his maxims, and in 1828 it seemed that if he did not undertake it there was no one else capable or willing and the Whigs would come in at last.

The Tories had done well enough under Lord Liverpool's Premiership. He was not a man of first-class ability, but he was capable and honest and had the great merit of being able to get on with other men and to hold his party together without apparent effort. In 1827 he had a stroke, and Canning succeeded him, but this at once caused a split in the party. Not only did none of the Tories like Canning but also those who opposed Catholic emancipation distrusted his soundness on the question. Wellington, Eldon, Peel and four others resigned from the Cabinet. Canning, who was quite conscious of his reputation and unpopularity, had tried to ensure the safety of his administration by forming a coalition with the Whigs, but Grey refused to have anything to do with him, and of those who joined him, only Brougham and Russell were men of real ability. The King was furious with Wellington for his resignation, the more so because it was becoming evident that no one except the Duke had the determination and the prestige to form a strong Cabinet and keep it in order.

He would not have Wellington if he could avoid it so made the unhappy choice of Goderich, of whom it was said that he was "as firm as a bulrush". Goderich had little to recommend him and did not impress his colleagues by his habit of bursting into tears whenever he came up against a difficulty. (He was also commonly known as "Goody Goderich".) He formed a Cabinet, though Wellington and Peel still held sternly aloof, and, having wrestled with the task of governing for less than six months, resigned and wept himself out of office.

For a short time there was parliamentary chaos and no one could be induced to take office. The Whigs would not risk it, preferring to look cynically on while the Tories blundered and failed. No Tory was anxious to undertake the task when such important matters as emancipation and reform were so dangerously near. Nor did any man of either party wish to lead a government under so raffish and untrustworthy a master. But the King's government must be carried, and His Majesty turned to the one man whom he knew he could always trust, whom he called "Arthur." Wellington unhesitatingly agreed to form a Cabinet. In January 1828 he became Prime Minister.

XXXVI

THE WELLINGTON administration lasted for two years and was almost uniformly unsuccessful. Probably Wellington would not have been an outstanding Prime Minister at any time, but he could hardly have had a time less suitable for a man of his views and temperament. It was an age of change and he hated change, of growing democracy and he despised democracy. The routine of office and its thousand petty annoyances were an intolerable burden to one who had known, all his life, the simple and direct life of the Army. Before he had been in office for more than a few months, he complained that half of his time was wasted by "assuaging" what gentlemen call their "feelings." He did not care for most of his colleagues and especially not for Peel, which was additionally unfortunate as Peel led the Commons, which duty threw him into constant contact and consultation with the Prime Minister. Wellington once went so far as to remark that they were a most unfortunate combination because, "I've got no small-talk and Peel's no gentleman."

Short-lived as it was, the Wellington administration had its triumphs. Greatly against its leader's inclination, it repealed the Test Acts, which had excluded dissenters from public offices and from the universities, on grounds once expressed by Dr. Samuel Johnson in the words, "Why, sir, a cow is a very good animal in the field but we turn her out of the Garden." It also granted Catholic emancipation, a proposal so repugnant to the Prime Minister that the wits said that he had risen in the Chamber and given the order, "My Lords, right about face!" This belated act of justice increased the unpopularity of the Cabinet and, most unfairly, since he hated it more than anyone, of the Duke. A strong hatred of the Papacy was and remains one of the very few political convictions which can always be relied on to arouse the people of Britain. So strong was the feeling at this time in some quarters that Croker, the diarist, told a friend, "The Duchess of Richmond had a number of rats under glass cases in her drawing room," to whom she gave the names of the "Apostates," those who voted for the Emancipation Bill.

The bill also caused Peel's resignation, but his short time in office had given him the chance of setting on foot his most famous enterprise, the formation of a corps of civilian police. They were first tried in the metropolitan area, where their blue uniforms and top hats caused much amusement and not a little indignation to the mob, who christened them "Blue Lobsters," and later "Peelers," or "Bobbies," after their originator.

Another of Wellington's handicaps was his growing distaste for King George IV and the uncertainty about the character of the Duke of Clarence who would succeed him. Sir H. Cooke wrote to Lord Fitzgerald that the betting in the London clubs was "an even chance that Clarence will be in a strait waistcoat before the King dies," but in June 1830 those who had risked their money on the Duke of Clarence's probable lunacy lost it when the King died and Clarence succeeded him as William IV.

The new King may not have been eligible for a strait waistcoat but he was decidedly odd, though this rather endeared him to his people, since his oddities, being harmless, seemed preferable to the vicious sanity of his predecessor. The new King, who had served for many years in his father's Navy, retained much of the manner and all of the vocabulary of the quarter-deck—his first recorded remark as King was, "This is a damned bad pen!" when signing a document at the first meeting of his Privy Council. He was a genial and unpretentious person who saw no reason why his elevation to the throne should affect his habits or behaviour. It seemed to him quite a normal thing to go for a stroll through London unattended, to walk arm-in-arm with any friend whom he chanced to meet and to hail a hackney cab when he felt tired. Such actions were as natural to him as opening the window of his coach and spitting into the road on his way to open Parliament, and to the end of his life he never lost the habit of getting drunk at public dinners and making, while in that state, the most injudicious of speeches.

He had many and solid virtues. He really meant to do his duty, if someone would tell him what it was, and though he entertained violent prejudices against individuals, he tried to deal fairly with both political parties. By temperament and habit he was a strong Tory and Churchman—when receiving the homage of a newly consecrated bishop, he said, "Bishop, I charge you, as you shall answer before Almighty God, that you never, by word or deed, give any encouragement to those damned Whigs who would upset the Church of England." His wife, Queen Adelaide, was an even stronger Tory and was suspected, probably without any justification, of making all his political decisions for him. William was a devoted, though not a legitimate, father and cared for his brood of ten Fitzclarences by giving them peerages or commissions in the Army. It must be set to the Queen's credit that she was invariably kind to the slightly unorthodox family over which she came to preside.

It was hard on William that it should have been he who would have to carry the burden of such an immense constitutional change as parliamentary reform. His Tory principles made the idea repugnant to him, and intellectually he was not fitted for long and delicate negotiations. Yet Britain might have fared worse under an abler king. William hated the idea of reform, which he equated, in his muddled mind, with Jacobinism and revolution. He did not give up hope until the last minute of somehow being able to strangle it before it became law. Also, he underestimated both the quality and the numbers of those who were pressing for it, seeing them as a turbulent crowd of artisans, all wearing red caps of liberty with a guillotine hidden somewhere round the corner. He visualized a Reform Parliament as something like the French Assembly during the Revolution. He was, in fact, one of a small number of men like Wellington and Eldon who refused to think of reform as a possibility.

Yet no intelligent and unprejudiced person in that year of 1829 could seriously question the need for reform, so ridiculous and anachronistic had Britain's electoral system become. It stood in that year almost as it had been laid down after the "Glorious Revolution" of 1688. When William and Mary came to the throne, Britain was almost entirely an agricultural country, so it was not amiss that the men who were to govern her should be men of the countryside—the old title of Knights of the Shire was still applicable. The growth of population, especially in the cities, had rendered the system farcical within the next hundred years. In 1829 such great cities as Leeds, Manchester, Sheffield and Birmingham returned no member to Parliament, while the county of Cornwall returned forty-four, of whom eighteen came from the area of twenty-eight by twelve square miles surrounding Liskeard. Yorkshire returned the same number of members, two, as a small borough like Sudbury, and the whole of Scotland returned only forty-five.

All counties had two members each. Most of these counties and the big towns, which had been burghs at the time that the system was adopted, had "scot and lot" elections which roughly meant that any rate-payer of the amount of forty shillings a year had the right to vote. But the bulk of members were returned by the "close" or "rotten" boroughs. These were constituencies which were the property of an individual who either represented it himself in Parliament or sent his nominee. These boroughs were bought and sold without shame or concealment, and their patrons were generally willing to sell the seats to any aspiring candidate. In 1829 the average price of a seat seems to have been about £6,000 during the life of the Parliament following the election, though more cautious buyers sometimes preferred to pay from £1,500 to £1,800 a year in case that Parliament should not run its full term.

Many of these "close" boroughs were notorious. The Sudbury voters invariably met before an election to agree on a price for their votes, the list price at the beginning of the century being £30 each. Shoreham, in Sussex, was, as Lord Winchelsea remarked, "a whore who is anyone's for their money." At Haslemere in Surrey, the voting was in the hands of a colony of Cumberland miners whom Lord Lonsdale had settled there for no other reason than to protect his interest and to vote as he told them. The notorious Old Sarum, which had once been the subject of one of Edmund Burke's most famous attacks, consisted of bare ploughed fields and seven voters who returned their two members. Sir T. R. M. Butler, in his *Passing of the Great Reform Bill,* writes: "Thus the main anomalies of the system were three; many insignificant places returned members while many important towns did not; even in large towns the members were often elected by a tiny fraction of the population; counties and Parliamentary Boroughs in England, regardless of their relative importance, returned alike two members."

There was no system of ballot, so that every voter was watched by his candidate's or his opponent's agent as he went to the polling booth, which opened a wide field for bribery and intimidation. (In a notorious election at Newark, the Duke of Newcastle evicted all his tenants who did not vote for his candidate.) Election then lasted for two or three weeks, during which time the countryside was regaled with what were called the "Three B's"—beer, bands and bribery. It was considered quite fair for a candidate's agent to make a number of the opposing side's voters dead drunk and then to lock them up in a coach-house until the poll was over.

In many cases this enormous expense was borne by the candidate, in others by the owner of the borough, or jointly by him and the candidate. Durham County was not a closed constituency and the Lambton interest was strong there, but Lord Durham, who as John George Lambton had contested it, calculated that his last election expenses amounted to some £30,000. The electoral system had once been fairly realistic, but now it was farcical, since the man who could afford the greatest sum for expenses was the most certain of a seat. The most damning accusation which can be brought against it is surely this: In England and Wales there were, in all, 513 constituencies. Of these, 300 were either controlled or owned outright by members of the House of Lords.

It was the law in those days that a general election should follow the accession of a new king. It was also the custom, as it is today, that each session of Parliament should be opened by the King with the "Speech from the Throne," which was written not by him but by the incoming Cabinet and foreshadowed the legislation which they proposed to introduce during the life of that Parliament and especially during the first session. All Britain—or all of that part of Britain which concerned itself with politics—eagerly awaited William IV's speech, knowing that it would embody the policy of the Duke of Wellington and his colleagues. Everyone knew that the Duke was opposed to reform. He had made no secret of it. Equally, most people believed that there would be some reference to it in the Speech from the Throne. The more forward-looking members of his own party, no less than the Whigs, believed that he would make some concession, some token offer to meet the general demand.

Some years earlier, Lord John Russell for the Whigs had made out a case for the disenfranchisement of the close borough of Grampound on account of some more than usually blatant instance of corruption, and Castlereagh, for the Tories, had had the sense to accept it without argument. Surely, the Whigs and a large section of the Tories felt, the Duke would have the political wisdom to do the same sort of thing. There were many close boroughs where the representation was so absurd that he could throw them to his enemies, as travellers in sleighs across the Russian steppes are said to cut a horse loose to appease the pursuing wolves. There was Gatton, which had one voter and two members; Winchelsea, with seven voters, and Rye with fourteen, each returning two members; Aylesbury, which could be bought for £7,000 and Hastings for £6,000; Old Sarum, which Cobbett called "the accursed hill," where, as Burke said, "The representatives, more in number than the voters, only serve to inform us that this was once a place of trade and sounding with the busy hum of men, though now you can trace the streets only by the colour of the corn, and its sole manufacture is members of Parliament." It seemed to both Tory and Whig alike impossible that Wellington should be unaware of the intense feeling in the country or, if he were aware of it, so crassly stupid and indifferent as not to make some sort of attempt to throw a sop to the clamouring reformers, however worthless any such a concession might later prove to be. A closely packed and excited House waited tensely for the Speech from the Throne. When it was delivered there was no reference to reform, and Earl Grey, the Leader of the Whigs in the Lords, rose on November 2, 1830, to fire the first shot in the coming battle. In accordance with custom and tradition, he first thanked His Majesty for his gracious speech and then regretted that it contained no reference to reform.

In a tense and silent House the Duke of Wellington rose to reply to Earl Grey. Even now it was not too late, so some, more hopeful than others, thought, for him to indicate that he proposed to make some sort of concession to public demand. But those who dared to hope or who feared this had never seen the Duke taking up a defensive position which he proposed to hold to the last man and the last round. Compromise was not in his nature and had never been his habit, and whatever may have been his shortcomings, a lack of courage physical or moral was not among them. Earl Grey's speech was to him like the advancing skirmishers of the enemy and, after his custom, he opened fire with cannon and small arms. So far was he from contemplating the least shadow of reform that he treated the House to a panegyric on the British electoral system as it stood at that day. It was, he declared, as near perfect as lay in the wit of man to attain perfection, and it was impossible to improve on it. Not only that but, had it not already existed and had he been charged with inventing a system, he would not dare to claim that he could think of one so faultless but his effort would be to devise one as near as possible to the pattern. He ended, to the shocked amazement of his party and the barely concealed delight of his opponents, by saying, "Under these circumstances, I am not prepared to bring forward any measure of the description alluded to by the Noble Lord. And I am not only not prepared to bring forward any measure of this nature, but I will at once declare that, as far as I am concerned, and as long as I hold any station in the government of this country, I shall always feel it my duty to resist such measures when proposed by others."

The Duke sat down again in the shocked and silent House. To the Whigs it was as though he had found his position surrounded on all sides and his troops outnumbered by a thousand to one and had still decided to hold out. The Tories felt more as though he had turned his own guns round and mowed down his own infantry.

His Grace was not usually susceptible to atmosphere, yet even he began to wonder, as he sat down again, whether he had said something amiss. He turned to Lord Aberdeen, the Foreign Secretary, who sat beside him, and asked, "I haven't said too much, have I?" (The fact that he asked the question showed how far he was from the world and the ways that he knew.) Aberdeen answered grimly, "You'll hear about it"; and, when another Peer, arriving late, asked Aberdeen what the Duke had said, Aberdeen answered, "He said we're going out."

Lord Aberdeen was right. After that candid statement of policy, delivered with such appalling abruptness, there was no hope left for the Tory government—not even the few months' delay which a few minor concessions, a few worthless sacrifices might have won them. The only member of it who did not seem disturbed was the Duke himself, who remarked a few days later to Lady Jersey, whom he met at a party, "Lord we shall not go out, you will see, we shall do very well."

"Never," wrote Lord Howick to his father Earl Grey on November 24, "was any administration so completely and so suddenly destroyed; and, I believe, entirely by the Duke's declaration; made, I suspect, in perfect ignorance of the state of public opinion."

XXXVII

S O IN 1830 the Whigs got the chance for which they had waited for
more than a quarter of a century and, having got it, seemed uncertain what to do with it. The only thing on which they were all agreed
was that they were pledged to introduce parliamentary reform. Beyond
that point the party split into small factions, each of which had its own
opinion about the best way and time to proceed. The cause of reform
had always been bedevilled by the multitude of self-styled experts who
were prepared at any time to lay down the principles which the bill must
follow, but who were very far from being prepared to consider any suggestions from anyone else. The leaders of the party in the Lords, Earl
Grey and Lord Holland, felt that it would be a mistake to hurry. "Reform will come," Grey said to Lord Durham, his son-in-law, "but not
in our time." Durham was young, able, self-opinionated and violently
quarrelsome and he was determined that reform should come in his time
and also in his own way.

Lord Brougham, who became Lord Chancellor in the new Cabinet,
was as determined as Durham but had his own recipe for reform and
had only with difficulty been prevented from introducing it as a Private
Member's Bill and robbing the government of the credit. Lord John
Russell was the technician of reform, which had been his lifelong study.
He knew more about the electoral system of Britain than anyone else in
his party, but he felt no great urgency about it. He was not unlike a man
who never gets a picture painted or a book finished because he can always think of some new detail which will improve it.

K

Separately their approaches were far apart. Together they made a formidable combination, and it was they, more than anyone else, who prepared the bill and forced it through Parliament, who persuaded the King to accept it and, most difficult task of all, outmanoeuvred the peers who tried to kill it. Sir T. R. M. Butler refers to "the statesmanship of Grey, the wisdom of Russell and the will of Durham" as the powers which drove the enterprise to its conclusion. Russell had the greatest part in drafting it, Grey steered it through the tedious and hazardous negotiations, and Durham, at the worst moments of crisis, threw the whole weight of his determination and the flame of his spirit into forcing the others to persist when they might have compromised and passed a truncated measure. It was not for nothing that he was known as "Radical Jack."

There was nothing radical about Grey's Cabinet when he announced their names. He had stated that while he believed that there was enough wisdom and force in his own class to manage the country he was "not averse from recognising merit in the commonalty, if he should meet with it." There was not much danger of that, for it was commonly said, "He loved the people but he loved them at a distance." He was shy and solitary, finding all his happiness on his own estates at Howick in Northumberland, disliking the rough and tumble of political life and detesting London.

He did not happen to meet with any merit in the commonalty, largely because he never met the commonalty. His Cabinet was said by statisticians to comprise the owners of more acres of land than any previous administration. Nor did Grey share the views of Thomas Jefferson who, when President of the United States, publicly thanked God that he could find positions for men of ability without having to employ his relations. Grey was happy to find room for six of his, so that his Cabinet was derisively known as "The Grey List." Yet it is only fair to remember that among his selections were five future Prime Ministers.

It was typical of the friendly and informal way in which the Cabinet was managed that when Grey had allotted all the offices still no one knew whose job it was to be to draft the Reform Bill. Characteristically he first mentioned it to Durham, his son-in-law, one winter evening as they were leaving the House. As he and Durham walked through the foggy night in Westminster, Grey casually said to him, "Oh, by the way, Lambton, I wish you would take charge of our reform bill," and, when Durham agreed, asked as casually if he minded letting Russell help him.

The invitation was casual but there was nothing casual in its acceptance, nor in the putting in hand of the work. Durham enthusiastically agreed to Russell as a colleague and himself asked for two more men,

Sir James Graham and Lord Duncannon. Graham, a Scotsman, had a good knowledge of the electoral problems of his own country. Duncannon was not only an excellent fellow but a connection by marriage of the Greys and the Lambtons. So there came into being the later famous "Committee of Four" who, in a matter of two months, overturned an electoral system which had sufficed Britain for something like a century and a half.

In January 1831 the committee had finished their work and presented their report to the Cabinet, who were delighted with the rapidity with which the task had been done, though when they read it and had time to think about it they were almost frightened by its drastic overturning of the whole tradition and basis of the British electoral system. Lord Durham and his colleagues had made a clean sweep of the system of close boroughs, ignoring the vested rights of their owners and the privileges of the electors. There was to be no constituency in Britain without a free election, and the seats which had belonged to the boroughs were to be distributed among the counties and the large towns, to conform with the growth and distribution of the population. There was a provision for the restriction of the right to vote to householders and ratepayers of a certain annual value—it had never been the idea to open the franchise to all the people, not perhaps for many years, when they might be expected to be educated to the idea and the responsibility of voting. As it was, the scheme was enough almost to terrify even the strongest supporters of reform like Grey and Holland, though the half-hearted were not displeased with it, believing that so wholesale a measure stood no chance of acceptance, which would save them all a lot of trouble.

The bill would have been more drastic still if Durham had had all his way, but he was ill when the Cabinet met and unable to take part in the discussions. It had been his particular desire to make voting by ballot a part of the bill and to hold elections triennially. He knew—and later events proved his wisdom—that unless every man in secret could vote as he pleased, it would never be possible to eliminate bribery from elections, and he believed that the people ought to have the right to decide on who should govern them at regular and not too distant intervals. In these, as in many other things, he was years ahead of his time, and as he was not there to fight for his views—which he would undoubtedly have done, being a notable fighter—the Cabinet thankfully took the opportunity of shelving his wilder ideas.

The bill was, they thought, drastic enough without any added frills, and there was no doubt that the King would never give his consent to any measure which included vote by ballot. As it stood, it was revolutionary, and the task of getting it through Parliament, especially the

Peers, and accepted by the King was terrifying in its difficulty. They decided to present it to Parliament at the opening of the new session in March and unanimously agreed that Russell should introduce it. Althorp would have done his best, but they had seen his best in recent financial debates and wanted no more of it. There could hardly have been a better choice than Lord John Russell. He was the chief draughtsman of the bill and he knew more about elections than any other man living. He was no great orator but he was capable of lucid and patient explanation and he was a man of unshakable courage and determination. He was, as a Tory member later remarked, "A little fellow not weighing eight stone," and his height was no more than five feet and two inches, but packed into that tiny body was a spirit and a calm self-assurance equal to any responsibility. According to Sidney Smith, he had once declared that though he knew nothing of naval matters, he would cheerfully take command of the Fleet if he thought it his duty to do so.

All political London was astir on that night of March 1, 1831, when Russell was to introduce the bill. In the great Whig houses the rooms were ablaze with the light of candles and all the curtains were drawn back, so that every window illuminated the streets, where restless and excited crowds moved up and down through the long hours of darkness, waiting for the latest news of some great matter which most of them did not begin to understand. In the lighted rooms the friends of reform sat at their dining tables for hour after hour and were prepared to sit as long as the debate should continue. In the precincts of Westminster were crowds of messengers and servants, whose duty it would be to run to the houses with the latest news or even the newest rumour of what was happening inside the House. Only the great Tory houses stood dark and shuttered, thereby incurring the displeasure of the crowd, who beguiled the hours of waiting by throwing stones at the windows of unfriendly houses though, after the way of crowds, they were not too discriminating in their choice and lustily pelted several houses whose owners had no connection with politics or were away from London.

The house on Cleveland Place, where Lord Durham was lying, sick and despairing at the untimely death of his eleven-year-old son and heir, almost came in for their attention, but they were luckily diverted and joyfully marched across the Green Park to attack Apsley House, the home of the Duke of Wellington. They would gladly have razed it to the ground and buried its owner beneath it, for he had made no secret of his undying hatred of reform in any shape.

But His Grace knew something about mobs and more than something about the tactics of defence, and it had never been his habit to be taken unaware by an attacking force. Apsley House stood grim and dark, with every window shuttered, but what gave pause to the crowd was the sight of the cannons which stood on each side of the front entrance. They were cannons which had stood on the slopes of Mont St. Jean, at Waterloo in 1815, and beside each of them stood old soldiers, trained gunners, some of whom had fired their pieces on Napoleon's Imperial Guard when they came up the hill in a hopeless endeavour to save a lost fight. In all the darkness of the façade, the only glimpse of light was the dim glow of the port-fires which the gunners held ready at their master's orders. The mob looked and turned back and departed in search of more vulnerable targets.

All that night and through the early hours of the next day the Commons sat to hear and discuss the proposals of the First Reform Bill. Russell rose punctually at six o'clock in the evening, and his speech lasted for two and a half hours. The House had an early taste of his quality when, after he had explained the fate of the close boroughs, he was interrupted by a clamour from the members of "Names! Names!" As calmly as though he were reading out a shopping list, Russell began on the list of boroughs which were to be totally disenfranchised, but soon he was interrupted by a storm of protest and indignation. He waited till it had died down, then, smiling pleasantly, remarked, "More yet," and continued with his reading.

The debate raged and ran its course for seven nights. Day after day dawn came, and in the House the candles paled and the first grey light of morning showed the members, rough-chinned, white with fatigue and hoarse with emotion and shouting. It ended on the eighth night, when the House gave leave to bring in the bill.

The bill was read for the second time on March 21, and after a two days' debate was carried by one vote. Thomas Babington Macaulay, who had spoken for it on the last night, left, in a famous passage, a description of the scene when the House divided.

"The Tellers scarcely got through the crowd, for the House was thronged to the table, and all the floor was fluctuating with heads like the pit in a theatre. But you might have heard a pin drop as Duncannon read the numbers. Then again the shouts broke out and many of us shed tears. I could scarcely refrain. And the jaw of Peel fell and the face of Twiss was as the face of a damned soul; and Herries looked like Judas, taking his necktie off for the last operation. We shook hands and clapped each other on the back and went out, crying and huzzaing into the lobby. And no sooner were the doors opened than another shout answered that within the House."

The shouting died and cold reflection and calculation took its place. The friends of the bill had been jubilant, but now they could not hide from themselves the narrowness of their victory and the gravity of their future expectations. The bill had indeed passed its second reading, but by one vote only. It had yet to run the gauntlet of committee, when the experienced Tory debaters would assail it, clause by clause, and expend all their ingenuity and determination to maim if not to destroy it. Beyond that lay the perils of the third reading and beyond again, the greatest of dangers, its passage through the House of Lords. There sat the Tory peers, its strongest opponents, men who were as impervious to argument as they were indifferent to popular clamour. The bill's chief creator and one of the finest speakers among its friends, Lord Durham, was still prostrated by illness and grief, and Grey would sorely feel the lack of his help and, perhaps, the stiffening of his inflexible will.

There were the half-hearted among the Whigs—Richmond, Melbourne, Palmerston and their like—and the less obstinate of the Tories who would bargain and manoeuvre and try to substitute some token offer, some paltry compromise, rather than admit defeat. Above all was the grim figure of the Duke of Wellington, absolute in his opposition, unassailable in his prestige, a master of defence and counter-attack, with a long history of success against overwhelming odds and an inflexible belief in the rightness of his judgment and the worth of his order. And, last of all, less formidable perhaps but wholly incalculable, was the unhappy King William IV, resolute to do what he saw as his duty, hating reform as the work of Satan, mentally at a complete loss, a figurehead it might be, but one whose constitutional position and ill-defined powers must be won over before either side could claim a victory.

So, till April, matters stood with neither side able to claim the advantage, with tempers rising and schemers manoeuvring, while outside London, all over the lovely English countryside, now growing green and golden with spring, the people of England hung trembling on the verge of revolution. In all that countryside, in black and smoky towns and cities, among the grey stone of university cloisters, from the Northumberland moors to the Cornish mines, and from the fishing ports of East Anglia to the Welsh seaboard, there was one determination and one cry for "The Bill, the whole Bill, and nothing but the Bill."

XXXVIII

THE MORE the Whigs thought about their situation, the less they liked it. The margin of one vote by which they had carried the second reading was not only derisively small but was the result of pure chance. A Tory member called Calcraft, who had held a minor post in Wellington's administration, had suddenly been afflicted with a brainstorm or an inexplicable change of heart and had voted against his party. Even in those more tolerant days a member who did such a thing could expect no mercy from his colleagues, especially when the issue was one so great. So strongly was the unhappy Calcraft made to feel the enormity of his conduct and so deeply did he brood on it that within a few days he took his own life.

Grey was seriously perturbed about the effect on the King of so paltry a majority, especially as he had unwittingly given his master to expect a reasonable vote in the bill's favour. Indeed, during the next few weeks, one of Grey's weaknesses was to be a real danger to his cause. He was too kindhearted and too sensitive to the King's distress and perplexity to be able to force himself to bring to bear the pressure that was needed to prevent William from taking fright altogether and abandoning his government thus early in the struggle. Grey and the King liked each other, and because he liked and pitied the poor distracted old sailor, Grey inadvertently spared him as much as he could, and so gave him a mistaken idea of the danger of the situation.

It was significant that, at this time, Grey, suffering from anxiety and self-questioning which would not have troubled a nature less fine, allowed his feelings to appear before his colleagues in the Cabinet. In one unguarded moment he even burst out with a heart-felt cry of "Oh, damn Reform! I wish I had never heard of it." It was the sort of unguarded remark which any man might have thrown off in the stress of the moment, but the feeling which caused it was enough to give hint of encouragement to all those members of the Cabinet who were themselves less than lukewarm.

Palmerston and Melbourne openly advised the dropping of the bill, and even Grey began to talk gloomily of retiring to his beloved Howick, and leaving the world of politics to those whose hearts were in it. The position was saved by the determination of two members, Durham and Russell. At once they were at Grey, warning him of the disgrace which would be his and his party's if they fell away from their pledge to pass the bill. Durham was still too ill to attend Cabinet meetings but he wrote to Grey, using all his passion and eloquence, straining to their limits his influence over the older man and his family affection. The Cabinet, he urged, would be everlastingly disgraced if they betrayed their cause and their friends. If the King were reluctant to help his ministers, he must be plainly warned that not only his honour but the safety of the throne depended on his playing the man. Durham, who thoroughly understood his father-in-law's nature, knew the danger which lay in that gentleness and sympathy for others.

It was at this point, and probably on Durham's suggestion, that the idea first rose of prevailing on the King to promise to create enough peers to ensure the passing of the bill through their House, if there were no other way of doing it. Grey knew how repulsive the idea would be to the King, but he also knew the strength and single-heartedness of his son-in-law. In the state of perplexity from which he suffered, a strong lead such as Durham gave him had immense influence. Indeed, at the moment, Radical Jack Durham's single-heartedness and will were the predominant influence in the Cabinet. Grey was hesitant, half of the others were ready to give in. The feeling was negative and timid, and in such an assembly the victory was likely to go to the man who knew what was needed, was resolute to get it and cared not in the least how unpleasant he made himself till he won his point. It was, as Sir T. R. M. Butler wrote, the "will of Durham" which rallied the Whigs and soon it was "the wisdom of Russell" which gave to that will practical expression.

The Cabinet decided that it would be at least advisable to review the bill and to see what, if any, alterations could be made to temper its severity and to increase its chance of passing. Naturally it was Russell who was called on to do the reviewing, a task which he undertook with alacrity. He was determined, as was Durham, that there should be no retreat from the government's pledge, but while introducing the bill to the Commons, he had noticed one or two minor points which might be altered to its advantage. Russell loved his bill as an artist loves his work and was only too glad of the chance of making it yet more perfect.

The Cabinet were less enthusiastic when they read the revised draft and found that such alterations as Russell had made were only in small matters of detail and that the general effect of them would be rather to stiffen than to moderate it. Since they themselves had no suggestions to make, they adopted the revised bill, hoping little for it but bowing to the pressure of the two men who had fathered it, and who would fight to the end for it. They were not surprised when, on being presented to the House in committee, it was defeated in a vote about one clause by eight votes. The clause which the Tories had selected for attack was one of the small points which Russell had altered in his amended draft.

The Tories had gained a tactical victory, but in their obstinacy and blind hatred of the bill, they had made a grievous miscalculation in their general strategy. They had openly declared their determination to kill the bill, and by means of a petty gain in a matter of detail, they exposed themselves openly to the whole country as the party who would stop at no trickery, however paltry, and miss no opportunity, however insignificant, to destroy the principle and to flout the desires and demands of the people of England. And it was the people who would now decide the issue, for the Tories' short-sighted little snatch at a victory had given to the Whigs the one advantage which they had so far lacked and which they could now fairly claim. Now that they had been beaten on a vote in the Commons, they had a perfect right to ask the King to dissolve Parliament and to appeal to the country in a general election.

But His Majesty had had enough. He had, most reluctantly, accepted the principle of reform because he thought that Parliament wanted it, and he held it to be his constitutional duty to support them. But now Parliament had clearly shown that they did not want it and the King, growing wearier and ever more muddled, decided that Grey had misled him about a possible majority for the bill. He seems also to have imagined that Grey had promised him that there would never be any question of a dissolution during the crisis. To his mind dissolution could only mean one thing, the end of royal authority and the giving over of the country to the Jacobin horde. He refused Grey's request, and so moved was he that he composed what Peel said was the only poem of his life,

> *I consider dissolution*
> *Tantamount to Revolution.*

The next forty-eight hours passed for both Whig and Tory in a mounting hysteria. Grey, Brougham and Durham, now restored to health, gave the King no peace. They were in an intolerable position, for they would not resign until they had secured the King's promise of full support. Nor could they be defeated in the House, since the Tories refrained from putting any motion to a division for fear that they might win it. They derived far more enjoyment from watching a powerless and frustrated Whig administration trying to hold on to office, to deal with the ordinary routine needed for the day-to-day running of the country, and at the same time trying to cajole or frighten the King into supporting them.

His Majesty equivocated, gave a promise and withdrew it, made piteous appeals to Grey to spare him and in every way drove his advisers nearly insane. As it was, it was the Tories whose lack of sense and good feeling turned the King away from them and into the hands of their enemies. The simple pleasure of baiting an impotent administration had somewhat gone to their heads, and they conceived themselves strong enough to try an offensive move. Lord Wharncliffe gave notice of his intention to move a prayer to the King asking him not to grant a dissolution. In his present mood it was all that His Majesty needed to drive him into violent action. Wharncliffe's motion, though it was perfectly constitutional and proper, appeared to him as a studied insult, and the Whigs seized their chance. Under renewed pressure from Grey, Durham and Brougham, the King agreed to come in person to the House and dissolve Parliament.

The new Parliament, when it met in November 1831, showed an overwhelming majority in the Commons for reform, yet the reformers were not much happier about their position. The Commons would, of course, pass the bill but there were still the Lords, who were as intractable as ever. The Duke of Wellington and his colleagues cared not in the least for public opinion and were still as determined as ever not to let reform reach the statute book. Like the crafty soldier that he was, Wellington prepared to fight an infinitely patient withdrawal action, hoping to find an opportunity once again to hold the bill up in committee. But Durham was back in the fight now, and, with his support, Grey hardened himself to demand from the King the only thing which now could help him, a creation of new peers, numerous enough to be sure of carrying the bill through their House.

In January 1832, the bill passed the Commons for the second time with a majority of 116, and Grey managed to extract from his master a promise that "The King will not deny to his Ministers the power of acting at once up to the full exigency of the case." Even now the King was to change his mind again. When the Peers rejected the bill and Grey reminded him of his promise, William completely lost his head, repudiated his given word and accepted the resignation of the Whig Cabinet.

The temper of the country had been steadily rising during these tedious and largely futile negotiations, and it was now close to active revolution. There was little rioting—the situation was too serious for that—but Francis Place confidently foretold a rising of the whole people if there were to be any more delay or obstruction to reform. In barracks up and down the country troops stood to arms, momentarily expecting to be called out to suppress a riot, while their officers wondered, with a little chill at their hearts, whether their men would obey an order to fire.

Samuel Bamford, the author of the *Autobiography of a Working Man,* was then serving in the Scots Greys, who were stationed at Birmingham, and wrote a vivid description of those days of madness which were later known as "The May Days." All leave was cancelled and the men were confined to barracks, while the horses of one troop at a time stood in the stables saddled and bridled ready for action. One Sunday, Bamford remembered, the men were fallen in and marched to the armourers' shop where stood the grindstones for sharpening their swords. An order which the younger men had never heard and did not understand was given to "rough-sharpen" the blades. The object of it was to leave a rough and jagged cutting edge which would inflict terrible wounds. The older soldiers were able to tell the frightened youngsters that the last time that the Greys had "rough-sharpened" their swords was on the eve of Waterloo.

The demonstrations and the efforts at pressure did not come only from the class whom the King thought of as Jacobins. Francis Place had the inspiration to call for a run on all the banks so as to threaten the country's credit, and his phrase, "To stop the Duke, go for gold," became one of the slogans of the day. The provincial banks soon began to report heavy withdrawals of gold, and at Birmingham alone £20,000 was withdrawn in one day. On the seventeenth of May the *Manchester Correspondent* reported gleefully that 620 depositors had given notice to withdraw sums amounting to £16,700. Much of this financial pressure was deliberate and tactical, but the run on the banks showed signs of falling into a real panic, when, at last, Grey announced the government's resignation.

The Bank of England fought the threat with the help of the Barings and Rothschilds and the other anti-reform bankers, but the next phase of the financial attack on the country began almost at once with the beginning of a general refusal to pay taxes until the bill should have been passed. In thousands of houses all over the country there were window bills announcing curtly, "No taxes paid here," and young Lord

Milton, Earl Fitzwilliam's heir, told a cheering House of Commons that he had "asked the tax-gatherer to call again."

The popular newspapers were unrestrained in their language and some of them went so far as to threaten the King and to speak of the possibility of a republic in Britain. "We are Monarchists," the *New Weekly Messenger* said on May 19, "but if monarchy can only subsist with Wellingtons, Cumberlands, Lyndhursts, ambitious bastards, and German women for its ministers and its loves, with rotten boroughs, enormous pensions, and desolating taxes for its appendages, let monarchy go to the right-about and the lesser evil of Republicanism be dominant in England."

Henry Cockburn recorded in his diary the thoughts which were entering the heads of very many of his countrymen during those "May Days." "I never before actually felt the immediate pressure of a great popular crisis. There was nothing to distract the attention or to break the terrible silence—nothing but grave looks and orderly public meetings, unconquerable resolution and the absolute certainty that, if any accident had made resistance begin anywhere, it would have run like an electric shock in a moment."

It is always helpful to a movement if hatred can be concentrated on an individual enemy, since men can more readily hate one man than a number of men, and either more readily than a cause or a doctrine. It was convenient that at that time of crisis there should have been ready to hand an individual whose power and prestige and whose uncompromising nature concentrated on himself a nation's loathing.

That tall spare figure and that arrogant face with the high-bridged nose, those familiar garments of blue frock-coat, white trousers and cravat, personified for the people of England all the sins and faults of Wellington's party, nor was he made more attractive by his obvious contempt for his enemies. Day after day he would mount his horse at Apsley House and, unattended except by one groom, ride slowly down to Westminster, calling perhaps at the Horse Guards on the way. He was abused, threatened, even pelted, yet there was something about his face and his upright seat on his horse which forbade the mob, who reviled him, to approach too near to his person. For a time, Wellington was, and must have known himself to be, the most hated man in the kingdom.

He cared as little for the people's hatred as for their adulation. He was single in mind, devoted entirely to his idea of what was right and honourable, utterly careless of his own reputation and even of his life. Again and again the crowd gathered outside Apsley House, and sometimes there were stones thrown, though there were iron bars on the windows now. In one of the upstairs rooms his Duchess, who had been Kitty Pakenham, had lain dying during the last days of April, hearing in her last moments of consciousness the shouting of the crowd outside the closed gates, behind which the Waterloo guns still stood, while their gunners waited not far away. If Wellington had ever hated the mob, he had cause to do so now when their ribaldry and their threats assaulted his wife's ears in her last hours of life. She died on April 21, and the Duke gave no sign of weakness, becoming a little more stern, sitting a little more upright on his horse and glancing round him with increased contempt. Night after night he sat in his place in the Lords, as watchful and calm as ever he had been at Vimeiro or Salamanca, intervening in debate as seldom and as briefly as he could, and all the time exerting his immense power of will to hold his supporters together and stiffen them for the fight. He advised on all troop movements in the country, distributing the small available Regular Army among the most dangerous spots. He knew that most of his own party disliked and distrusted him now, seeing him as a betrayer of the Tory party and the monarchy. There were by this time few Tories who did not realize that some measure of reform must be granted to stave off a revolution. There were many who hoped to get into power and then to grant such a measure and thereby establish their own party and not the Whigs as the people's friends. He still had allies in the House, but by a strange irony most of them came from the most recent creations of Pitt's Premiership, who were still sensitive enough of their recent elevation to seek to justify it by looking down on their neighbours.

They were, of all men, the least likely to be welcome allies to that stern aristocrat, the Duke of Wellington, and many of the older aristocracy had turned against him and were either openly supporting reform or were ready to compromise. He was supported by most of the bench of bishops, always ready to oppose any movement toward liberty or humanity. They, too, were strange allies for him, but he was used to strange allies. He had suffered from them all his life, in India, in Portugal, in Spain. Perhaps, in his singlemindedness, he did not realize how many of his fellow peers were cursing his obstinacy and the way in which he was ruining the prospects of his party and perhaps the safety of their own order. If he did not, he was soon to have an opportunity. In May, Grey resigned, the Whigs were out, and Britain was without a government.

King William was now in a state bordering on insanity, which the hearty abuse of his subjects did nothing to allay. Only a short time ago he had been King Billy, the people's friend; now he was tyrant and oppressor. All over the country, inn signs which bore the image of the "King's Head" or the "King William" were torn down and burnt. Meanwhile the papers raged at him in phrases which would surely have involved their publishers in prosecutions for sedition had anyone had the time to bother with them. And, in the middle of all this, he had to find an immediate solution for the country's problem, since there was no government and even the ordinary legislation needed for the everyday supplies and finance of the country was at a standstill. The King's first suggestion, which commended itself to no one but its author, was that the late Whig administration should continue to govern without holding office. With some wild idea of keeping Grey's assistance, he very handsomely offered to make his brother Bishop of Hereford. But Grey, who was seldom unwilling to provide for his family, had just appointed his brother to the living of St. Botolph, Bishopsgate, and even the King's further offer to let him hold both the incumbency and the bishopric failed to move the Prime Minister.

The Whigs were out, and out they would stay until they got the King's promise, in writing, to create enough new peers to pass the bill. There was no hesitancy among their leaders now. They were too deeply committed to the fight, and their tempers were rising as they saw themselves wantonly obstructed by their master in spite of his previous promise to help them. The only alternative—and it was not a hopeful one—was the return to power of the Tories. If they could form an administration and make up their minds to pass some measure of reform, they might yet pacify the country and deliver the King. His Majesty consulted Wellington, who gave him little encouragement, though he suggested that either Peel or Lord Lyndhurst might be able to get together some sort of administration, if only a temporary one, to keep the wheels running. Peel refused to have anything to do with the idea. He had been called a turncoat at the time of Catholic emancipation and he was not minded to incur the same charge over reform.

Lyndhurst was willing to try, though not hopefully, but by that time both Wellington and the King had come to the conclusion that he would stand little chance. He had made himself more than usually ridiculous in a speech during the reform debates, by claiming to speak for the greater part of the people of England, who, he said, were against the bill. Being unkindly pressed by his fellow peers for details, he had admitted that he had got the information from his bootmaker in St. James's Street. Lyndhurst had asked him what he thought of reform, and the tradesman, who was no politician but a good man of business, who knew that the customer was always right, had replied that he did not expect any large increase of trade if the bill were to pass. Even the other Tory peers were inclined to disregard this somewhat fallacious claim, and the situation was too dangerous for experimenting with a man who had just notably made a fool of himself in public and might do the same again at any moment. In despair, the King begged the Duke to form an administration.

Wellington never thought of refusing. It was his simple creed that

"The King's Government must be carried on." As he had said, many years before, he was "nimmukwallah."' He had eaten the King's salt and he was the King's servant, whose duty it was to serve in any capacity and any place to which he might be called. But he knew how hopeless a venture he was undertaking. His immediate need was for a strong man to lead the Commons, a task for which Peel was ideally suited, but once again Peel declined to have any share in the business. Rather hopelessly the Duke trailed his net again but brought up nothing more promising than Sir Henry Hardinge, an old Peninsula comrade, and Manners Sutton, the Speaker. Sutton was willing to consider the Chancellorship of the Exchequer for himself or, failing that, the Foreign Office. When he found that all the Duke was willing to offer was the leadership of the House of Commons, he withdrew his offer to help.

Hardinge would have followed his chief anywhere, as he had followed him in Spain and Portugal and Belgium, but even with the addition of the aging Eldon as Lord Chancellor, it could hardly be considered a strong team. The Duke persisted but the plain fact was that no one wanted to take office in an administration which would start at the height of unpopularity and would probably last no more than a few weeks. In addition to this, most of the party had lost confidence in the Duke as their leader after the egregious blunder of his reform speech in the previous year and in face of his almost idiotic refusal to see that there was no alternative to passing a reform bill except revolution.

Politically, the impasse was now complete. On May 14 the Tory leaders met at Apsley House and acknowledged their political bankruptcy. Next morning Wellington informed the King of his failure. There was nothing else to do but to recall the Whigs. The King sent for Grey, who at least had always been kind and understanding; but while the courtesy and kindness were still there, it was a new Grey whom the King now saw, with a new obstinacy and a new reluctance to listen to evasions. Grey already felt hurt at the King's treatment of him and suspicious of his latest offer. The feeling changed to anger and disgust when he learned that the King still refused to create new peers. (It was likely, too, that Grey's new determination had been much stiffened by the return to active life of Radical Jack.) There were no waverers in the Whig councils now. Even these like Richmond, Palmerston and Melbourne had realized that there could be no more compromise and no giving way. If the Duke had achieved nothing else, he had united the Whig party.

Meanwhile the temper of the country was rising, and there were more demonstrations and more talk of violence. Cam Hobhouse told Francis Place that arrangements had been secretly made for getting the King and Queen out of the country should it be necessary. In the smoky towns of the North Country, sullen and dangerous workmen watched the dragoons who patrolled the streets and heard the rumble of gun wheels as the batteries were moved to points near to their eventual positions. The situation was too serious, the issue too great, for partial or sporadic resistance. If it came at all it would come all over the country, and it would not be easily stopped.

Still Britain had no government and the runs on the banks went on. It seemed that there could be no way out except by the last road of armed combat. And yet at, if not after, the eleventh hour a way was found. As is the usual way of English politics, it was a way of compromise, and a way so simple that it seemed strange to many that they had not themselves thought of it. Who did, in fact, think of it was and remains uncertain, but the origin of the plan seems to have been a remark made in the Commons by Mr. Baring the banker, a remark of which nobody took very much notice at the time. Mr. Baring had suggested as a possible solution that the Whigs should remain in office and pass the bill but should not ask for the creation of new peers, on condition that the House of Lords should refrain from voting against the government.

Later the King claimed to have found this way out of the impasse, which is almost certainly untrue. Many historians have given the credit to General Sir Herbert Taylor, the King's private secretary, who, if he did not think of the plan, had a large part in bringing it into being. The King warmly approved of the idea and at once wrote to Wellington to ask him to refrain from voting and to persuade the other Tory peers to do the same. At the same time he gave permission to Taylor to write to several other peers, a permission which Taylor interpreted so literally that before long every Tory peer had received the same request.

It was as well that Taylor acted as he did, vastly though he exceeded his instructions, for there was to be no support for the plan from the Duke of Wellington. He had received the King's personal request and, uncompromising as ever, had replied with icy correctness that he would "as a private individual" refrain from voting, but that it was not a course which he thought it proper to recommend to his colleagues, whom he left to the prompting of their individual consciences. The Duke was beaten at last and he knew it. He had thrown the whole weight of his prestige and his will into the fight only to find himself betrayed by his master, abandoned by his colleagues and hated by the people at large.

He did not attend the sitting of the House when the bill received its third reading, while the opposition benches were empty and the division a formality. On June 7, 1832, the Reform Bill received the Royal Assent and became law. That night, from behind the barred windows of Apsley House, the Duke looked out on an England to which he had given his life and which would never again be the England that he had known.

EPILOGUE

1832-1852

WELLINGTON was sixty-three in 1832 when the passing of the First Reform Bill interrupted his active career as a politician. He had still twenty years of vigorous life before him during which he would be Commander-in-Chief of the Army, a member of several Cabinets and, very briefly, both Home and Foreign Secretary. Twice he might have returned to the Premiership, but on both occasions he refused, advising his sovereign to send for Peel, as a Prime Minister in those modern days ought to be in the Commons. (Privately he remarked that he was damned if he was going back to the task of "assuaging what gentlemen are pleased to call their feelings.") But he was always assiduous in his place in the Lords and spoke when the subject of debate was one of which he had special knowledge. Obviously his most congenial and most frequent topic was the Army, and to the end of his life he continued to resist any scheme of improvement and to defend flogging and the purchase of commissions. He still held that "The King's business must be carried on," but now it seemed permissible for someone else to do it, and he had had enough of the vagaries of royalty. It had been his unkind fate to serve two kings, both of whom adored him and neither of whom he could tolerate. Much as he had disliked George IV, he found William IV even more trying. He was a worthier man but his mind was incurably muddled, and Wellington had no patience left for obscure thinkers. He wrote, in a letter to Lord Ellesmere, that most people in England thought that commanding an army was the same as commanding a fleet, adding a little sourly,

"One of these is our most gracious Sovereign." He was happier when Victoria came to the throne, finding her charming and touching in her youth, so that with Lord Melbourne he did much to help her through her early years of rule and to teach her the business of being a Queen.

He was undergoing the slow process by which the English never fail to remind their national heroes that they are as other men, mortal and fallible. Like others of his sort, he passed from adulation to unpopularity, from that to acceptance and, in the fullness of years, to the dignity of an institution, a popular and respected figure about London, an indispensable part of every ceremony and public occasion. And, like others, his popularity grew with the waning of his powers and the consequent lessening of any danger of his becoming a public nuisance instead of a public figure.

He was always there to be consulted if anything went wrong or anyone lacked knowledge or precedent. As time went on and he became a little less active, his importance as a general counsellor only increased. As he said himself, there was always the Duke of Wellington to see to things and everyone expected him to know everything. Difficulties and problems of all sorts were brought to him, and he generally knew the answer, which he gave in his laconic way and without undue consideration for the inquirer's feelings. Before the Queen's coronation, Lord Albemarle brought his own problem to the Duke for solution. He was Master of the Horse and held that, as such, he had the right to ride in the royal coach in the coronation procession. Some ill-disposed people, he found, were disputing that right, and he looked to the Duke to justify him. It can have given him small comfort to be roundly told, "Her Majesty can make you go inside the coach or outside the coach or run behind the coach like a damned tinker's donkey." The Duke had little patience with importunity and made no pretence of showing it. A persistent agricultural reformer who tried to interest him in colleges for teaching farming in the county of Kent was bleakly told, "There is nothing that I know less about than agriculture and I own no land in Kent," with the further comment that he owned land in several other counties and had no intention of setting up agricultural colleges there.

Naturally the War Office and the Horse Guards were the most untiring applicants for his advice. He was Commander-in-Chief in 1826 and 1827 but not again for twenty years thereafter. His place was taken by Lord Hill, who had been one of his divisional generals in Spain and who, apparently, still regarded himself as a subordinate. Appointments to command were Hill's main anxiety, and when in doubt he referred them to Wellington, who did his best to help whenever he could, though not without showing some signs of asperity—he had never asked for advice when he commanded an army. So, when Hill asked him to suggest three names for command in India, Wellington wrote down the name of Charles Napier three times on a piece of paper and returned it to the Horse Guards. He was even less accommodating about the command in Burma, recommending Lord Combermere and replying to the objection, "But I thought that your Grace always considered Lord Combermere a fool," with, "So he is a fool, and a damned fool. But he can take Rangoon."

General Hardinge, when he commanded in 1852, was even more devoted to his former chief and openly admitted that when he had to make a decision he always first asked himself what the Duke of Wellington would have done in his place. It was perhaps natural but it was not healthy for the Army, since it meant in effect that nothing which had not been done in the Duke's time could be considered twenty years later. The British Army payed dearly for the system when they embarked for the Crimea with the equipment and organization which had sufficed for the Peninsular War fifty years earlier, and then only because a great soldier commanded the Army. (It must always be a matter for regret to a historian that Wellington did not live for a few more years to try conclusions with Miss Nightingale.)

Even when he gave a slightly grudging consent to experiments with the rifle as a replacement for the musket—after all the old Brown Bess had been good enough at Salamanca and Waterloo—he insisted that it must still be called a "musket" or all the private soldiers would get ideas above their station and want to be called "riflemen" and to dress up in "Jack-a-Dandy uniforms."

Once, by pure chance, he bequeathed to the Army a name and a tradition which may well last as long as his own. The War Office was preparing a manual of military law and wanted a typical soldier's name for the defendant in certain trials—a sort of military equivalent of John Doe and Richard Roe. The united intelligence of the Horse Guards and the War Office being unequal to the invention of a suitable name, the question was inevitably referred to the Duke. From his long and full memories, he dredged up the name of a man who had been his servant in Spain and told them to call the mythical character by the name of Thomas Atkins.

He had another reminder of old days at the Queen's coronation when the Marshal the Duke of Dalmatia, whom he had faced in Spain as Marshal Soult, came to represent the King of France. They had never spoken to each other, though they found, on comparing notes during a walk in St. James Park, that they had caught sight of each other in the Pyrenees in the year 1814, when they were on opposing mountain tops.

He found that, as he grew older, he became every year busier and more in demand, not for events or causes of national importance but at the behest of individuals, many of whom showed an astonishing familiarity in approaching him and a complete lack of the feeling that he had done his part and might now be allowed to rest. Since it was his absurd pride to answer every letter that he got, his correspondence grew overwhelming, and there was displayed an increasing tone of impatience in those famous notes of his, written in the third person and presenting "F.M. the Duke of Wellington's compliments." Sometimes he misread the letter of application or misspelled his answer, as he did when he told the Archbishop of Canterbury, who had requested the honor of being allowed to see the avenue of Waterloo beeches at Strathfield Saye, that "If he comes to his house he can see the breeches which the Duke wore at Waterloo, though His Grace cannot imagine why he would want to see them." There must have been hundreds of these stories in circulation and probably as many more have been invented later by devotees of the legend who cannot bear not to add to it. It is difficult today to know which are the genuine and which are the false, since he had the rare quality of being in fact exactly like his legend. If some of them are false, they all deserve to be true. Undoubtedly the shortest of all of them is a true one—"Compliments. The Duke has received your letter. Wellington."

He was loaded with honours and titles—surely no man ever held more —being a peer and a field-marshal in half the countries of Europe, but there were certain smaller distinctions which were pressed on him and he never liked to refuse. Oxford University made him their Chancellor, and when he accepted, he found rather to his dismay that he would have to make a speech in Latin at his installation. He knew, he said, no more Latin and Greek than a fourth form boy, so he turned for help to his physician, for the rather odd reason that any man who wrote out prescriptions must be a classical scholar. As it happened, Sir Henry Halford, the doctor, was something of a scholar, though either he failed to instruct the Duke in pronunciation or the Duke did not remember his lessons. As was noted earlier, he startled the dons of Oxford with two glaring false quantities in the names Carolus and Jacobus.

Sometimes the honours which were offered to him were sinecures, like the Rangership of the Queen's Parks and the Wardenship of the Cinque Ports. But where other men would thankfully recognize a sinecure for what it was, Wellington could not deny himself the performance of any duties which might be attached to any post that he held. He inspected his parks with regularity and met one of the few defeats of his life at the hands of an old woman who had established herself with squatter's rights in a pie stall and refused to be moved from it.

He loved the Wardenship of the Cinque Ports not least because it gave him the official residence at Walmer Castle, a house which he came to like almost as much as Strathfield Saye. He used it more regularly toward the end of his life when he had had to give up hunting and found that Hampshire had thereby been robbed of something of its charm for him. He lived happily at Walmer Castle in what he considered the height of luxury, though most of his guests found the house intolerably cold and the furniture scanty.

Occasionally there were problems of real importance to engage his attention, and when they were, as they often were, military matters he spoke with all his old authority and brevity, so that ministers who waited on him for advice were apt to wonder whether they were ministers after all and not importunate staff officers. When there was rebellion in Canada in 1837 and the Earl of Durham was going out to deal with that and Canada's many other problems, Wellington spent some time with him discussing the best dispositions for the troops in the event of further trouble. It is true that he had never been to Canada, but all military problems are one and most of them admitted his unfailing solution —to keep his own troops on a reverse slope and "to know what is going on on the other side of the hill." Thereafter he kept a watchful eye on Canada—an eye which a battalion of the Guards found to be upon them from the other side of the Atlantic. Lord Durham, whose mission was a brilliant success, was sacrificed to party feeling and Melbourne's selfishness and recalled in something like disgrace. The Guards battalion in Quebec, anxious to show their respect for him, held a dinner at which he was guest of honour and at which speeches were made which seemed to reflect on the government's wisdom and propriety in recalling him. Communications in those days were slow, and no doubt the officers thought that they were safe in expressing their personal loyalties. They were, after all, most of them, too young to have served under Wellington and to know that he missed nothing, and they had probably forgotten all about it when a rebuke in Wellington's best manner reached Canada some months later. They learned that they ought not to have had the dinner, ought not to have invited Lord Durham to it and certainly ought not to have made speeches suggesting that the government were fallible. It seems perhaps a little hard, especially when we know that Lord Durham had confined his speaking at the dinner to proposing Wellington's health, but discipline must be maintained even at the distance of a few thousand miles. And, when Lord Durham came home and was subjected to the vilest forms of party persecution, Wellington, although he was a

Tory and Durham a Whig, refused to take any part in the game. He knew more than most men about the lonely life of a proconsul and the irrationality of home governments, though as a lifelong supporter of regulations and accuracy he voted in favour of Lord Brougham's bill, which was passed to correct a technical legal error committed by Lord Durham while in Canada. His Grace did not care for Brougham and had the rare distinction of having reduced him to silence in the Lords. Brougham, in the flood tide of his masterly oratory, was suddenly brought up short by the sight of Wellington's raised and admonitory finger and his almost gentle rebuke, "Now, now, mind what you say next."

In 1848 there was trouble near at home, and again Wellington was called on to advise and, very nearly for the last time, to command troops in action. The Chartists were marching on London to present a monster petition, and the Cabinet, remembering the days of the Gordon Riots, had visions of London in flames and chaos. There were a few battalions of infantry and some guns in London, and his anxious colleagues begged Wellington to draw up a defence scheme. He was seventy-nine in that year and his colleagues were finding him increasingly deaf and testy, so that he was not altogether welcome at meetings where everything that was said had to be repeated for his benefit.

But it was a very different kind of Cabinet meeting that he attended to discuss the Chartist danger. The long table in the Cabinet room was covered by his maps, and he stood over them with a pointer while he explained his plan and gave his orders. Men remarked afterward how unusually strong his voice was and how decisively he told them what to do. Perhaps, like an old man dreaming dreams, he had felt himself carried back to the Peninsular days and fancied himself surrounded not by anxious and dark-coated ministers but by the men whom he had commanded half a lifetime ago—Somerset and Uxbridge, Hill and Picton, Beresford and Graham. It was remarked that even his deafness did not trouble him that day, though there is, after all, little to be wondered at in that. He was giving his orders and it had never been his habit to encourage discussion or questioning of them.

His plan, when he detailed it, surprised some of his hearers, who thought that a military man must delight in the use of force. But it was, like all his actions, sensible, practical and undramatic in that it left the keeping of order to the civilian police and the special constables and held back the troops south of the river—he had always liked reverse slopes—only to be used as a last resort. For all his lifetime of soldiering, there was never a man less in love with military dominance in civil affairs. It had always lain at the root of his insistence on the sale of commissions, which would prevent the formation of a class of career officers who might someday become a military danger, and behind his addiction to the wearing of civilian clothes off-duty and his encouragement of the same practice by his officers. He had spent his best years in fighting the power of a military dictator, and he was having no trace of any such thing in his London. As it turned out, he was justified, for the police had little difficulty in keeping order, and the troops were not summoned to cross the river at any moment in the day. It was his victory—his last and not his least important or creditable.

In 1851 The Great Exhibition in Hyde Park was to usher in the era of peace, prosperity and industry. Britain had not been at war with any European power since Waterloo, and the Duke still presided at the War Office with the help of his old Peninsular veterans, principal among whom were Lord Fitzroy Somerset and Sir Henry Hardinge. There was intermittent fighting in Britain's overseas possessions, but the army at home had nothing to do and suffered from a lack of occupation and a thoroughly unimaginative command. The cavalry were almost wholly obsessed with sartorial problems, becoming every year more tightly breeched, more lace-encrusted and more fantastically crowned with busby or helmet. The infantry carried out the old drills with the old musket, though the new rifle was beginning to find supporters. Even such a modest routine was too much now for Wellington, and at last he tried to lay down his command, making the ill-advised suggestion that it should pass to the Prince Consort, who had the sense to refuse it.

In February the troopship *Birkenhead* struck a rock off the coast of Africa and sank with a loss of 454 lives. The reports told a high story of courage, of men standing in their ranks while the bands played, and of calmness and dignity in the face of certain death. Wellington spoke of the tragedy in the House of Lords with some emotion, but men who heard him remarked that he spoke entirely of the troops' steadiness and discipline and never mentioned the word "courage." He had always taken that for granted in himself or any other soldier, seeing it less as a virtue than as the inevitable result of strict discipline. In all his life he had never recommended men for decorations for courage in action, believing that no less was to be expected of a soldier, who should be mercilessly punished for not displaying it and not rewarded for doing what he was told to do.

That speech was almost the last service which he was to do for the Army, and he spent the greater part of the spring and summer at Walmer Castle. Europe was still at peace but he read the papers which were sent to him from the Cabinet and War Office, and as he did so, he must have had moments when he felt himself carried back to an earlier day and a less hopeful world—for there was to be an Emperor in France again and his name was Napoleon. The French, always the most politically fickle of people, having experimented with royalty and republic were once again feeling their need for an absolute master, though in that year of 1852 he still appeared in the mild guise of a constitutional President. But all the signs and portents were there. In January, Napoleon, soon to be the Emperor Napoleon III, was installed at Notre Dame as Prince-President, and took up his residence in the Tuileries.

It was the high flood of Bonapartism. "Liberty, Fraternity and Equality" were officially proscribed as slogans, and from the streets the new names were erased and replaced by the old hagiography of the First Empire. The eagles were returning to the standards, and within a few years the Imperial Guard and the Cuirassiers would be out again in their uniforms of Austerlitz and Borodino and Waterloo. As a final gesture of reverence for his ancestry, the new Napoleon decreed that the birthday of his uncle, Napoleon I, on August 15, should in future be observed as the only national holiday in France.

Thoughtful men who read the signs were set to worrying about the new France and to wondering whether they would, sooner or later, be put to the task of destroying another empire.

But that at least could not be laid on the shoulders of the man who had done more than most men to break the power of the First Empire. On September 14, 1852, the Duke of Wellington died at Walmer Castle.

INDEX

Tone, Wolfe, 42, 43
Tooke, 38
Tories. 19-20, 50, 51, 86, 246, 250, 252-253, 254, 266, 268, 269, 274, 275, 285-286, 289, 290, 291
Torquemada, 202
Torrens. Colonel, 166
Torres Vedras, 162, 168, 170, 171, 172, 174, 175, 178, 179, 183-184, 197, 201, 208
Total War, concept of, 28, 95
Toulon, France, 24
Toulouse, 215. 217, 218
Townshend, Charles, 5, 6
Trafalgar, 111, 113, 127
Trant, 171
Treasonable Practices Act, 38
Trevelyan, Sir George, 39
Trident, 93, 94
Trim, Ireland, 4, 23
Trinity College (Dublin), 3
Tudors, 19
12th Dragoons, 23
Tyrconnel, Lord, 42

Ulm, 96, 116
Uxbridge, Lord, ix, 109, 235

Valencia, 145
Valladolid, 144, 209
Vellore, 65, 66
Versailles, 11, 17
Victor, Marshal, 155, 157, 159, 160, 161, 176-177, 178, 183
Victoria, Queen, 296
Victory, 100, 101, 104, 106, 108-112
Vienna, Congress of, xi, 7, 119, 226-227
Villeneuve, Pierre, 76, 80, 94, 97, 98, 100, 101, 103, 110
Vimeiro, Portugal, 140
Vitoria, 208, 210, 216, 217, 263
Voltaire, 13

Waal, 25, 26
Wagram, 168, 182
Wales, Prince of, 116
Walmer Castle, 299, 301, 302
Walpole, Robert, 38
Waters, Colonel, 158
War of 1812, 127, 185-187, 203
War Office, 296, 297
Washington, George, 6
Wasp, 186
Waterloo, 10, 26, 32, 66. 181, 230-237
Wellesley, Arthur, see Wellington, Duke of
Wellesley, Arthur (son), 224-225
Wellesley, Charles (son), 224
Wellesley, Gerald (brother), 4, 6
Wellesley, Long (nephew), 41

Wellesley, Richard, Lord Mornington (brother), 3-4, 5, 6, 7, 14, 17, 22, 23, 43, 47, 49, 53, 55, 56, 123-124
Governor-General of India, 60-68, 74, 75
Wellesley, Waleran de, 55
Wellesley, William (brother), 23
Wellington, Duke of
birth date, vi, 3, 12
birthplace, 3
Chancellor of Oxford University, 6
Chief Secretary for Ireland, 124, 132
Colonel, 43-44, 47
commissions purchased by, 21-23
Congress of Vienna and, 226-227
death of, vi
diplomatic missions, 219-225
education, 3-7, 9
father, see Mornington, Baron
first war experiences, 24-27, 40
Governor of Seringapatam, 70-71
hatred for, 288-289, 293
Major-General, 71-72, 75
marriage, 124, 130
Master General of the Ordnance, 240, 255
meets Nelson, 102-104
member of Parliament, 124
mother, see Mornington, Lady
Napoleon's abdication and, 215-217
opposition to reform, 17, 282
Peninsular War and, 132-185, 197
Prime Minister, 269, 270
rules for public speaking, 6
titles and honours bestowed on, 259, 298-299
Waterloo and, 230-237
wife's death, 289
Wesley, see Wellesley
West Indies, 43, 76, 79, 100
Whigs, 15, 17, 18-19, 50, 86, 87, 90, 205, 206, 246, 250, 254, 267, 269, 272, 274, 275, 277, 283, 284, 286, 289-292
Wilberforce, William, 222
William IV, King, ix, 42, 244, 245. 247, 271-272, 274, 282, 283, 285-287, 290-292, 295
William and Mary, 272
Winchelsea, Lord, 273
Windsor, England, 14
Wittgenstein, 202
Wolfe, James, 33
Wordsworth, William, 85
World War I, vii
World War II, vii

York, Duke of, 24, 25, 34, 40, 41, 125, 136
Yorkshire, 15, 82, 204
Ypres, 36

Printed in Great Britain by
Lowe & Brydone (Printers) Ltd., London